THE
AGA
BOOK

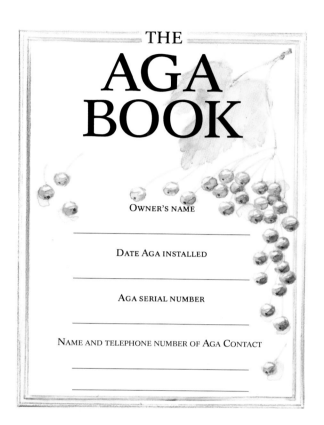

OWNER'S NAME

_____

DATE AGA INSTALLED

_____

AGA SERIAL NUMBER

_____

NAME AND TELEPHONE NUMBER OF AGA CONTACT

_____

_____

This book has been a joy to write and I would like to thank
my team of friends who helped me:
Debbie Woolhead, Sheila Inglis, Joanna Drew, Penny Tetley,
Miranda Hall, Jenny Hopkirk, Susan Middleton,
Deborah Murdock, Annabelle Christie and Jill Bull.
Special thanks also to my friends at Aga, especially Dawn Roads,
Aga's Home Economist, and Hazel Jordan.

The Aga Book is published by Aga-Rayburn,
Glynwed Consumer and Foodservice Products Limited,
PO Box 30, Ketley, Telford, Shropshire TF1 4DD.
Tel: 01952 642000
Aga is a trademark of Glynwed International Plc.
© Glynwed International Plc.
PRODUCED BY CHARLES BARKER CONNECTIONS
DESIGNED AND ART DIRECTION: *Sandy Bradley*
TYPOGRAPHIC DESIGN: *Mark Richards*
Set in Concorde by Technique Typesetting Ltd.
PHOTOGRAPHY: *Sandy Hedderwick*
HOME ECONOMIST FOR PHOTOGRAPHY:
Sheila Bretherton • Wendy Strang
WATERCOLOUR ILLUSTRATIONS: *David Westwood*
TECHNICAL ILLUSTRATIONS: *Alan Hancocks*
CO-ORDINATOR: *Gill Derry*

The publishers of The Aga Book would like to thank the following
companies for their generosity in loaning ceramics, porcelain,
kitchenware, fabrics, furniture and surfaces for use in photography.

FOOD PHOTOGRAPHY
DAVID MELLOR James Street, Convent Garden, London.
W.H FRALEY & SONS Gas Street, Birmingham.
LONDON ARCHITECTURAL SALVAGE & SUPPLY COMPANY
Mark Street, London.
FIRED EARTH Twyford Hill, Oxford Road, Adderbury, Oxfordshire.
DESIGNER'S GUILD Kings Road London.
CASA FINA Regent Street, Royal Leamington Spa, Warwickshire.

Printed by Pentagraph Ltd
Macclesfield, Cheshire SK11 7JB
Telephone: 01625 619257

Eighth Reprint 1999.

AGA

THE
AGA
BOOK

by
MARY BERRY

2 oven Aga - Golden Yellow

4 oven Aga with optional electric hob - Claret

2 oven Aga - Royal Blue

LIVING WITH AN AGA

Until I owned an Aga I never quite understood how Aga owners could be so ecstatic about a cooker. Now I totally understand and am devoted to mine. I have withdrawal symptoms when, once a year, I turn it off for servicing.

When asked to explain my thoughts and feelings about the Aga, a variety of images flash through my mind.

I see myself coming downstairs on a cold February morning, walking straight to the warm heart of the kitchen, the Aga. Leaning against it as I get my thoughts straight for the day, meanwhile moving the pile of sheets that have been airing all night on top of the Simmering Plate's insulated cover.

Then I see one of the boys coming in after getting soaked on the golf course. No problem, the damp clothes go up to dry in the warm air above the Aga. I can also see the happy look on the face of someone snuggling into an Aga-warmed jacket before going out!

I can recall the Mallard duck that hatched out in the cupboard next to the Aga, what excitement that was. I can see Bumble, our much loved black retriever and indeed his son too, stretched out beside the Aga and being told to move over because I wanted to cook.

So far I haven't even started on all the meals I've cooked on the Aga, seeing delicious dishes coming out of its seemingly limitless depths, enjoying the sheer space of its big Boiling and Simmering Plates, after the confines of an ordinary cooker.

Life has changed over the last few years and we now want meals which are healthier, with less fat, more fibre and often with shorter cooking times; meals which span the much loved basics of British cookery but also include a wider international range than in the past. The Aga is still the ideal cooker to match these aims and this book is intended to help you achieve the very best.

I have enjoyed writing the Aga book more than any book I have ever written, I think because I am devoted to my Aga and testing the recipes over the past 2 years has been an indulgence for me – certainly not for one moment a chore.

It is said of the House of Commons that it's like joining the best club in the country. I think owning an Aga is a bit similar; certainly when you meet another Aga owner it is like discovering an instant friend.

Mary Berry

CONTENTS

INTRODUCTION
6

SOUPS & STARTERS
17
Hearty soups, essential stocks, elegant starters, tempting pâtés and terrines.

VEGETABLE DISHES
67
Vegetables cooked simply the Aga way or made extra special for vegetarian meals.

PUDDINGS
115
Indulgent desserts and puddings to drool over.

MEAT DISHES
27
Sumptuous roasts, tender casseroles, family favourites and celebration specials.

SAVOURIES & SAUCES
81
Sweet and savoury sauces to bring meals alive and ideas for savoury nibbles.

PRESERVES
125
The tang of home-made marmalade and the taste of summer preserved in jams, jellies and chutneys.

POULTRY & GAME
51
From the richness of venison to the lightness of chicken – with lots in-between.

LUNCHES & SUPPERS
89
Lunch in a hurry and suppertime classics.

BREAKFASTS
137
Inventive ideas to start the day the Aga way.

FISH & SEAFOOD
61
Fish at its simple best or dressed with the lightest sauces.

HOME BAKING
97
Cakes to be proud of, sweet things to tempt you and unforgettable home-made bread.

INDEX
142

As you probably know, your Aga is a cast-iron heat storage cooker. It's quite unique and deserves a brief explanation.

Whatever the heat source, be it gas, oil solid fuel or electricity, the heat is conducted under the hotplates and around the ovens.

Logically then, the hotplate above the heat source is the Boiling Plate, whereas the one over the ovens is the Simmering Plate.

On the two oven Aga the top oven is hot and ideal for roasting and baking; the bottom Simmering Oven is less hot and superb for slower cooking.

Aga cookers with four ovens have a slightly different layout. The top right oven is for roasting, the bottom right for baking, the top left is for simmering and the bottom left for plate warming.

The cast-iron parts of your Aga retain the heat superbly, helped by the efficient insulating material packed into the casing.

The Aga is thermostatically controlled and as you cook the lost heat is automatically restored.

The externally-vented ovens not only prevent cooking smells returning to the kitchen but give you superb cooking results – neither soggy nor dried out.

OLDER AGA COOKERS

If you have an older Aga timings may vary from those in the book; you may need to cook food longer. Make a note of the timings for your Aga in the margin when you cook a recipe for the first time

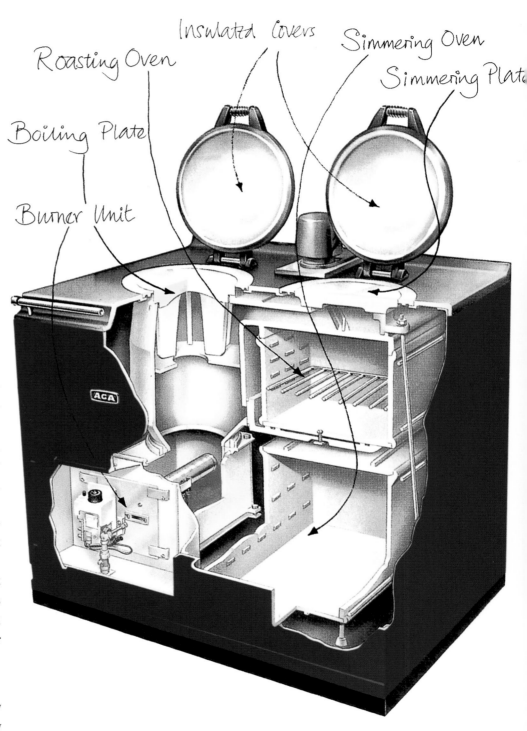

For the purpose of demonstration, the two oven gas-fired Aga is illustrated.

As the Aga works on the principle of storing heat within the cooker, the aim is to cook as much as possible in the ovens so that the heat is retained. Use the Boiling and Simmering Plates as little as possible and keep the insulating lids closed when the plates are not in use.

For example: Instead of frying bacon on top of the Aga, fry it on the floor or grill it at the top of the Roasting Oven. The grill racks now available for your new Aga cooker allow fat to drip off meats and provide a healthier method of cooking. Pans or casseroles can be brought to the boil on the Boiling Plate then transferred to the Simmering Oven to cook. Christmas pudding cooks to perfection in the Simmering Oven. The steam disappears up through the oven vent, instead of filling your kitchen and the pan does not boil dry so quickly, if at all.

No smells when cooking in Aga ovens; they disappear through the flue or vent pipe, unlike an ordinary cooker where smells waft through the house. Indeed, don't leave the sausages cooking in the Roasting Oven without a timer to remind you to take them out – you won't smell them burning – so effective is the seal of the doors! My Aga flue comes out by the parsley bed by the back door so only when picking parsley do I know whether I am burning something in the oven! There is much less problem with condensation in the kitchen if you use the Aga ovens. Because an Aga kitchen is always warm, you may find a condensation problem disappears.

Aga ovens are much more roomy than an ordinary cooker and you can fit in many more pans and dishes because of the marvellous design of the Agaluxe pans. With their flat lids, you can pile the pans one on top of another as well as side by side. Caution: if you are cooking really large quantities, filling the oven completely, do allow longer cooking time.

Many ordinary cookers have just one oven. It is such a bonus with the Aga to have two or even four ovens ready to cook. For instance when cooking a roast, you can transfer it to the Simmering Oven if your visitors are delayed or if it seems to be browning too quickly.

And, of course, because the Aga's cast iron ovens retain their heat, you can open the door to peep at soufflés and cakes without them collapsing.

The Heat Indicator

Exact temperatures become less important as you get used to your Aga. (Forget what you did with your previous cooker and follow the Aga methods.)

All you have to do is check the Heat Indicator first thing in the morning, or after several hours without cooking. If the mercury is on the single black line your Aga has its full amount of stored heat.

During cooking the mercury will drop back, but don't worry this is normal and the heat is automatically restored.

You need only adjust the control when the Aga is installed or first switched on after servicing. Then just note the position of the mercury for 2-3 mornings and advance or retard the control, as described in the operating instructions, until the mercury consistently reaches the centre line.

The Aga Hotplates

The surface area of both the Boiling Plate and the Simmering Plate is large so you can cook in several pans at the same time.

THE BOILING PLATE: Use the Boiling Plate when a fierce heat is required, i.e. boiling green vegetables, grilling meat in the Aga grill pan, deep fat frying (if you must!), brisk stir-frying and of course for toast and boiling the kettle fast for that welcome cup of tea.

THE SIMMERING PLATE: Use the Simmering Plate for a more gentle heat; for sautéing vegetables, boiling milk, making sauces and using as a griddle for Scotch pancakes.

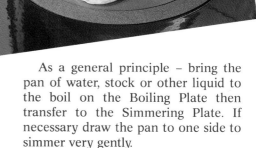

As a general principle – bring the pan of water, stock or other liquid to the boil on the Boiling Plate then transfer to the Simmering Plate. If necessary draw the pan to one side to simmer very gently.

Remember that heat escapes when the Boiling and Simmering Plate covers are lifted, so use the ovens as much as possible and close the covers promptly when not using the plates.

THE WARMING PLATE: (4 oven Aga only) This oblong plate is a useful spot for placing hot baking tins straight from the oven, very handy for serving from, and for warming the tea pot or sauce boats.

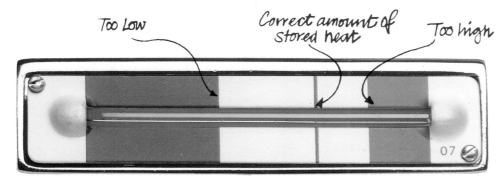

Too Low   Correct amount of stored heat   Too high

The Heat Indicator.

2 ▪ FOR TWO OVEN AGA OWNERS

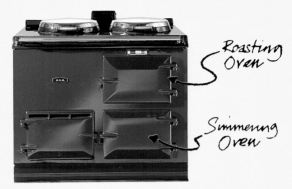

Roasting Oven

Simmering Oven

THE ROASTING OVEN: I bet when your Aga was delivered, like me, you asked your Aga Distributor the temperature of the Roasting Oven. It is very hot, hotter than the hottest setting of an ordinary oven – wonderful for getting crisp pork crackling, for browning dishes topped with cheese and for cooking the everyday things like pies and sausages.

The top of the oven is the hottest, so just right for Yorkshire pudding, grilled foods, puff pastry and savouries, whereas roast meats cook best in the middle and roast and baked potatoes, quiches and bread, are best cooked on or near the floor of the oven.

Unlike an ordinary cooker the floor of the Roasting Oven is hot so it can be used for shallow frying in a cast iron dish, or for browning the bottom of quiches or plate pies.

Consult the recipes that follow for details, but I find that for most pies, crumbles, sponge-topped puddings and some less tender roasts, start cooking in the Roasting Oven, cook until golden – in the case of the meat until crisp and brown – then transfer to the Simmering Oven till cooked through. You can always slip a roast back into the Roasting Oven to crisp up the top.

To create a moderate oven simply use the cold plain shelf and the Aga Cake Baker as described later.

Excess moisture and cooking odours are drawn into the flue or vent pipe, leaving little or no kitchen smells.

THE SIMMERING OVEN: This has a fairly gentle heat with the top of the Simmering Oven the hottest part.

Almost without exception everything that is cooked in the Simmering Oven must be started elsewhere, either in the Roasting Oven or on the hotplates. For example a casserole can be brought to the boil on the Boiling Plate, covered and transferred to the Simmering Plate for 5 or 10 minutes then put in the Simmering Oven. Likewise use the oven method for root vegetables, as described in the chapter on vegetables. Wonderful stocks for soups are also produced in this oven.

Rich fruit cakes cook long and slow in the Simmering Oven, as do excellent meringues. No need to start cooking elsewhere first.

Your new Aga comes complete with one large and one half-size roasting tin, two grill racks, two oven grid shelves, a plain shelf, a wire brush and the Aga toaster.

THE ROASTING TINS I use these not just for meat but to hold casseroles or spillable dishes like fruit pies. They are extremely useful for cooking large traybake cakes, lasagne, moussaka etc. for party quantities. The large tin takes a 28lb (13kg) turkey, the half-size tin is for smaller roasts, potatoes etc. The large tin can also be used to protect small items such as little cakes or biscuits when cooking in the Roasting Oven.

Halfsize Roasting tin

Large Roasting tin

Cold plain shelf

Oven Grid shelf

Aga ovens have runners on the sides for the tins to slide directly along, plus non-tilt lugs near the front, to stop them tilting too far.

THE GRILL RACKS are made to be used in either of two positions in the roasting tins. The high position is for grilling bacon, sausage, fish etc at the top of the Roasting Oven. The lower is for roasting meat and poultry. Another use for them is for cake cooling racks.

THE GRID SHELF is designed to be non-tilt, so when pulled forward it cannot come right out. This shelf fits all ovens – I usually keep it in the Roasting Oven on the lowest set of runners as this is the position I use most. Extra shelves, grid or plain are available from your local Aga Distributor.

THE PLAIN SHELF fits all the ovens and is used firstly to cut off the top heat from the Roasting Oven (mostly in the two oven Aga) preventing food getting too brown, i.e. biscuits, cakes and custards. Slide it onto the second or third set of runners from the top, above the food being cooked on the grid shelf below. Immediately after use take the plain shelf out of the oven and store with the roasting tins so that it is always cold and ready to use. The second use is as a baking sheet for biscuits, bread rolls and scones etc.

The Aga Toaster

THE AGA TOASTER looks like a big wire ping pong bat and works brilliantly. It's a joy to use. Sandwich the slices of bread – up to four at time, any thickness you like – between the two frames. Place the toaster directly on the Boiling Plate and allow the toast to brown, then turn over. Use the toaster for crumpets, toasted sandwiches and teacakes too. For quicker toast, close the lid. N.B. For new bread, heat the toaster on the plate first, this prevents the bread sticking.

▄4▄ FOR FOUR OVEN AGA OWNERS

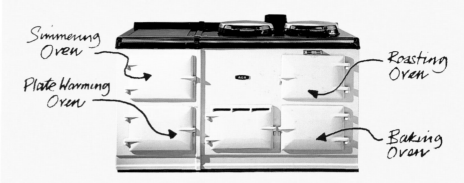

THE ROASTING OVEN: Hotter than the hottest setting of an ordinary oven the Roasting Oven is wonderful for getting crisp pork crackling, for browning dishes topped with cheese and for cooking the everyday things like pies and sausages.

The top of the oven is the hottest – just right for Yorkshire pudding, grilled foods, puff pastry and savouries, whereas roast meats cook best in the middle, and roast and baked potatoes, quiches and bread, are best cooked on or near, the floor of the oven.

Unlike an ordinary cooker the floor of the Roasting Oven is hot so it can be used for shallow frying in a cast iron dish or for browning the bottom of quiches and plate pies.

Excess moisture and cooking odours are drawn into the flue or vent pipe leaving little or no kitchen smells.

BAKING OVEN: Its moderate temperature is ideal for cakes, biscuits and other foods not requiring a high temperature. Meat can be roasted here too.

As with the Roasting Oven, the top is hotter than the bottom and this will affect the positioning of various foods. For instance small cakes, lasagne, fatless sponges towards the top; baked fish, crumbles, brandy snaps, roulades around the centre and Victoria sandwiches, shortbread etc. towards the bottom.

Many items cooked in the Roasting Oven can be cooked in the Baking Oven, but for a longer time.

THE SIMMERING OVEN: This has a fairly gentle heat.

Almost without exception everything that is cooked in the Simmering Oven must be started elsewhere, either in the Roasting Oven or on the hotplates. For example a casserole can be brought to the boil on the Boiling Plate, covered and transferred to the Simmering Plate for 5 or 10 minutes then put in the Simmering Oven. Likewise use the oven method for root vegetables, as described in the chapter on vegetables. Wonderful stocks for soups are also produced in this oven.

Rich fruit cakes cook long and slow in the Simmering Oven, as do excellent meringues. No need to start cooking elsewhere first.

PLATE WARMING OVEN: As the name suggests this is ideal for heating plates and serving dishes. However it can also be used for resting joints before carving, holding sauces and keeping covered meals warm for the late-comer.

Although cooler than the Simmering Oven it may be used in somewhat similar ways.

THE AGA WITH MODULE OPTION: The Module is a conventional cooker in the Aga style, which is purchased and installed only with your new Aga cooker. This has a separate instruction booklet and is used as other cookers.

When cooking on an Aga, a good pan with a heavy base is essential; the Aga range is recommended. Anyone who has previously coped with flimsy pans with warped bases will now discover how much better it is to cook with the right equipment. You will see the illustration showing how the transfer of heat from the flat Boiling Plate is very effective as long as the whole base of the pan or kettle is in as perfect a contact as possible.

If you feel anxious about the expense of buying a whole new set of cookware, may I make two points. First, ask your Aga specialist to check your existing pots and pans. Solid cast-iron casseroles may well be useable and if you have good quality pans with a thick base you may be able to use these too. I use good quality cake tins for sponge sandwiches etc. You can also use Pyrex and earthenware dishes in the Aga ovens. My second point is that when you have invested in the Aga pans you have virtually made a one-off purchase which can last you the rest of your cooking days! They often do end up as hand-me-downs many years later.

The Aga pans certainly have many more advantages apart from their ability to boil very quickly. They can be used on both the hot-plates and in the ovens.

They have flat top lids for stacking in the Simmering Oven or for storage; rounded corners for easy cleaning and an attractive finish.

The items of the cast-iron Aga cookware with ground bases are for maximum efficiency and are finished in the same vitreous enamel as your Aga with a choice of matching or contrasting colours. They can also be used on the hotplates or in the ovens.

My own choice of Aga pans was:

The largest Aga pan (20 pints/11 litres) that goes into the Simmering Oven - brilliant for preserving, bulk cooking of casseroles, batches of Bolognaise sauce, and good to use for vegetables when you have a crowd. Such a good buy as it has a lid too.

Two large shallow stacking pans (6 pints/3.5 litres) for steaming vegetables, casseroles, sauces and umpteen other uses.

Two small stacking pans (1¾ pints/1 litre) for sauces, boiling eggs, reheating small amounts, and boiling milk.

One deep pan (3½ pints/2 litres) for boiling green vegetables and steaming puddings.

An Aga kettle. It's amazingly fast.

The Aga Cake Baker (for 2 oven Aga cooker) for large cakes. Don't forget you can use the pan lid as a 9 pint (5 litre) saucepan.

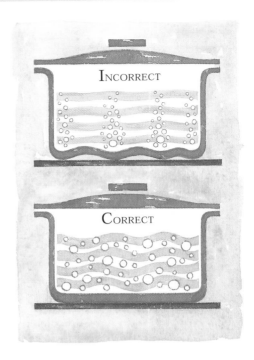

The Aga grill pan.

The Aga cast-iron gratin dish, an ideal shape for frying trout or for scalloped potatoes or baking fish stakes.

The Aga omelette pan.

The oval and round Aga casseroles which can be used on the hotplates before transferring to the oven.

The Aga Grill Pan

Although most grilling can take place at the top of the Roasting Oven I find steaks are best cooked in the Aga grill pan on the Boiling Plate. This method of intense under heat grilling, just like the barbecue, gives a succulent steak, because the natural juices are sealed into the meat, not lost in the pan.

The Aga grill pan is made of cast-iron for evenness of cooking and heat retention. It has a ridged base to intensify the heat.

To get the most effective use, gradually heat up the grill pan until it is really hot. Put the meat into the grill pan and press down with a wooden spatula, to ensure full contact with the base. Allow 2 minutes each side or longer if you prefer your steak well done.

An alternative way to use the grill pan is on the floor of the Roasting Oven. Don't forget to use an oven cloth or pan handle cover to remove it from the oven as the handle will be hot!

The grill pan has a strong surface so put to soak after using or boil up hot water with a detergent, brush the ridges well with a nylon brush and rinse thoroughly.

The Aga Cake Baker

FOR USE WITH TWO-OVEN MODELS

This Aga pan creates a moderate oven within the Roasting Oven to bake cakes requiring over 45 minutes cooking time, easily and conveniently.

It consists of a deep 9 pints (5 litre) pan and lid together with a cake rack and three sizes of cake tin, 6in., 7in. and 8in. (15, 18, 20cm).

The pan and lid should be placed on the floor of the Roasting Oven to preheat whilst the cake is being made. Line the cake tin in the normal way and place in the cake mixture, put the cake tin in the rack making sure it sits level. Take the hot pan out of the oven and lower the cake tin, in its rack, into the pan. Replace the lid and put back onto the floor of the Roasting Oven.

If you are converting a recipe, generally cook for a shorter time than in an ordinary oven.

The cake baker pan and lid can also double up as a saucepan for steamed puddings or vegetables, or as a stew pan. It's a versatile extra for your Aga.

The three cake tins and the cake rack slide neatly into the cake baker for easy storage.

I strongly recommend that, if possible, you make room for the family to eat in the kitchen – the Aga becomes the centre of the house, everyone wants to congregate around its friendly warmth.

I think it is essential for anyone with an Aga to consider how it will fit in with other kitchen equipment. For instance, I would not be without my food processor or my freezer. You will find that the Aga with its special qualities, has a great deal to offer – and this has a bearing on how you use the rest of the kitchen.

Although you bought your Aga for its cooking excellence you will find there are many other benefits of owning an Aga.

Keeping Food Hot

If you like entertaining, owning an Aga will make this even more of a pleasure; you can complete the meal and leave it in the Simmering Oven while you join your guests for drinks.

Use the plain shelf in the Simmering Oven to give you an extra level. Remember to position the course you need to serve first at the front, things for later on at the back. If you have several sauces and want to keep them hot for a long time, cover, then stand them in the Simmering Oven.

Family Celebrations

The Simmering Oven is so useful whenever you want to cook a turkey for lunch – at Easter and Christmas or whenever you have a family get-together.

The bird cooks in the Simmering Oven overnight for a slow-cooked succulent meat with a lovely golden-brown appearance. Instead of the Christmas morning rush to get the turkey on, you can enjoy opening your stocking in the calm knowledge that the Aga is looking after the turkey for you.

A large Christmas fruit cake also cooks to perfection in the Simmering Oven. Also cook the Christmas pudding here as the kitchen will not get steamed up.

Airing & Drying – with the help of the Aga

Because the Aga provides a steady dry warmth, the kitchen can become a really effective airing cupboard! You may consider installing one of the ceiling-hung wooden rail dryers in a farmhouse kitchen; these have pulleys enabling them to be whisked up out of the way, making use of the warm air at the top of the room.

I have a wooden shelf running along the wall above the Aga and I hook clothes on hangers to air and just tidy them away if friends are staying or we are entertaining in the kitchen.

Ironing – a hated chore

I use my Aga to cut down on the amount of ironing I have to do. The following ideas are for using the chrome lid of the Simmering Plate – not the Boiling Plate. Please be careful to ensure that clothes do not drape over the handles of the insulated lids and take care not to obstruct the ventilation slots in the left hand door, if putting items on the chrome rail.

Football shirts, sweat shirts, tea towels, bath and hand towels, socks: spin then fold and press creases firmly by hand and put to press on the Simmering Plate, turn once – looks perfect!

Sheets: wash, spin then fold and hang over the chrome rail at the front of the Aga. When almost dry transfer to the lid of the Simmering Plate for the final pressing.

Help with the drying up

Many cooking items are too big or too odd shaped to get into the dishwasher for washing and drying effectively. Your Aga with its constant warmth can help.

Baking trays, graters, the food processor blade – any or all of these, when washed, can be stood on tea towels at the back of the Aga to get thoroughly dry. It is a helpful anti-rust precaution too.

Drying Herbs and Flowers

The gentle dry warmth rising from your Aga is perfect for drying flowers and herbs. Hung in neat bunches they can look very attractive and add a lovely subtle aroma to the whole kitchen.

House Warming and the Aga

On really cold nights leave the kitchen door open. You will be amazed how the warmth given out by the Aga will help keep the chill off the entire house.

The Aga and the Freezer

The Aga and the freezer go hand-in-hand. Certainly a microwave oven is the fastest way of thawing food from frozen, but the steady warmth of the Aga can do this more quickly than you would think. For instance: If you need bread for a couple of slices of toast, stand your frozen unsliced loaf on end behind the Boiling Plate. In 15 minutes or so you can cut off slices.

It is important that joints, and especially poultry, are allowed to thaw thoroughly either at room temperature or in the fridge.

Softening & Melting by the Aga

When foods need to be softened, or when bowls need to be warmed, use the work surface beside the Aga. Butter from the fridge softens quickly here.

Stand a bowl and beater here for 15-30 minutes before whisking up a sponge or roulade, or creaming fat and sugar. Break chocolate into a bowl and leave it on the Aga surface behind the Simmering Plate to melt. Let meat stand beside the Aga for 10-15 minutes to come to room temperature before cooking, do not use it from the fridge cold.

To make jam spreadable for Victoria sandwiches stand the jar in the Simmering Oven, or if time allows soften slowly in the jar standing at the back of the Boiling Plate for 1 hour.

9 out of 10 pets prefer Aga

Just like humans, dogs and cats find the Aga a joy, they congregate around it.

To cook their food: bring bones and meat, just covered with water to the boil on the Boiling Plate. Transfer to the Simmering Oven until the meat is tender. I use the cooking liquid as well, to moisten dog biscuits. Never throw away bread crusts, or the tail end of a loaf, cut them up and put them on a plate or in the small roasting tin and dry in the Simmering Oven or on the back of the Aga then use instead of dog meal. Save bacon rinds. Leave in a tin in the Simmering Oven till crisp and then put out for the birds – that is if you can do so before the children eat them!

TIMETABLE FOR ROAST BEEF

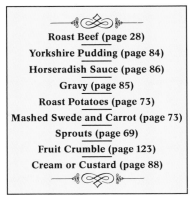

Roast Beef (page 28)
Yorkshire Pudding (page 84)
Horseradish Sauce (page 86)
Gravy (page 85)
Roast Potatoes (page 73)
Mashed Swede and Carrot (page 73)
Sprouts (page 69)
Fruit Crumble (page 123)
Cream or Custard (page 88)

First thing in the morning, prepare crumble and put to one side. Prepare vegetables. Mix Yorkshire Pudding. Slide cold shelf into the Simmering Oven to give a centre shelf. Stand gravy boat at back of Aga to warm.

10.30 Cook Crumble.

11.15 Bring potatoes to the boil, drain. Bring carrot and swede to the boil. Simmer 5 minutes, drain, then transfer, covered, to the Simmering Oven for about 1 hour. Remove crumble and put to one side.

11.25 Put small rack at one end of large roasting tin. Put meat on rack. Season. Put fat or oil in tin ready for potatoes. Lift tin to floor of Roasting Oven – meat towards back of oven.

11.30 Put potatoes in fat in roasting tin. Turn potatoes from time to time.

12.30 For 8 Individual Yorkshire Puddings. Put a knob of fat into each pudding pan. Heat in Roasting Oven then pour in batter. Cook for about 15 minutes on 3rd set of runners. Arrange on ovenproof serving dish, put to one side. Put plates and serving dishes to warm in Simmering Oven on shelf and on oven floor.

12.35 Bring water to boil for sprouts and cook then drain. Put in serving dish in Simmering Oven. Remove carrots and swedes, mash, season, add butter and then put in serving dish in Simmering Oven.

12.40 Remove meat onto serving dish to rest with roast potatoes. Put in Simmering Oven.

12.50 Make gravy. Reheat Yorkshires for 5 minutes on floor of Roasting Oven. Put crumble in Simmering Oven to reheat, with pudding plates.

1pm Serve lunch.

ROAST BEEF

To cook lunch for eight people I roast a boned forerib 5lb (2½kg) in weight. It is cooked 15 minutes to the lb (450g) – i.e. 1¼ hours. The result is pink in the middle. If you like it very rare do 12 minutes to the lb (450g) or well cooked, a little longer. If you are cooking a very small joint under 2lb (1 kilo) add 15 minutes to the normal roasting time.

THE YORKSHIRE PUDDING If you wish, you can very satisfactorily cook the Yorkshire Puddings ahead, first thing in the morning, then reheat them in the Roasting Oven for 5-10 minutes before serving. I do mine in deep individual Yorkshire pudding pans, four to the tin. Two of these go on the grid shelf and the two tins take ½pt (300ml) liquid, 4oz (100g) flour etc. quantity. The small half-sized roasting tin takes this quantity too – cook for 15 minutes longer.

ROAST PORK

To cook lunch for six people I roast a piece of pork, boned leg, 4½lb (2kg) in weight. It is cooked 25 minutes to the 1lb (450g) totalling 1¾ hours. The result is perfect and still moist, with plenty of crispy crackling. There should be enough left over to serve cold the following day.

The stuffing quantities are sufficient for the half-sized roasting tin.

ROAST LAMB

Roast lamb is usually cooked on the bone. Follow the timetable for roast pork but alter the meat roasting time to 15-20 minutes per lb (depending on whether you like lamb pink or well done). Obviously change the vegetables to use the best of the season. Perhaps serve apple pie as the pudding (see page 119). Cook before the roast as with the fruit crumble in the Sunday Lunch Roast Beef menu.

TIMETABLE FOR ROAST PORK

Roast Pork (page 28)
Stuffing (page 84)
Apple Sauce (page 85)
Gravy (page 85)
Roast Potatoes (page 73)
Red Cabbage (page 80)
Runner Beans (page 69)
Treacle Tart (page 119)
Proper Custard (page 88)

First thing in the morning, make treacle tart, put to one side. Prepare vegetables, then prepare apples for apple sauce, adding a squeeze of lemon juice. Prepare red cabbage. Prepare stuffing and put in half-sized roasting tin then slide cold shelf into Simmering Oven to make a centre shelf. Stand gravy boat at back of Aga to warm.

10.30 Cook Treacle Tart and put to one side when cooked. Parboil potatoes for 3-4 minutes, then drain.

10.50 Prepare meat for roasting.

11.00 Put small rack at one end of large roasting tin. Put meat on rack. Season. Lift tin onto 3rd set of runners in Roasting Oven.

11.25 Put fat in tin ready for potatoes.

11.30 Put potatoes in fat in roasting tin and transfer to floor of Roasting Oven. Turn them from time to time.

11.45 Bring red cabbage to boil, then transfer to floor of Simmering Oven.

11.55 Make custard. Put in jug at back of Aga to keep warm.

12.00 Prepare Apple Sauce and place pan in Simmering Oven.

12.15 Cook stuffing in Roasting Oven with tin on 2nd set of runners.

12.30 Transfer Apple Sauce to dish. Keep warm in Simmering Oven with plates and serving dishes.

12.35 Cook beans. Transfer to the Simmering Oven in serving dish.

12.45 Transfer meat onto serving dish with potatoes, then make gravy.

12.50 Finish cabbage, check seasoning, transfer to serving dish. Transfer stuffing to dish in Simmering Oven.

1pm Serve lunch. Put Treacle Tart in Simmering Oven to re-heat together with pudding plates and custard.

I love the shining glossy top of my Aga so I am careful when lifting pans from the plates. Don't drag pans off to one side or gradually the top surface will be scratched and will become matt and dull. Do remember to explain this to anyone helping you in the kitchen. Keep a damp cloth near enough to be able to wipe up spills quickly, especially if you are cooking something like jam or chutney.

Aga Cleaning

This is something I enjoy enormously about the Aga – the fact that there is so very little cleaning to do. Anyone who has grappled with cleaning a greasy ordinary oven will be delighted to hear that this is now a thing of the past when you own an Aga.

OVENS

The continuous heat in the ovens means that food spills carbonise and these can eventually be brushed out. If you are an experienced cook and do not spill much, quite honestly years may go by before you even need to brush out the ovens. I prefer to use an old dust pan and brush. The wire brush provided helps to rid the oven of any burnt on spills. To spring-clean inside the ovens remove the shelf if in position. Use the wire brush provided to clean out the sides, roof and base of cast-iron ovens, working quickly. All very easy.

TOP AND FRONT

The Aga is a wonderful strongly made cooker, it will keep its shine providing it is cherished. Wipe over the Aga top surface and front with a warm soapy cloth and polish up with a dry cloth. If milk or fruit juice, or anything containing acid is spilt on the Aga, wipe off immediately.

Do not use abrasive cleaning materials. If there is a mark to remove which will not come off with the warm, damp cloth as above, then try a proprietary mild cream cleaner. If after many years use there is a build up of a greasy deposit – and this should, really, never happen if you keep to the wiping programme – then I advise you to use a soap-filled wire pad very lightly and carefully as this should remove the grease but not the enamelled surface itself. Wipe off any streaks on the front plate around the oven doors. To spring-clean doors, first lay a towel on a strong work surface, then using oven gloves, lift the door off the hinges, lie it on the towel with the inside uppermost. Leave it to cool a little then clean it with a soap-filled wire pad. Turn the door over and wipe the front with a warm soapy cloth, rinse and wipe with a plain wet cloth. When dry, I polish with a silicone polish. Replace the door. Never immerse the doors in water as they contain insulating material. Because they are continuously hot the hotplates will carbonise most food spills.

HOTPLATES: The wire brush is provided to keep the hotplates clear of any burnt on particles, which would interfere with the contact between the base of the saucepan and the hotplate.

The inside linings of the insulated lids can be wiped over with a damp soapy cloth or use a cream cleaner. For more stubborn marks use a soap-filled pad. Open the lids and allow them to cool a little before cleaning, a quick way that the heat from the hotplate can be deflected downwards is to carefully place the grid shelf over the hotplate with the cold plain shelf on top, whilst cleaning takes place.

THE INSULATED COVERS: these lids are shiny and if you want to rest the hot roasting tin on them, even for a moment, always slip a cloth underneath first, this avoids them getting scratched. A word of warning, do brief the family, and any other friends that help, not to put roasting tins or saucepans on the lids. To clean, wipe over with a damp soapy cloth, followed by a wet cloth then polish up with a clean dry cloth.

Servicing

To keep your Aga running efficiently it is recommended that it is regularly serviced by your local Aga Authorised Distributor: refer to the operating instructions supplied with your particular model, or contact your Aga Distributor. Your Authorised Distributor has specially trained staff and carries the full range of genuine Aga spares.

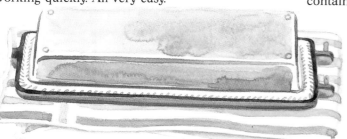

When I am doing demonstrations, or broadcasting, around the country, many of the same questions crop up from Aga owners. Here are just a few.

Q **Should you switch the Aga off when you are going away for a weekend?**

A I leave the Aga switched on if I'm away just for the weekend. The stored heat system is so efficient that this is perfectly safe, the cooker will not overheat. But I do save money by turning the central heating off. The Aga being left on means there is still a source of gentle warmth in the house, keeping it aired and warm. This is a boon when I am away for a winter weekend but you won't be surprised to hear that it is often useful in summer too, when the weather turns cold or damp – or both! With water heating models, turn to low or pilot.

Q **Away for a week or more – turn the Aga off or not?**

A Although Aga generally recommend extinguishing the cooker during periods of extended absence, if I am going away for a week I turn the control down and then turn it back up again to its original position on my return.

For two weeks, or more, I would really leave it on very low simply because I so like to come back to the warmth which somehow seems to welcome us back home. (Unfortunately this does not apply to the solid fuel model).

Q **Doesn't your kitchen get very hot leaving the Aga on in summer?**

A Strangely enough, I have never found this. Of course with the sort of family life I lead, children or dogs are constantly coming in and out of the kitchen which we use as a living room as well. It is also a fairly big, airy room.

Q **Is the Aga expensive to run since it is on day and night, seven days a week?**

A The exact consumption will be supplied by your Aga Distributor for you to judge this. In my experience I haven't noticed an expensive new way of life – quite the contrary I find any extra expense is amply rewarded by the warmth provided in my kitchen.

Q **I have many cherished family recipes and other recipes from cookery books. They usually have different temperatures for baking and cooking. How do I adapt them for an Aga?**

A Quite easily. Check with a similar recipe in this book and adapt accordingly. It is easier when you haven't knobs to twiddle and adjust. Of course, with a 4-oven Aga you have the advantage of a moderate oven which is right for baking sponges for instance. But I cook very successfully with a 2-oven Aga using the cold plain shelf or the Aga Cake Baker. Check with my recipes to see how the cold shelf can be put in above a sponge cake to cut off top heat in the Roasting Oven, creating a moderate oven beneath.

To batch bake, you will need to cool the plain shelf before re-use. To do this plunge in cold water, or prop up outside – it cools in a very short time.

Q **Can I have my Aga integrated into a fully fitted kitchen?**

A Yes, and I think a gap is to be avoided – it's a dirt trap as some spills are unavoidable and cleaning a narrow space is so difficult, but I and plenty of friends have kitchen cupboards built up to the Aga and have experienced no problems; do tell your designer this. Do work out the best use of the cupboards next to the Aga as they will be warm ones. Divided vertical storage for the roasting tin, cold shelf and baking tins is useful to have near the Aga. It keeps tins dry and takes up little space. I've found it is an ideal place to store tea towels as they are kept aired. It is nice, too, for tea, sugar, coffee. My jar of caster sugar with a vanilla pod in it is ready for baking and soufflé making too, as there is no fear of these becoming clogged by damp.

USING THE AGA BOOK

I hope that this book will help you to enjoy the very special culinary pleasures of an Aga. Like all good guides it sets out to make your path as easy as possible. So there are symbols to denote cooking on the 2 oven and 4 oven Aga so that you can see at a glance which applies to you.

Cooking and timing in a 2 oven Aga

Cooking and timing in a 4 oven Aga

The recipes are in imperial and metric measures. Do not mix the two as conversions are not exact.

The runners are counted from the top of the oven downwards.

Where flour is in a recipe this means plain, unless otherwise stated.

As you know Aga cookers are available in gas, oil, electric and solid fuel models. Although they all work on exactly the same principle timings may vary a little, depending on the flue, installation and model.

SOUPS & STARTERS

WONDERFUL SUMMER SOUP P.19 · CARROT AND ORANGE SOUP P.20 · CHICKEN AND WATERCRESS TERRINE P.26

A good soup is one of the quickest, most satisfying ways I know of conjuring up an instant meal or a delicious first course. Stocks can happily simmer away in the Aga for hours (without steaming up the kitchen or creating all-pervading smells in the house), then if you like they can be frozen until you need them.

Aga-baked terrines and pâtés are wonderful. Rich and moist, they make a fabulous light lunch served with freshly baked granary rolls or crisp Aga toast.

INGREDIENTS

GOOD BEEF STOCK

**as many sawn beef marrow bones as
you can get into your largest pan
water to cover
salt and black pepper
2 onions, quartered
1 carrot
2 sticks celery
sprig of thyme, bay leaf and a few
parsley stalks**

INGREDIENTS

LIGHT STOCK

**chicken, turkey or veal bones
2 onions
1 carrot
2 sticks celery
water to cover
salt and black pepper
sprig of thyme, bay leaf and a few
parsley stalks**

GAME STOCK

**carcass of game birds
giblets
2 onions
2 sticks celery
water to cover
salt and black pepper
sprig of thyme, bayleaf
and a few parsley stalks**

INGREDIENTS

FISH STOCK

**1lb (450g) white fish bones and
trimmings
salt and freshly ground
black pepper
1 onion, peeled and quartered
1 stick celery
water to cover**

INGREDIENTS

FAMILY STOCK

**left over joint bones, cooked
chicken carcasses
left over root vegetables
water to cover
salt and freshly ground
black pepper**

STOCKPOT

One of the great joys of an Aga is always having stock on hand as it freezes well.

THE STOCKPOT AND STOCK. *Use the largest* Aga pan you have with a well fitting lid. Make overnight in the Simmering Oven, the gentle, controlled heat will extract all the goodness from the bones. After straining off the stock, the bones can be thrown away.

WHICH BONES TO USE. *Best are* beef, veal, poultry and game including all the giblets. You can use non-fatty pork, lamb and mutton bones for broth. Don't include the following in stock: starchy vegetables, mixed raw and cooked bones (use for separate stocks), extra fat, cooked green vegetables – they become overcooked, especially cabbage and sprouts.

GOOD BEEF STOCK

Roasting Oven: put the bones into the large Aga roasting tin. Cook in the Roasting Oven for about 45 minutes to brown the bones. Lift out of the oven and transfer to your largest pan, add the remaining ingredients. Bring to the boil and simmer for 10 minutes.

Simmering Oven: cover with a lid and transfer to the floor of the oven overnight. Next morning, skim off any fat and strain.

LIGHT STOCK OR GAME STOCK

For the method see Good Beef Stock – without browning the bones first.

FISH STOCK

Choose the bones and trimmings of white fish, avoid strong oily fish.

Wash bones and trimmings, add other ingredients. Bring to the boil, skim. Bring to the boil again. Cover.

Simmering Oven: transfer to the floor of the oven for 1 hour. Strain. Cool and store covered in the fridge for up to 3 days.

FAMILY STOCK

No need to brown the bones in the Roasting Oven for this. Add water and continue as for Good Beef Stock but cook in the Simmering Oven just for 2 hours.

VEGETABLE STOCK

Good to use for sauces to accompany vegetables. Remember vegetable stock does not keep well. Use within three days. Ingredients could include root vegetables, though not too much of the strongly flavoured ones like swede, parsnip, carrot and leeks. Also, the outer leaves of green vegetables could be added for the last 20 minutes. Roughly chop the vegetables, cover with water, season and bring to the boil. Simmer 5 minutes then cover with a lid.

Simmering Oven: transfer to the floor of the oven for about 3 hours. Strain and use.

TO KEEP STOCK FRESH

Stock keeps for up to a week in the refrigerator or 3 months if kept in the freezer. Take from the fridge and bring to the boil for 5 minutes every other day then cool and return to the fridge.

WATERCRESS SOUP

*Most watercress soups are based on potatoes, this one has more onion instead,
I find it lighter.*

SERVES 6

Heat the butter and oil in a large pan and gently fry the onion for about 10
minutes until soft and transparent. Sprinkle in flour and cook for a minute, add the
stock a little at a time and bring to the boil, stirring until thickened. Wash the
watercress, removing any limp pieces, and reserve a few of the brightest leaves to
chop as garnish just before serving. Add the watercress to the pan with the
seasoning. Bring back to the boil, cover and simmer gently for about 5 minutes.
Reduce the soup to a purée in a processor or blender then return to the pan.
Blend in milk. Slowly bring back to the boil, stirring. Taste to check seasoning and
serve with the reserved chopped watercress sprinkled on top.

INGREDIENTS
1oz (25g) butter
1 tablespoon sunflower oil
1 large onion, chopped
1½ tablespoons flour
1 pint (600ml) light stock
2 bunches watercress
salt and freshly ground black
pepper
1 pint (600ml) milk

QUICK VEGETABLE SOUP

*Even though in the recipe I have put finely sliced, if you have a processor it is so
quick and easy using the blade. If you have no homemade stock, add a 14oz
(397g) can of chopped tomatoes and chicken stock cubes.*

SERVES 8-10

Soften onion, carrots and celery in the fat for about 5 minutes, tossing
constantly. Add mushrooms and stock. Bring to the boil and simmer for about 5
minutes. Season to taste and serve piping hot.

INGREDIENTS
1 onion, finely sliced
4 carrots, finely sliced
5 sticks celery, finely sliced
a little butter or chicken dripping
2oz (50g) button mushrooms,
finely sliced
3 pints (1.75lt) good stock
salt and freshly ground
black pepper

to garnish
a little single cream

RED LENTIL SOUP

Buy lentils which do not require soaking overnight before they are used.

SERVES 4

Heat the butter and oil in the deep pan and quickly fry the onion, carrot
and celery for about 5 minutes until the onion is soft. Add the stock, lentils and
seasoning, bring to the boil then cover and simmer for 5 minutes.

2▮
▮4▮ Simmering Oven: stand the pan on the floor of the oven and leave to
cook for about 45 minutes or until the lentils are tender.

Reduce the soup to a purée in a processor or blender then return to the pan.
Reheat until piping hot. Taste to check seasoning and serve with croûtons.

INGREDIENTS
1oz (25g) butter
1 tablespoon sunflower oil
1 large onion, sliced
1 large carrot, sliced
2 sticks celery, sliced
1½ pints (900ml) light stock
4oz (100g) red lentils
salt
1 level teaspoon paprika pepper
good pinch cayenne pepper

WONDERFUL SUMMER SOUP

*Delicious served hot or cold. Take care not to overcook the soup otherwise it will
lose its bright green colour.*

SERVES 6

Heat the butter and oil in a deep pan and gently fry the onion for about 10
minutes until soft. Roughly chop the lettuce and add to the pan with the
watercress, sorrel and spinach. Cook for a few more moments then stir in the flour,
cook for a minute then gradually blend in the stock. Bring to the boil, stirring until
thickened. Season to taste. Cover and simmer for about 10 minutes or until the
watercress is tender.
Reduce the soup to a purée in a processor or blender then return to the pan. Stir
in the milk and reheat until piping hot to serve. Taste to check seasoning and serve
with a swirl of cream.

INGREDIENTS
1oz (25g) butter
1 tablespoon sunflower oil
1 onion, chopped
1 lettuce, or outside leaves
of a lettuce
1 bunch watercress
about 14 sorrel leaves
a handful of fresh spinach
2oz (50g) flour
1½ pints (900ml) light stock
salt and freshly ground
black pepper
½ pint (300ml) milk

to garnish
a little single cream

1oz (25g) butter
2 tablespoons sunflower oil
8oz (225g) green peppers, seeded
and diced
2 onions, chopped
1½oz (40g) flour
¾ pint (450ml) light stock
salt and freshly ground black
pepper
¾ pint (450ml) milk

to garnish

a little single cream

1oz (25g) butter
1 tablespoon sunflower oil
2lb (900g) carrots, scrubbed and
sliced
2lb (900g) onions, sliced
3 pints (1.75lt) light stock
salt and freshly ground
black pepper
6oz (175g) carton concentrated
frozen orange juice

to garnish

2 tablespoons freshly chopped
parsley

2oz (50g) beef dripping
1lb (450g) onions, finely chopped
2 level teaspoons sugar
1oz (25g) flour
2 pints (1.2lt) beef stock
salt and freshly ground
black pepper

to serve

4 slices French bread
2oz (50g) Gruyère cheese, grated

GREEN PEPPER SOUP

It is important to sieve the soup after processing in order to remove the skin.

SERVES 4

Heat the butter and oil in a deep pan and add the peppers and onions and cook gently for about 5 minutes on the Simmering Plate, stirring occasionally. Stir in the flour and cook for a minute. Blend in the stock and bring to the boil, stirring until thickened. Season well, then cover and simmer for 5 minutes.

2▪ Simmering Oven: stand the pan on the floor of the oven and cook for
▪4▪ about an hour or until the vegetables are tender.

Reduce the soup to a purée in a processor or blender, then sieve back into the pan and add the milk. Bring to the boil, taste and check seasoning and serve with a swirl of cream.

CARROT AND ORANGE SOUP

Served with garlic bread it also makes a light special lunch when the weather is gruesome.

SERVES 8 GENEROUS PORTIONS

Heat the butter and oil in a large pan on the Simmering Plate. Sauté the carrots and onions in the pan with the lid on for about 10 minutes. Pour on the stock, season and bring to the boil. Cover and simmer for 5 minutes.

2▪ Simmering Oven: stand the pan on the floor of the oven and leave to
▪4▪ cook for about 45 minutes until just tender.

Reduce the soup to a purée in a processor or blender then return to the pan. Stir in the orange juice, reheat until piping hot. Taste to check seasoning and garnish with chopped parsley.

FRENCH ONION SOUP

Use good beef dripping; adding any sediment to the soup later. If dripping is not available use butter and oil instead.

SERVES 4

Heat the dripping in a deep pan on the Simmering Plate, add the onions and sugar and fry gently, stirring occasionally until golden brown. Be careful not to let them burn otherwise the soup will taste bitter. This will take about 10 minutes.

Stir in the flour and cook for a minute, then gradually blend in the stock and bring to the boil, stirring until thickened. Season and cover with a lid, simmer for 5 minutes.

2▪ Simmering Oven: stand the pan on the floor of the oven and leave to
▪4▪ cook for about 40 minutes. Taste and check seasoning.

Toast the bread on one side, then sprinkle the cheese on the untoasted side and put on the grid shelf in the Roasting Oven to melt. Place slice of bread in each soup bowl then pour over the soup. Serve at once.

Soup à la Reine

*This is a superb soup and no-one would ever guess it was based
on the humble parsnip.*

Serves 6

Heat the butter and oil in a deep pan and add the parsnips, garlic and onion and fry gently on the Simmering Plate for about 10 minutes. Stir in the flour and the curry powder and cook for a minute, then add the stock and seasoning and bring to the boil, stirring. Cover and simmer 5 minutes.

2 / 4 Simmering Oven: stand the pan on the floor of the oven and leave to cook for about 40 minutes or until the parsnips are tender.

Reduce the soup to a purée in a processor or blender then return to the pan. Reheat and taste to check seasoning. Serve with a swirl of cream and a few snipped chives sprinkled on top.

INGREDIENTS

**2oz (50g) butter
1 tablespoon sunflower oil
1lb (450g) parsnips, cubed
1 fat clove garlic, crushed
1 onion, chopped
1oz (25g) flour
1 rounded teaspoon curry powder
2 pints (1.2lt) good stock
salt and freshly ground
black pepper**

to garnish
**¼ pint (150ml) single cream
a few snipped chives**

Oven Baked Aga Croûtons

For flavour, croûtons cooked in butter taste the best.

Melt the butter in the small roasting tin. Toss the cubes of bread in the butter.

2 / 4 Roasting Oven: place the tin on the floor of the oven and cook for about 6 minutes until golden brown. Keep turning the cubes at intervals to prevent them browning too quickly. Drain on kitchen paper and store in the freezer. Reheat before serving.

INGREDIENTS

**Bread, cut into cubes
Butter or oil (or mixture)**

Melba Toast

Slices brown or white bread.

Toast the slices of bread in the Aga Toaster on the Boiling Plate. Remove crusts with a sharp knife then cut the bread in half horizontally through the doughy middle. Put the slices of toast into a roasting tin.

2 / 4 Roasting Oven: hang the tin on the lowest set of runners and allow the bread to toast to a rich golden brown. This takes about 10 minutes but do watch to check it doesn't overbrown.

Leave to cool on a wire rack and store in an airtight tin. If necessary re-crisp in the Roasting Oven for 2 minutes before serving.

Garlic Bread

A large French Stick needs more butter.

Lay a large piece of foil on a work top. Make wide diagonal cuts through the bread. Beat the garlic and seasoning into the butter until soft and smooth. Spread the garlic butter on each side of the bread slices and ease it back into its original shape on the foil. Spread any remaining butter over the crust. Wrap the foil round the bread.

2 / 4 Roasting Oven: with the grid shelf on the highest set of runners cook for about 6 minutes until crispy and the butter has just melted.

INGREDIENTS

**1 French stick
2 fat cloves garlic, crushed
salt and freshly ground
black pepper
3oz (75g) butter**

MOULES À LA MARINIÈRE P.23
UPSIDE DOWN PRAWNS P.23
GARLIC MUSHROOMS P.23

MOULES À LA MARINIÈRE

Do ensure that every mussel is tightly closed before they are cooked. This means that they are all alive and that there are no bad ones. Open mussels should be tapped, if they close they may be used.

SERVES 4

Scrape and clean each mussel with a strong knife to remove all the seaweed, mud and beard. Wash thoroughly in several changes of water, then drain. *Melt the butter* in a deep pan, add the onion and fry gently until soft. Add the herbs, pepper, wine, salt and mussels, cover with a lid and transfer to the Boiling Plate and cook quickly for about 5 minutes, shaking the pan constantly until the mussels open. Lift the mussels out, and keep warm in a covered dish in the Simmering Oven.
Remove and discard the herbs from the cooking liquor. Drop the creamed butter into the stock a little at a time and whisk until the sauce has thickened. Taste to check seasoning, pour over the mussels and serve sprinkled with chopped parsley.

INGREDIENTS

**4 pints (2.3lt) fresh mussels
1oz (25g) butter
1 onion, finely chopped
4 stalks parsley
2 sprigs fresh thyme
1 bay leaf
freshly ground black pepper
½ pint (300ml) white wine
salt
1oz (25g) butter creamed with
½oz (15g) flour**

t o   g a r n i s h
chopped parsley

UPSIDE DOWN PRAWNS

A simple rice salad with prawns.

SERVES 6

Cook the rice in plenty of boiling salted water, as directed on the packet, until just tender. Rinse well with warm water and drain very well. Alternatively follow the Aga oven method (see page 72).
When the rice is as dry as possible, turn into a large bowl and stir in the prawns, pepper, peas and mayonnaise and mix well. Add seasoning to taste. Brush 6 ramekin dishes of ¼ pint (150ml) capacity with oil and divide the mixture between them, pressing the rice down firmly.
Leave in a cool place until required then turn out onto individual plates and garnish each with chicory leaves and serve with cucumber sauce (see page 87).

INGREDIENTS

**6oz (175g) long-grain rice
6oz (175g) peeled prawns
1 red pepper, diced and blanched
4oz (100g) cooked peas
6 tablespoons good mayonnaise
salt and freshly ground
black pepper**

t o   g a r n i s h
chicory leaves

GARLIC MUSHROOMS WITH CREAM

Choose small white button mushrooms for this recipe.

SERVES 4

Trim the ends of the mushroom stalks. Melt the butter in a large pan on the Simmering Plate and add mushrooms and garlic and cook gently for about 5 minutes. Season well, stir in the cream and simmer gently for a further 5 minutes or until the mushrooms are tender. Divide between four small warm serving dishes or ramekins and serve at once with warm granary rolls.

INGREDIENTS

**12oz (350g) small button
mushrooms
1½oz (40g) butter
1 fat clove garlic, crushed
salt and freshly ground
black pepper
¼ pint (150ml) double cream**

GAME TERRINE P.25
FARMHOUSE PÂTÉ P.25
RILLETTES DE CAMPAGNE P.25

RILLETTES DE CAMPAGNE

Best described as "potted pork," this typically French dish is simple and inexpensive to make and will keep for up to a week in the refrigerator. Serve as a starter with crispy French bread or as a light lunch or supper dish with a green salad.

SERVES 6-8

Cut the pork into small chunks and put into a pan with the cider, thyme, cloves, nutmeg, garlic and seasoning. Bring to the boil and cover with a lid.

2▆ Simmering Oven: transfer to the floor of the oven for about 4½ hours
▆4▆ until falling apart. Remove and discard the stems of the thyme and the cloves and tear the meat into shreds using two forks. Alternatively shred in short pulses in a food processor with the plastic blades. Don't over-process, check the seasoning then divide between six or eight ramekin dishes or a terrine and pour over the liquid remaining in the pan. Chill until set then melt the butter and pour over the pork mixture. Leave to set. Garnish with fresh thyme.

INGREDIENTS

2lb (900g) belly of pork, with the bones and rind removed
5 tablespoons cider
bunch fresh thyme
3 cloves
½ teaspoon freshly grated nutmeg
2 cloves garlic, crushed
salt and freshly ground black pepper
2oz (50g) butter

to garnish
fresh thyme

GAME TERRINE

Use whatever game is available according to the season in this pungent and robust terrine. If preparing jugged hare save the saddle for this or use venison which can generally be bought frozen in supermarkets. Any game bird will be delicious and substitute duck or goose livers for the chicken livers as a variation.

SERVES 8

Well grease a 2pt (1 kilo) terrine.
Soak the pheasant in the marinade overnight. Next day, pick out the meat from the marinade, strain off the liquid and soak the bread in it. Slice any pheasant breast into thin strips and process the rest. Process the livers to a purée, then process the other meats, taking care not to make them too fine. Put all the meats into a large bowl, except the bay leaves, and add the bread, mix together with the rest of the ingredients. Lay the bay leaves in a line down the centre of the loaf tin. Spoon into the terrine. Cover with foil and stand in the small roasting tin, half filled with boiling water.

2▆ Roasting Oven: with the cold plain shelf on the second set of runners and the grid shelf on the floor of the oven, cook for about 1¾ hours.
▆4▆ Baking Oven: hang the tin on the third set of runners, for about 2 hours. Leave to cool in the tin weighted down with a couple of tins of baked beans.

MARINADE

2 fl oz (50ml) red wine or sherry
1 bay leaf
1 clove garlic, split into four
1 scant tablespoon oil
a little sliced onion

INGREDIENTS

8oz (225g) boned raw pheasant
2 slices wholemeal bread
8oz (225g) chicken livers
8oz (225g) belly of pork, with bones and rind removed
8oz (225g) bacon pieces
1 egg, beaten
salt and freshly ground black pepper
2 cloves garlic, crushed
1 teaspoon ground nutmeg
1 generous tablespoon chopped fresh thyme
3 bay leaves

FARMHOUSE PÂTÉ

Very quick coarse pâté to make if you own a processor, but if not, this can easily be done with a mincer.

SERVES 8

Line a 2lb (900g) loaf tin with foil and grease lightly.
Process the livers, steak and pork, turn into a large bowl and mix with the herbs, seasoning, egg and the sherry. Line the loaf tin with the bacon and fill with the mixture. Cover with foil and stand in the small roasting tin half filled with boiling water.

2▆ Roasting Oven: with the grid shelf on the floor of the oven and the cold plain shelf on the second set of runners, cook for about 1¾ hours.
▆4▆ Baking Oven: hang the tin on the third set of runners and cook for about 1¾ hours. Leave to cool in the tin and chill well before turning out.

INGREDIENTS

4oz (100g) chicken livers
8oz (225g) pigs liver
4oz (100g) braising steak
12oz (350g) belly of pork
2 cloves garlic, crushed
1 tablespoon chopped fresh mixed herbs or 1 teaspoon dried herbs
salt and freshly ground black pepper
¼ teaspoon ground mace
1 small egg, beaten
1 tablespoon sherry
6oz (175g) thin rashers of streaky bacon, rinded

**6 rashers streaky bacon,
rind removed
1 egg
4oz (100g) brown bread
4 tablespoons brandy
1lb (450g) chicken livers
1 clove garlic, crushed
salt and freshly ground
black pepper
good pinch freshly ground nutmeg
4oz (100g) bacon pieces, cut into
small pieces
4oz (100g) melted butter**

**12oz (350g) raw breast of chicken
1 tablespoon lemon juice
Salt and freshly ground
black pepper
2 bunches watercress
1oz (25g) shallots or spring onions,
chopped
½ teaspoon freshly grated nutmeg
2 heaped teaspoons flour
1 egg
2 tablespoons double cream**

s a u c e
**¼ pint (150ml) plain yogurt
¼ pint (150ml) good mayonnaise**

t o   g a r n i s h
a little chopped watercress

SMOOTH CHICKEN LIVER PÂTÉ WITH BRANDY

SERVES 10

Stretch the six rashers of bacon with the back of a knife on a board, then use them to line the base and sides of a 2 pint (1.2 litre) loaf tin or terrine.

Break the egg into a processor or blender and add the bread, broken into small pieces, the brandy and half the chicken livers. Reduce to a purée and then transfer to a bowl. Next put the garlic, remaining chicken livers, seasoning, nutmeg and bacon pieces into the processor and reduce to a purée. Add to the first batch of mixture and stir in the melted butter. If you have one of the large processors you may be able to do this in one batch. Turn into the prepared tin or terrine and cover with foil, stand in the small roasting tin, half filled with boiling water.

2 Roasting Oven: with the grid shelf on the floor of the oven and the cold plain shelf on the second set of runners, cook for about 1¼ hours.

4 Baking Oven: hang the tin on the second set of runners and cook for about 1½ hours.

The pâté is cooked if the juices run clear when the centre is pierced with a skewer.

Remove the pâté from the oven and leave to become quite cold before turning out onto a serving dish.

CHICKEN AND WATERCRESS TERRINE

Deceptively easy but dramatic in appearance, this is a good starter, or lunch.

SERVES 8 AS A STARTER OR 4 FOR LUNCH

Line a 1lb (450g) loaf tin with foil and grease. Divide the chicken into two. Cut half of one portion into thin slices and process the remainder of that portion in a food processor, season with salt, pepper and lemon juice and leave on one side. Pick over the watercress and dry thoroughly. Saving a small bunch for the sauce, process the remainder briefly. Cut the second portion of chicken into chunks and add to the processor with the watercress, add the shallots, nutmeg, flour, egg and seasoning. Process, then lastly add the cream.

Spoon half this mixture into the prepared tin, lay the chicken slices carefully on top and cover with the plain processed chicken. Top with the remainder of the watercress and chicken mixture. Cover with foil. Stand in the small roasting tin half filled with boiling water.

2 Roasting Oven: with the grid shelf on the floor of the oven and the cold plain shelf on the second set of runners, cook for about 40 minutes.

4 Baking Oven: hang the tin on the third set of runners and cook for about 40 minutes.

Leave to cool in the tin and chill well before turning out. Garnish with watercress.

For the sauce: process the saved bunch of watercress and mix all the ingredients together and season to taste. Serve the terrine in thin slices with a little of the sauce.

MEAT DISHES

ROAST BEEF P.28 · YORKSHIRE PUDDING P.84 · HORSERADISH SAUCE P.86 · GRAVY P.85

*M*ost of us are avoiding using too many animal fats in cooking these days. With an Aga, food can often be cooked without using any extra fat at all. Trim the surplus from meats before casseroling – the long slow cooking process itself will create succulent chunks of meat in a rich sauce. Stir-frying, too, is particularly successful on the Aga Boiling Plate. Use one of the large Aga pans, the 22 pint one makes an excellent 'wok.' The high temperature achieved in this quick flash-fry method gives wonderful results.

MEAT ROASTING

There are two methods of roasting, normal and slow roasting. Coarser cuts are better cooked slowly and better cuts are best cooked normally.

Meat Thermometer: *It is difficult to give exact cooking instructions when cooking meat, because a long thin piece of meat will cook considerably quicker than the same weight of a thick dense rolled joint. I now recommend the use of a meat thermometer to check the internal temperature of the meat so you can gauge the degree of doneness.*

Season the meat, place in the small or large roasting tin and on a grill rack if you like.

2 Roasting Oven: hang the tin on the lowest set of runners in the Oven.

4 Before carving leave meat to rest for 15 minutes in the Simmering Oven. A long thin joint such as a boned and rolled loin of pork or lamb will take less time than a solid leg of pork or lamb pound for pound.

Slow Roasting: the times for the slow roasting method are as follows: Cook in the Roasting Oven as below for about 30 minutes, or until beginning to brown then transfer to the Simmering Oven for double the remaining cooking time. In the case of best cuts of beef, lamb, veal and pork, bring back to the Roasting Oven to crisp before serving. Less tender beef roasts such as silverside or brisket – transfer to the Simmering Oven for 1 hour to the lb (450g).

Normal Fast Roasting Method:

ROAST BEEF

These times give a pink medium rare centre. If you like it well done, add 5 minutes per lb (450g).

on the bone – 12 minutes per lb (450g)
off the bone – 15 minutes per lb (450g)
fillet – 10 minutes per lb (450g)

I have found a 2lb (900g) thick end of fillet takes 30 minutes in the Roasting Oven for a pink middle and 40 minutes for a 4lb (1.8kg) thick end of fillet for the same. If you like it well done increase the time a little.

ROAST VEAL

Cook as for beef for 20 minutes per lb (450g).

ROAST LAMB

When roasting lamb, sprinkle the top surface with dried rosemary or pierce little holes with a sharp knife and insert slithers of garlic inside.

pink – 15 minutes per lb (450g)
well done – 20 minutes per lb (450g)

ROAST MUTTON

Mutton is difficult to buy but it is worth searching for. I buy mine from a country butcher; it is inexpensive and full of flavour.

Trim excess fat off the joints before cooking. To slow roast a large shoulder or leg, cook in the roasting tin overnight in the Simmering Oven loosely covered in foil, then it will be done by the morning. I take it out and drain off all the juices and fat from the tin. Once the fat has set then I can use the juices for gravy and re-heat the joint and brown it in the Roasting Oven for half an hour before lunch. I serve it with caper, mint or onion sauce.

I stew the smaller cuts of mutton. They take double the time for lamb.

ROAST PORK

Pork crackling is wonderful when it is just right and very crisp. First see that the skin is freshly scored, then brush with oil or rub over with a butter paper. Sprinkle with salt at the end of the cooking time, or if you prefer at the beginning, roast at the top of the Roasting Oven until the skin bubbles. If it is an awkward shape with some of the crackling under the joint, remove all the skin with a sharp knife before roasting and roast separately.

Cook for 25 minutes per lb (450g).

GRILLING

Steaks and chops can be grilled using the Aga grill pan. See page 10. Bacon and sausage can be grilled at the top of the Roasting Oven, use the grill rack placed in the meat tin. See pages 8/9.

BOILED BEEF AND DUMPLINGS

Remember to ask the butcher to brine the meat for you. The beef is simmered slowly to avoid shrinkage. We serve mustard sauce (page 85) with it.

SERVES 8-10

Wash the beef in cold water and if necessary soak overnight (ask advice from your butcher about this) to remove excess salt. Place the beef in a large pan and cover with cold water. Cover with a lid. Bring to the boil then simmer 30 minutes.

2 / 4 Simmering Oven: transfer to the floor of the oven and cook for 3-3½ hours.

Lift the pan onto the Boiling Plate and add the vegetables, bring to the boil and return to the Simmering Oven for about a further hour until the meat and vegetables are tender.

Lift the beef out onto a serving dish and arrange the vegetables around the meat. Keep warm in the Simmering Oven.

Place the flour in a bowl with the suet, seasoning and herbs, mix well. Add enough water to make a soft but not sticky dough. Form into 8-10 small balls.

Place the meat stock pan on the Boiling Plate and add the dumplings. Transfer to the Simmering Plate and cook for about 30 minutes until well risen. Drain the dumplings and arrange with the meat and vegetables and keep warm.

Prepare the mustard sauce using ½ pint (300ml) beef stock and ½ pint (300ml) milk and serve with the meat.

CHASTLETON POT ROAST

This cuts well cold so makes a delicious sandwich in brown bread with mustard. Leave vegetables in big pieces.

SERVES 6

Heat the oil in a large pan and quickly brown the meat on all sides on the Boiling Plate. Thickly cut the vegetables and tuck down the sides with the bouquet garni. Pour over liquid and season. Cover with a lid.

2 / 4 Roasting Oven: with the grid shelf on the floor of the oven cook for 20 minutes.

Simmering Oven: transfer to the bottom of the oven with the grid shelf on the floor and cook for 2½-3 hours or until the meat is tender.

Put the meat onto a serving plate and strain off the vegetables and keep both hot. Skim fat off the remaining juice. Mix flour with 1 tablespoon of this fat and add to the juice. Bring to the boil stirring until thickened. Check seasoning and serve with the meat and vegetables.

INGREDIENTS
3½lb (1.5kg) boned and rolled salted silverside
1lb (450g) small whole onions
1lb (450g) small whole carrots
8 sticks celery, sliced
8 medium potatoes, halved
2 tablespoons chopped parsley

HERB DUMPLINGS
4oz (100g) self-raising flour
2oz (50g) shredded suet
salt
1 tablespoon freshly chopped herbs
6 tablespoons cold water

INGREDIENTS
1 tablespoon oil
2½ lb (1.25kg) silverside of beef
8oz (225g) onion
8oz (225g) carrot
8oz (225g) parsnip or celeriac
3 sticks celery
bouquet garni
small glass red wine or stock
salt and freshly ground black pepper
1 dessertspoon of flour

IRISH STEW P.43
BEEF WELLINGTON P.31
HORSERADISH BEEF P.31

BEEF WELLINGTON

Cook the beef fillet first for 10 minutes per lb (450g) or, if you like it very rare, 8 minutes per lb (450g), then chill and wrap in pastry. Leave to chill in the refrigerator until needed then glaze and cook until golden.

SERVES 6-8

Melt the butter in the small roasting tin. Trim any fat off the fillet, lift into roasting tin and roll in the butter.

2 / 4 Roasting Oven: hang the tin on the top set of runners and cook for about 20 minutes turning the meat over once so that it is browned on both sides. Lift out onto a plate and cool completely.

Add the sliced onion to the juices in the tin and stand on the floor of the Roasting Oven to cook, stirring from time to time until golden, add the mushrooms and cook for 2 more minutes. Lift out of oven, season and leave to cool.

Roll out the pastry to a rectangle 14 x 16 inch (35 x 40cm) depending on the size of the meat. Place half the mushroom mixture down the centre of the pastry then place the meat on top, flat side uppermost. Season well. Cut a 1½ inch (3.5cm) square from each corner of the pastry for decoration and keep on one side. Fold the pastry around the meat, so that it is sealed inside. Turn over and stand on a baking sheet. Brush liberally with beaten egg. Use the left over pastry to decorate the top with leaves or lattice. Chill in the refrigerator for up to 24 hours before baking.

2 / 4 Roasting Oven: with the grid shelf on the floor of the oven cook for about 25-30 minutes until pale golden brown. Make a good gravy from the reserved onions and mushrooms to serve with the beef.

BEEF IN HORSERADISH CREAM

This is one of my favourite buffet party dishes and the flavour of the sauce is really different. It can all be prepared well in advance and then the horseradish cream stirred in at the last minute.

SERVES 6

Cut the meat into 1 inch (2.5cm) cubes. Turn into the large Aga casserole and heat gently on the Simmering Plate until the fat begins to run out of the meat. Move to Boiling Plate and fry until meat has browned on all sides. Add the onion, curry powder, ginger, sugar and flour and cook for a minute. Stir in the stock and bring to the boil, stirring until thickened. Add Worcestershire sauce and seasoning, cover with a lid and simmer for about 5 minutes.

2 / 4 Simmering Oven: transfer to the floor of the oven for about 4 hours until the meat is tender.

When ready to serve, stir in the horseradish cream and turn into a warm serving dish. Sprinkle with parsley and serve at once.

INGREDIENTS

1½ lb (675g) chuck steak
2 tablespoons oil
good knob of butter
8oz (225g) onions, sliced
8oz (225g) carrots, sliced
1½ oz (40g) flour
¾ pint (450ml) pale or brown ale
**1 rounded tablespoon demerara
sugar**
1½ level teaspoons made mustard
**salt and freshly ground black
pepper**

INGREDIENTS

2lb (900g) stewing steak
1½oz (40g) flour
**salt and freshly ground
black pepper**
2 tablespoons sunflower oil
8oz (225g) onions, chopped
2 cloves garlic, crushed
4oz (100g) mushrooms, sliced
1 green pepper, seeded and sliced
1 tablespoon apricot jam
½pint (300ml) red wine
¼ pint (150ml) stock

INGREDIENTS

**2 rounded tablespoons ground
coriander**
1 rounded teaspoon ground cumin
1 level teaspoon ground turmeric
1 level tablespoon garam masala
2 fat cloves garlic, crushed
**1 piece finely chopped fresh root
ginger (about the size of a walnut)**
salt
3 tablespoons oil
2 large onions, chopped
14oz (397g) can tomatoes
1 good tablespoon tomato purée
2lb (900g) chuck steak, cubed
¼ pint (150ml) water

INGREDIENTS

**4 slices topside or silverside
(each about 6oz (175g))**
1½ oz (40g) flour
**salt and freshly ground
black pepper**
2 tablespoons sunflower oil
1oz (25g) butter
2 large onions, finely sliced
2 sticks celery, sliced
14oz (397g) can tomatoes
2 teaspoons tomato purée
1 teaspoons Worcestershire sauce
¼ pint (150ml) stock

CARBONNADE OF BEEF

A good casserole that the Aga does so well.

SERVES 4-6

Cut the meat into strips ½ inch (1cm) thick. Heat the oil and butter in a pan, add the meat and brown quickly on the Boiling Plate. Lift out and keep on one side. Add the onions and carrots to the pan and fry until golden brown. Sprinkle in the flour and cook for a minute. Blend in the ale and bring to the boil, stirring until thickened. Add the remaining ingredients and return the meat to the pan. Bring to the boil, cover and simmer for 5 minutes.

Simmering Oven: with the grid shelf on the floor of the oven cook for 3-4 hours or until the meat is tender. Taste and check seasoning before serving.

BEEF OXFORD

Perfect for supper on a cold winter's day. I like to serve this with jacket potatoes, of course, cooked in the Aga!

SERVES 6-8

Cut the meat into 1 inch (2.5cm) cubes, put in a polythene bag with the flour and seasoning, toss until evenly coated. Heat the oil in a large Aga pan and fry the meat quickly on the Boiling Plate to brown. Add the remaining ingredients and bring to the boil. Simmer for 5 minutes and cover with a lid.

Simmering Oven: transfer pan to the floor of the oven and cook for about 4 hours or until the meat is tender. Taste and check seasoning before serving.

MILD INDIAN CURRY

This authentic recipe is not overpoweringly strong, but has a deep rich colour, superb flavour and is so simple to make. It freezes well so make enough for another day. Thaw slowly before reheating.

SERVES 6

First mix all the spices together then add the garlic, ginger and salt. *Measure the oil* into a large pan, add the onions and fry until golden brown. Add all the spice mixture, tomatoes, purée and cook without a lid, stirring until the oil starts to come through slightly. Add the meat, cover with a lid and simmer for about 15 minutes. Remove the lid, add the water, cover and bring to the boil.

Simmering Oven: transfer to the floor of the oven and cook for about 3 hours or until the meat is tender.

SWISS STEAK

Especially popular with those who like a good slice of very tender beef.

SERVES 4

Cut beef into 8 pieces. Mix together the flour, salt and pepper and toss the meat in this mixture, pressing it so that most of the flour is used. Measure the oil and butter into a pan and fry the meat quickly on all sides on the Boiling Plate until browned. Lift out and place in a casserole dish.
Add the onions and celery to the fat remaining in the pan and fry until golden. Add any remaining flour and cook for a minute then stir in the tomatoes, purée, Worcestershire sauce and stock, bring to the boil then pour over the beef. Cover.

Simmering Oven: cook on the floor of the oven for 3 hours or until the beef is tender.

BAKED MARROW – THE BEST WAY I KNOW!

*Make in the small roasting tin for 4 or double the recipe and use the large tin for 8.
I nearly always prepare this ahead – say in the morning, cover it and then put
it in the fridge for later in the day.*

SERVES 4

Turn the minced beef into a pan and heat on the Simmering Plate to draw out the natural fat then transfer to the Boiling Plate and fry quickly with the onion. Add stock, bring to the boil, cover and simmer 20 minutes. Remove from the heat, add breadcrumbs and season well.

Peel the marrow with a potato peeler. Cut into rings, about 8 usually fills the small roasting tin. Scoop out and discard the seeds from each slice. Butter the roasting tin. Blanch the marrow rings in boiling salted water for about 5 minutes until still just crisp and drain well. Arrange the rings in the roasting tin.

Divide the mince mixture between the rings, piling it on top. Stir the Dijon mustard and nutmeg into the sauce and spoon over each ring. Scatter with cheese.

2▪ / ▪4▪ Roasting Oven: with the grid shelf on the second set of runners. Cook for about 30 minutes or until golden brown and bubbling. Serve with garlic bread.

INGREDIENTS

**1lb (450g) raw minced beef
1 medium onion, chopped
¼ pint (150ml) beef stock
2 tablespoons fresh white
breadcrumbs
salt and freshly ground
black pepper
1 medium marrow or overgrown
courgette!
1 teaspoon Dijon mustard
a little freshly ground nutmeg
¾ pint (450ml) white sauce
(see page 85)
4oz (100g) well-flavoured
Cheddar cheese, grated**

THURLESTONE BEEF

*So called because it is a big casserole and I take half the casserole on holiday
with me for the first night and leave half in the freezer at home.
It is lovely to come back to when I'm into piles of washing and ironing the day
after we return!*

SERVES 12

Take your largest pan with a lid, add the oil and meat and heat on the Simmering Plate to let out any natural fat from the meat. Transfer to the Boiling Plate, add bacon and fry quickly to brown the meat. Sprinkle in the flour and curry powder and mix well. Add the remaining ingredients and bring to the boil, stirring from time to time. Cover with a lid and simmer for 10 minutes.

2▪ / ▪4▪ Simmering Oven: transfer to the floor of the oven and cook for about 5 hours or until the meat is tender. Taste and check seasoning and serve with buttered noodles with added freshly chopped parsley.

INGREDIENTS

**3 tablespoons sunflower oil
4lb (450g) stewing steak, cut into
1 inch (2.5cm) pieces
3 rashers streaky bacon, snipped
3oz (75g) flour
1 heaped teaspoon curry powder
8 celery stalks, chopped
2 onions, chopped
2 fat cloves garlic, crushed
1lb (450g) carrots, cut into pencil
strips
¼ pint (150ml) port
2 x 14oz (397g) cans chopped
tomatoes
1½ pints (750ml) stock
salt and freshly ground
black pepper**

GINGERED SPICED BEEF

*If your family enjoys kidney beans, add a 16oz (450g) can red kidney beans, bring
back to the boil, then return to the oven for the last 30 minutes of cooking.*

SERVES 4

Mix flour, seasonings, ginger and chilli seasoning together in a polythene bag and use to coat the meat. Measure the oil into a large pan and brown meat quickly on the Boiling Plate. Add any flour left in the bag to the meat. Add tomatoes, mushrooms, Worcestershire sauce, sugar, vinegar and garlic. Bring to the boil. Simmer for 5 minutes then cover with a lid.

2▪ / ▪4▪ Simmering Oven: transfer to the floor of the oven and cook for about 4 hours or until the meat is tender. Taste and check seasoning and serve with boiled rice and a crisp green vegetable.

INGREDIENTS

**1oz (25g) flour
salt and freshly ground
black pepper
2 level teaspoons ground ginger
¼ teaspoon chilli seasoning
2 tablespoons sunflower oil
1½lb (675g) good stewing beef,
cubed
14oz (397g) can tomatoes
6oz (175g) button mushrooms,
sliced
1 tablespoon Worcestershire sauce
2 level tablespoons muscovado
sugar
2 tablespoons vinegar
2 cloves garlic, crushed**

Ingredients (St. Anne's Beef)

**2lb (900g) chuck steak
3 tablespoons sunflower oil
1oz (25g) butter
1½oz (40g) flour
1 pint (600ml) beef stock
3 tablespoons Worcestershire sauce
4 tablespoons redcurrant jelly
8oz (225g) button mushrooms
salt and freshly ground
black pepper**

**8oz (225g) prunes
a little sunflower oil
3lb (1.5kg) chuck steak, cubed
2oz (50g) flour
2 tablespoons soy sauce
3 tablespoons clear honey
4 tablespoons vinegar
¾ pint (450ml) water
salt and freshly ground
black pepper
8oz (225g) button mushrooms**

**scant 2 tablespoons sunflower oil
3lb (1.5kg) bladebone steak, or good
stewing steak, cubed
1¼lb (550g) shallots, peeled
1 teaspoon sugar
1 fat clove garlic, crushed
3½ fl oz (100ml) red wine
2 tablespoons wholemeal flour
1¼ pints (750ml) beef stock
salt and freshly ground
black pepper**

stir-fry
**knob butter
10 sticks celery, chopped diagonally
4oz (100g) walnut pieces**

ST. ANNE'S BEEF

Such a good casserole for a hot buffet. Serve with pasta and a green salad or tiny new potatoes, if in season. For some this could be a little sweet so if you prefer add only 2 tablespoons redcurrant jelly.

SERVES 6

Trim the fat off the meat and cut into cubes. Take a large pan, measure in the oil and butter and fry the meat quickly until browned. Sprinkle in the flour, blend well then add stock and bring to the boil, stirring until thickened. Add Worcestershire sauce, redcurrant jelly and mushrooms. Cover, bring to the boil and simmer for 5 minutes.

Simmering Oven: transfer to the floor of the oven for about 4 hours until the meat is tender. Taste and check seasoning before serving.

HIGHGATE BEEF WITH PRUNES

For a crowd or to freeze.

SERVES 8-10

Soak prunes overnight then remove the stones. Measure a little oil into a pan, brown the meat in batches on the Boiling Plate, transfer to an Aga casserole with a slotted spoon, draining well. Sprinkle flour over meat and stir over the heat, add soy sauce, honey, vinegar, water and seasoning. Bring to the boil, stirring until thickened, cover and simmer for 5 minutes.

Simmering Oven: transfer to the floor of the oven for about 2½ hours. Remove from oven, stir in mushrooms and drained prunes, bring to the boil again and leave to simmer for 5 minutes, then return to the oven for a further 45 minutes or until the meat is tender. Check seasoning then serve.

BASSETBURY BEEF

Memorable beef casserole served with stir-fried celery and walnuts.

SERVES 8-10

Heat a little oil in the frypan and brown the beef a little at a time on the Boiling Plate, transfer to a large Aga casserole with a slotted spoon. Add the shallots and sugar to the pan and cook quickly, stirring well until beginning to brown, add garlic and cook for a further minute, transfer to the casserole. Add red wine to the pan, work in any sediment and set aside. Sprinkle flour over beef, stir well over the heat, add red wine, stock and seasoning, bring to the boil, stirring until thickened then cover.

Roasting Oven: place on the floor of the oven for about 10 minutes.
Simmering Oven: transfer to the floor of the oven for a further 3 hours or until meat is tender. Taste and check seasoning.

Heat the butter in a pan, add celery, stir well on the Boiling Plate for about 2 minutes then add the walnuts and continue to cook for a further minute or two. Serve with the beef.

LASAGNE

Always a firm favourite! Useful because it can be made in advance and reheated when necessary. Freezes well before the final cooking. Thaw before cooking.

SERVES 6

First make meat sauce: heat the minced beef gently in a large Aga pan on the Simmering Plate to allow the fat to run out, then move on to Boiling Plate and fry until browned. Add onions and bacon and fry for a further 5 minutes. Stir in the flour and then the remaining ingredients. Stir well, bring to the boil and simmer for 5 minutes. Cover with a lid.

2 / 4 Simmering Oven: transfer the pan to the floor of the oven for about 45 minutes or until the meat is tender. Taste and check seasoning.

For the white sauce: heat the butter in a pan on the Simmering Plate until melted, stir in the flour and cook for a minute then gradually blend in the milk. Bring to the boil, stirring until thickened. Add mustard, seasoning and nutmeg to taste.

To assemble the lasagne: take a shallow ovenproof dish, spread ⅓ of the meat sauce over the base of the dish, then ⅓ of the white sauce and ⅓ of the cheese. Top this with ½ the lasagne, arranging the sheets edge to edge so they don't overlap. Repeat these layers once more and then top with the last of the meat sauce, white sauce and finally the cheese.

2 Roasting Oven: with the grid shelf on the lowest set of runners cook for about 45 minutes until the cheese has browned and the pasta is tender. If necessary protect with the cold plain shelf.

4 Baking Oven: slide into the centre of the oven, or just below. Cook for about 45 minutes until the cheese has browned and the pasta is tender.

SWEET AND SOUR MEATBALLS

A delicious Chinese style dish which is good served with rice. If the meatballs are soft, it may be easier to chill them for a while before cooking as this makes them easier to handle.

SERVES 4

Put the minced beef and breadcrumbs into a bowl, add egg and seasoning and bind together. With lightly floured hands, divide the mixture and roll into 16 balls. Heat the oil in a large pan on the Boiling Plate and fry the meatballs until browned all over. Lift out with a slotted spoon and leave on one side.

Add the onion, carrot and leek to the pan, transfer to the Simmering Plate and cook gently for about 10 minutes. Measure the cornflour and sugar into a bowl and gradually stir in the water and then the ketchup, vinegar and soy sauce and add to the cooked vegetables. Bring to the boil, stirring until thickened. Season to taste. Return the meatballs to the pan, simmer 5 minutes then cover with a lid.

2 / 4 Simmering Oven: transfer the pan to the floor of the oven for about an hour or until the meatballs are tender.

8oz (225g) Gruyère cheese, grated
1oz (25g) Parmesan cheese, grated
6oz (175g) no-cook lasagne

meat sauce

1lb (450g) minced beef
2 large onions, chopped
4oz (100g) streaky bacon, snipped
1 rounded tablespoon flour
½ pint (300ml) stock
4 tablespoons tomato purée
2 fat cloves garlic, crushed
2 level teaspoons sugar
salt and freshly ground
black pepper

white sauce

2½oz (60g) butter
2oz (50g) flour
1 pint (600ml) milk
½ teaspoon Dijon mustard
salt and freshly ground
black pepper
a little freshly ground nutmeg

12oz (350g) raw minced beef
2oz (50g) fresh brown breadcrumbs
1 egg
salt and freshly ground
black pepper

sauce

1 tablespoon sunflower oil
1 onion, chopped
2 carrots, cut into pencil strips
1 leek, sliced
4 teaspoons cornflour
2 teaspoons sugar
½ pint (300ml) water
2 tablespoons tomato ketchup
1 tablespoon vinegar
1 tablespoon soy sauce

BEEF PAUPIETTES P.37
MEAUX PORK CHOPS P.46
RED CABBAGE P.80

PEPPER STUFFED BEEF PAUPIETTES

Pre-cooked cracked wheat is available in supermarkets and health food shops, it gives texture to the stuffing and tastes a little like brown rice, though easier to prepare. There is no need to tie up the meat rolls – I find that they hold together well if packed together fairly tightly and browned in the Roasting Oven.

SERVES 6

Beat out slices of silverside (with meat in a polythene bag) one at a time, cut in half and season. Cover cracked wheat with boiling water, leave to stand for 10 minutes, then drain well. Soften the onion in the butter, then add diced pepper, parsley, seasoning and cracked wheat. Divide the mixture between the slices of beef and roll up carefully. Oil the small Aga roasting tin and lift the paupiettes into the tin so that the fold is underneath, brush over the top of each with a little oil.

2 / 4 Roasting Oven: hang the tin on the highest set of runners and cook for about 20 minutes until browned, drain and save any liquid and return to the oven for a further 10 minutes, to finish browning.

To make the sauce: soften the onion in the butter, add flour and cook for a minute, then gradually add the red wine. Measure the saved liquid and make up to a pint (600ml) with the stock, add this liquid to the sauce and bring to the boil, stirring until smooth and slightly thickened. Lift paupiettes into a large shallow casserole, pour over the sauce and cover.

2 / 4 Roasting Oven: with the grid shelf on the floor of the oven, cook for 10 minutes.

Simmering Oven: transfer to the floor of the oven for 3-4 hours or until the beef is tender. Taste and check seasoning then serve.

CHILLI CON CARNE

If you like it very hot, add a little more chilli seasoning. Makes of chilli seasoning do vary so beware!

SERVES 4

Lightly fry the onion in the oil until soft on the Simmering Plate. Add the mince and transfer to the Boiling Plate to brown quickly. Stir in the chilli seasoning, sugar and salt. Sprinkle on the flour and cook for a minute. Add the tomatoes and beans and bring to the boil, stirring. Simmer for about 10 minutes.

2 / 4 Simmering Oven: transfer to the oven for about 1-1½ hours. Serve with boiled rice or Aga oven rice (see page 72).

PAUPIETTES
12 thin slices silverside of beef (about 2½lb (1.25kg) total weight)

RED PEPPER AND BULGAR WHEAT STUFFING
**1½oz (40g) Bulgar pre-cooked cracked wheat
1 onion, finely chopped
good knob butter
1 red pepper, seeded and diced
4 tablespoons freshly chopped parsley
salt and freshly ground black pepper
a little sunflower oil**

sauce
**1 onion, sliced
3oz (75g) butter
3oz (75g) flour
1 pint (600ml) red wine
about ½ pint (300ml) beef stock
salt and freshly ground black pepper**

INGREDIENTS
**1 onion, chopped
2 tablespoons oil
1lb (450g) minced beef
2 teaspoons chilli seasoning
1 teaspoon sugar
salt
1 tablespoon flour
14oz (397g) can tomatoes
14oz (397g) can red kidney beans**

1lb (450g) beef skirt
4oz (100g) ox kidney
1oz (25g) flour
2 tablespoons oil
1 large onion, chopped
½ pint (300ml) beef stock
**salt and freshly ground
black pepper**
4oz (100g) mushrooms, sliced

QUICK FLAKY PASTRY

8oz (225g) strong plain flour
**6oz (175g) hard margarine,
frozen for 1 hour**
**about 9 tablespoons or scant ¼ pint
(150ml) cold water**
a little beaten egg to glaze

1¼ lb (550g) skirt of beef
6-8oz (175-225g) ox kidney
1 onion, finely chopped
1 level tablespoon flour
**salt and freshly ground black
pepper**
1 tablespoon Worcestershire sauce
scant ¼ pint (150ml) water

SUET CRUST PASTRY

8oz (225g) self-raising flour
4oz (100g) shredded suet
salt
about 7-8 tablespoons water

STEAK AND KIDNEY PIE

Add more or less kidney according to the family's likes.

SERVES 4-6

Cut the steak and kidney into 1 inch (2.5cm) pieces, put in a polythene bag with the flour and toss until well coated. Measure oil into a pan, add the meat and onion and cook until browned. Stir in the stock, season and bring to the boil. Cover with a lid and simmer for 5 minutes.

2 / 4 Simmering Oven: cook on the floor of the oven for about 2½ hours then add the mushrooms and cook for a further 30 minutes until the meat is tender. Taste and check seasoning and turn into a 1½ pint (900ml) pie dish and allow to become cool. Put a pie funnel or handleless cup in the centre.

For the pastry: measure the flour into a bowl and grate the cold margarine into the bowl and add just enough water to make a firm dough. Lightly roll out to make a strip ½ inch (1cm) thick and 6 inches (15cm) wide. Fold the pastry in three and give it a quarter turn to the left. Roll it out again and repeat folding. Wrap in foil and chill in the refrigerator for 30 minutes. Roll out the pastry and use to cover the pie, seal and decorate the edges and use any trimmings to make pastry leaves for the top. Brush with beaten egg and make a small hole in the top for the steam to escape.

2 / 4 Roasting Oven: with the grid shelf on the floor of the oven cook for about 25-30 minutes until the pastry is golden brown and the meat heated through.

STEAK AND KIDNEY PUDDING

*We like plenty of gravy, so I cook a little extra kidney and onion to make
a good stock in a small pan in the Simmering Oven. Then I make
more gravy with this to serve with the pudding. If you have an Aga Cake Baker
use this as a saucepan and start off in the Roasting Oven.*

SERVES 6

Cut the steak and kidney into ½ inch (1cm) cubes, removing any fat. Trim the core from the kidney and roughly chop. Put the steak and kidney in a bowl with the onion, flour, seasoning and Worcestershire sauce. Mix together well. Grease a 2½ pint (1.4 litre) pudding basin.

For the pastry: put the flour, suet and salt into a bowl and gradually add the water and mix to a soft but not sticky dough. Take a third of the pastry and roll out on a lightly floured surface to a circle large enough to fit the top of the basin. Roll out the remaining dough and use to line the basin.

Fill the basin with the meat mixture and add the water. Dampen the edges of the pastry and cover with the pastry lid, pressing the edges firmly together to seal. Cover the pudding with a pleated piece of greaseproof paper and then a lid of foil. Stand the basin in a pan and pour in boiling water until it comes half way up the sides of the basin. Bring to the boil and simmer for 30 minutes.

2 / 4 Simmering Oven: transfer the basin, water and pan to the floor of the oven for about 6 hours until the meat is tender.

FIRST RATE MUTTON HOTPOT

Each year I seem to end up with mutton breasts, scrag of neck of mutton and middle neck in the freezer. In fact all the cheaper fatty cuts. This recipe is a delicious way of using them up. You could also use lamb if it is cooked for a shorter time in the Simmering Oven to begin with. It is not worthwhile making this just for 4, best to make for 8 then freeze half, but without the potatoes.

SERVES 8-10

Put the untrimmed meat in the large Aga roasting tin, pour over water and season. Lay a piece of foil loosely over the top.

2 / **4** Simmering Oven: hang the tin on the bottom set of runners in the oven and leave to cook overnight.

First thing next morning: take roasting tin out of oven, allow to cool and fat to set.

Remove fat, pour off the stock, simmer the onion and carrot in this until almost tender. Blend the flour with enough milk to make the thickness of pouring cream. Add some of the stock to this. Then add this to the pan. Bring to the boil, stirring until thickened. If necessary, thin down to a pouring consistency with more milk then season.

Take all the fat and bone away from the meat – the bones can be used for stock, if liked. Discard all the fat. Dice the meat and add to the sauce. Turn into a large, fairly shallow ovenproof casserole or dish. Slice the potatoes and arrange over the top so they are overlapping. Cover with a lid or foil.

2 / **4** Roasting Oven: with the grid shelf on the third set of runners, cook for about 1 hour, removing the lid or foil for the last 30 minutes or so until the potatoes are crisp and browned. Serve with a green vegetable such as beans or crisp cabbage.

INGREDIENTS

2 large breasts and 3lb (1.5kg) scrag
end neck of mutton on the bone
3lb (1.5kg) middle neck of mutton
on the bone
3/4 pint (450ml) water
salt and freshly ground
black pepper
2 large onions, chopped
1 1/2 lb (675g) carrots, sliced
2oz (50g) flour
milk
about 2 1/2 lb (1.25kg) potatoes

LAMB VERT

Wonderful bright green stuffed lamb – nothing could be simpler.

SERVES 4

Remove any excess fat from the joint. Lie on a board, skin side down. Loosen the eye of the meat back a little from the skin, season. Reserve a few sprigs of watercress for garnish. Remove the stalks and chop the rest of the watercress. Spread this over the end of the meat where the lean eye is, pushing it under the eye. Roll up from this end with the eye in the middle. Secure with string or fine skewers. Spread lightly with the butter, season and lift into the small roasting tin.

2 / **4** Roasting Oven: hang the tin on the third set of runners and cook for about 30-35 minutes until brown and crispy.

Transfer the joint to a plate and put in the Simmering Oven. Skim off any excess fat from the tin then work in the flour and add the remaining ingredients and bring to the boil, stirring to make a good sauce. Check seasoning.

Remove the string or skewers from the joint, carve into thickish slices and arrange on a warm serving dish, pour over a little of the sauce, garnish with the reserved watercress and serve the remaining sauce in a sauceboat.

INGREDIENTS

1 good sized best end neck of lamb,
boned
2 bunches watercress
1oz (25g) butter
salt and freshly ground
black pepper
1 heaped teaspoon flour
1/2 pint (300ml) stock
2 teaspoons Worcestershire sauce
2 teaspoons redcurrant jelly

INGREDIENTS

1½lb (675g) fillet of neck of lamb
2 tablespoons sunflower oil
1 large onion, chopped
2 fat cloves garlic, crushed
1 teaspoon ground turmeric
1 teaspoon ground cumin
1 teaspoon ground coriander
1 teaspoon flour
¼ pint (150ml) chicken stock
salt and freshly ground
black pepper
1 or 2 (5oz) (150g) cartons unset
natural yogurt
fresh coriander

INGREDIENTS

2lb (900g) boneless shoulder lamb,
cubed
a little sunflower oil
1½oz (40g) flour
4 fl oz (120ml) white wine
3 cloves garlic, crushed
1 pint (600ml) chicken stock
peeled rind and juice 2 lemons
3 generous sprigs thyme
salt and freshly ground
black pepper
2 egg yolks

t o   g a r n i s h
a little freshly chopped parsley
or mint sprigs

INGREDIENTS

1 tablespoon flour
salt and freshly ground
black pepper
1lb (450g) lambs liver
1oz (25g) butter
1 tablespoon sunflower oil
1 large onion, chopped
4oz (100g) streaky bacon, snipped
½ pint (300ml) stock
2 cloves garlic, crushed
14oz (397g) can tomatoes

KASHMIR LAMB

Fillet of lamb in a spiced piquant sauce. Sometimes fillet of neck of lamb is hard to come by so use lean shoulder of lamb instead. Serve with rice flavoured with saffron and a green salad with mint. If you like a lot of sauce add 2 cartons of yogurt or ½ pint (300ml) Aga yogurt (page 139).

SERVES 4

Cut fillet into discs the thickness of thick sliced bread. Measure the oil into a large pan, brown the meat on both sides on the Boiling Plate. Lift out into a small ovenproof casserole. Fry the onion in the remaining oil and add the garlic. Stir in the spices and flour then add the stock, stirring all the time. Allow to thicken, season and pour over the meat. Cover with a lid. Bring back to the boil.

2 Simmering Oven: transfer to the floor of the oven for about 1½ hours
4 until the meat is tender. Just before serving stir in the yogurt and mix well. Do not reboil. Garnish with fresh coriander.

LEMON LAMB FRICASSÉE

A velvety lemon sauce. Do try to use fresh thyme, preferably lemon thyme, this is very easy to grow and once planted it goes on for years.

SERVES 6

Heat a little oil in a pan and brown the lamb on the Boiling Plate a little at a time, transfer to a casserole dish with a slotted spoon. Sprinkle flour onto the meat, stir and cook for about a minute then add wine and garlic, and the chicken stock, a little at a time. Add peeled rind of the lemons (keep the juice to add later) and 2 sprigs of thyme. Season and bring to the boil, stirring until thickened, then simmer for 5 minutes. Cover with a lid.

2 Simmering Oven: transfer to the floor of the oven for about 1½ hours, or
4 until the lamb is tender. Drain off liquid and save, discard lemon rind and sprigs of thyme.

Strip thyme off remaining sprig, blend together with lemon juice and egg yolks. Bring the saved liquid to the boil, add a little of the hot liquid to the lemon and yolks, mix well and return to the pan. Whisking well, bring just to the boil, add remaining thyme and pour over the meat. Return to the Simmering Oven for about 20 minutes, check seasoning and skim off any excess fat. To serve, sprinkle with parsley or mint and serve with mashed potato to sop up the wonderful sauce.

ITALIAN LIVER

Quick and easy to make.

SERVES 4

Measure the flour and seasoning into a polythene bag and toss the liver in this. Heat the butter and oil in a large pan and fry the onions gently on the Simmering Plate for about 5 minutes. Add the liver and bacon and fry for a further 5 minutes. Stir in any remaining flour and gradually blend in the stock. Add the remaining ingredients and bring to the boil, stirring. Cover with a lid and simmer 5 minutes.

2 Simmering Oven: transfer to the floor of the oven for about 30 minutes
4 until the liver is tender and the flavours have had time to develop. Taste and check seasoning, serve with creamy mashed potatoes.

KASHMIR LAMB P.40
LEMON LAMB FRICASSÉE P.40
ORANGE MARINATED LAMB P.42

1lb (450g) raw minced shoulder of lamb
8oz (225g) onions, chopped
2 fat cloves garlic, crushed
1½oz (40g) flour
salt and freshly ground black pepper
a little fresh or dried thyme
14oz (397g) can tomatoes
3 aubergines

s a u c e

1½oz (40g) butter
1½oz (40g) flour
¾ pint (450ml) milk
grated nutmeg
1 level teaspoon made mustard
6oz (175g) Cheddar cheese, grated
1 egg, beaten

2 tablespoons oil
1½lb (750g) fillet neck of lamb, sliced in ¾ inch (2cm) slices
1½lb (750g) onions, chopped
2 fat cloves garlic, crushed
1lb 8oz (750g) can of tomatoes
2 teaspoons ground cumin
salt and freshly ground black pepper

Best end and loin of lamb in a piece, boned and rolled

m a r i n a d e

8 fl oz (250ml) orange juice from carton
2 tablespoons clear honey
2 tablespoons soy sauce
2 tablespoons vinegar
2 cloves garlic, crushed
2 heaped teaspoons dried rosemary
1 teaspoon ground ginger

g a r n i s h

orange wedges
rosemary

MOUSSAKA

Blanching the aubergines instead of frying them makes the dish lighter and healthier.

SERVES 6-8

Turn the lamb into a large pan and cook until the fat begins to run out, stirring to avoid sticking. Add the onions and garlic and fry until brown, about 15 minutes. Spoon off any excess fat. Add the flour, seasoning, thyme and tomatoes. Bring to the boil and simmer for 5 minutes.

Slice the aubergines and blanch in a pan of water for 1 minute. Drain then dry on kitchen paper.

To make the sauce, heat the butter in a pan, add the flour and cook for a minute then gradually blend in the milk, stirring well and bring to the boil. Add the nutmeg, mustard, seasoning and cheese. Cool slightly then stir in the egg.

To assemble the moussaka: Butter a large shallow ovenproof dish. Put half the meat mixture into the dish, cover with half the aubergines. Season. Repeat with the remaining lamb and aubergines. Pour over the cheese sauce.

2▆ ▆4▆ Roasting Oven: with the grid shelf on the floor of the oven cook for about 35 minutes until the top is golden brown.

CUMIN SPICED LAMB

A different casserole with a good thickened sauce. Best with brown rice. Even better when made a day ahead and reheated.

SERVES 6

Measure the oil into a large pan and brown the meat on all sides on the Boiling Plate. Lift out of the pan and put the meat on one side. Add the onion and garlic to the fat remaining in the pan and stir well. Cook on the Simmering Plate for about 10 minutes. Stir in the tomatoes, cumin and seasoning. Return the meat to the pan, bring to the boil and simmer for 5 minutes.

2▆ ▆4▆ Simmering Oven: cover and cook on the floor of the oven for about 1½ hours until the meat is tender. Check seasoning and serve.

ORANGE MARINATED LAMB

It is bliss to put a roast in the oven and for it to come out ready to serve with the delicious gravy-cum-sauce made in the roasting tin underneath. This is a top family favourite; sometimes I use boned leg of lamb opened out like a butterfly instead of loin of lamb. It takes longer to cook, about 60 minutes for a good sized boned leg; I add the marinade half way through in the same way as the recipe below.

SERVES 6

Make up the marinade the day before. Combine the orange juice, honey, soy sauce, vinegar, garlic, rosemary and ginger. Take two large freezer bags and put one inside the other. Put the lamb and the marinade into the bag, seal and leave for at least 12 hours in the fridge, turning occasionally. Remove the lamb from the marinade and save the liquid.

2▆ ▆4▆ Roasting Oven: put the lamb in the small roasting tin and hang the tin on the third set of runners. Roast for 20 minutes, then pour over the marinade and roast for a further 10-15 minutes, until the marinade has changed colour and become a dark gravy and when the lamb is pierced with a skewer the juices run clear.

To serve; skim off any excess fat from the gravy. Cut through the bones giving two chops each. Garnish. Serve with the gravy.

IRISH STEW

True Irish Stew is made using only lamb and potatoes, but I like to include carrots too.

SERVES 4

Cut the lamb into neat pieces and remove the spinal cord. Peel and slice the onions, carrots and potatoes. Arrange alternate layers of meat with layers of each vegetable, seasoning each layer with salt and pepper. Finish with a layer of potato, which should be neatly arranged to give an attractive appearance to the finished dish. Pour in sufficient water to half fill the casserole. Cover with a lid.

2❚ **❚4**❚ Roasting Oven: with the grid shelf on the third set of runners cook in the oven for about 15-20 minutes until boiling.

Simmering Oven: transfer to the floor of the oven for about 2½ hours.

Roasting Oven: remove the lid and return to the Roasting Oven for about 20-30 minutes to brown the potatoes.

Served with chopped parsley.

INGREDIENTS

3lb (1.5kg) scrag and middle neck of lamb
2 large onions
8oz (225g) carrots
1lb (450g) potatoes
salt and freshly ground black pepper

to garnish
chopped parsley

STUFFED BREAST OF LAMB

If you have fresh spinach in the garden or Swiss Chard use 1lb (450g) and cook it briefly first.

SERVES 4-6

To make stuffing: squeeze out all the liquid from the spinach and chop roughly. Put into a bowl. Fry bacon until most of the fat has run out, add walnuts and fry quickly on the Boiling Plate for 2 minutes, stirring all the time. Add to the bowl with the remaining stuffing ingredients and mix well.

Open out the breast of lamb, trim off any excess fat and season well. Spread stuffing thinly over the lamb then roll up starting from the narrower end of the breast. Secure with string or skewers. Place in a casserole just large enough to hold it and pour over the wine. Cover.

2❚ **❚4**❚ Roasting Oven: with the grid shelf on the floor of the oven cook for 20 minutes.

Simmering Oven: transfer to the oven for a further 2½ hours.

Lift meat out of casserole and put in a roasting tin then cook on the second set of runners in the Roasting Oven for 10 minutes. Skim off the fat from the juices in the casserole, season to taste and serve with the lamb.

INGREDIENTS

1 breast lamb, boned
¼ pint (150ml) white wine

10oz (275g) frozen leaf spinach, thawed
4oz (100g) streaky bacon, chopped
2oz (50g) walnuts, coarsely chopped
2oz (50g) brown breadcrumbs
1 egg, beaten
salt and freshly ground black pepper

SHERRIED KIDNEYS

Kidneys have become less popular over the years so are less expensive yet so good. Serve with rice or noodles.

SERVES 6

Cut kidneys in half lengthwise. Remove skin and core. Heat oil in a large pan. Briskly fry kidneys for a few minutes, turning once. Lift out with a slotted spoon and put into a casserole. Add onion to fat remaining in the pan and fry gently on the Simmering Plate for 5 minutes until soft and golden brown. Stir in flour and cook for a minute. Add tomato purée and blend in stock. Bring to the boil, stirring until thickened. Add sherry and season to taste. Add bay leaf, sausage, mushrooms and redcurrant jelly to sauce, bring to the boil then pour over the kidneys.

2❚ **❚4**❚ Simmering Oven: put casserole in oven for 10 minutes or until kidneys are cooked. Sprinkle with chopped parsley to serve.

INGREDIENTS

12 lamb's kidneys
2 tablespoons oil
1 onion, thinly sliced
1oz (25g) flour
1 teaspoon tomato purée
¾ pint (450ml) stock
6 tablespoons sherry
salt and freshly ground black pepper
1 bayleaf
6oz (175g) German smoked sausage, sliced
4oz (100g) button mushrooms
1 teaspoon redcurrant jelly

to garnish
chopped parsley

BOILED BACON AND GAMMON JOINTS

I have found that when the joints are cooked very slowly, they taste delicious, they are moist and lose very little weight due to shrinkage.

Soak joints in cold water from 6 to 12 hours according to size. Put a small upturned enamel plate in the bottom of a pan so that the joint won't come into contact with the bottom of the pan. Add the joint and cover with fresh cold water, cover, bring slowly to the boil then simmer for 20-30 minutes depending on the size of the joint.

2 Simmering Oven: transfer to the floor of the oven for the following
4 length of time:

2-3lb (900g-1.5kg)	about	1½ hours
4-5lb (1.75kg-2.25kg)	about	2 hours
6-7lb (2.75kg-3kg)	about	2½ hours
8-9lb (3.5kg-4kg)	about	3½-4 hours
10-11lb (4.5kg-5kg)	about	4½ hours
12-13lb (5.5kg-6kg)	about	5 hours
14-15lb (6.5kg-6.75kg)	about	5½ hours
16lb (7.25kg and over)	about	6 hours

Remove from the oven and take out the water. Test for doneness, spear with a skewer though to the centre, it should go through easily and juices run clear or use a meat thermometer. If the temperature is not reached, i.e. 75°C, return to the water, bring to the boil and return to the Simmering Oven until done. Cool a little and cut off any string. Peel off the skin, score fatty surface. Mix dry mustard powder and demerara sugar together and press onto the fatty skin. Cover all the lean meat with foil, stand in a roasting tin.

2 Roasting Oven: brown fairly near the top of the Roasting Oven
4 for about 10-20 minutes, according to size. Do keep an eye on the joint, and turn to get an even colour.

Serve hot with Mustard Dill Sauce leaving out the dill (see page 87).

PRESSED OX TONGUE

Removing the skin and any gristle and bone is not at all difficult but it is easier to do with rubber gloves on and also helps if the tongue is hot. Ox tongues now come trimmed, usually in a vacuum pack.

SERVES 10-12

Soak the tongue in water in the fridge for 24 hours, changing the water several times. Drain off the water and put the tongue into a large pan. Cover with cold water, add the onion, bay leaves and parsley and bring to the boil. Cover and simmer for 5 minutes.

2 Simmering Oven: transfer to the floor of the oven and cook for about
4 3½ hours.

To test if the tongue is cooked, pierce the thickest part with a fine skewer; it will feel tender if cooked. Drain, remove the skin, then the bones and gristle which come at the base of the tongue. Cut the tongue in half lengthways and put one half, cut side down into a 6 inch (15cm) cake tin or deep saucepan, curling it round to fit. Then arrange the second half, cut side up, on top, curling it round in the same way. Cover with a small saucer and press down hard until the juices run to the top. Put some heavy weights on top of the saucer and leave to become cold. Chill in the refrigerator overnight. Turn out onto a plate to serve.

INGREDIENTS

**1 salted and trimmed ox tongue
(about 3½lb (1.5kg))
1 onion, peeled and stuck with
1 clove
2 bay leaves
1 large sprig parsley**

BOILED BACON P.44
MUSTARD SAUCE P.87
COLD PRESSED OX TONGUE P.44
BROAD BEANS IN PARSLEY SAUCE P.72

1lb (450g) fillet of pork
2 tablespoons sunflower oil
1½oz (40g) butter
1 onion, finely chopped
1 tablespoon paprika pepper
good 1oz (25g) flour
½ pint (300ml) stock
5 tablespoons Madeira or sherry
1 tablespoon tomato purée
**6oz (175g) button mushrooms,
sliced**
**salt and freshly ground
black pepper**
¼ pint (150ml) double cream

4 lean pork chops
Meaux mustard
demerara sugar

1-2 pork fillets
12oz (350g) white cabbage
2 teaspoons cornflour
2 tablespoons sherry
2 tablespoons sunflower oil
**salt and freshly ground
black pepper**
**1 small red pepper, seeded and
sliced**
8oz (225g) beansprouts
6 spring onions, shredded
1 clove garlic, crushed
¼ pint (150ml) good stock
2 tablespoons soy sauce

PORK WITH MADEIRA AND CREAM

Very special and very quick to do. There is plenty of sauce with this so serve with creamy mashed potato, noodles or rice and a green salad or broccoli. If you are feeding six, just increase the pork to 1½lb (675g) and the sauce will stretch.

SERVES 4

Cut the fillet into ½ inch (1cm) discs, measure the oil into a large pan and brown the meat on both sides on the Boiling Plate – this will take about 10 minutes. Lift out with a slotted spoon.

Add the butter to the pan and fry the onion until tender on the Simmering Plate. Add paprika and flour and cook for a minute, then gradually blend in the stock, stir until a smooth and thickish sauce. Season to taste and stir in the Madeira, tomato purée and mushrooms. Return the meat to the pan, bring back to the boil and simmer for about 3 minutes until the meat is tender. Just before serving, stir in the cream.

MEAUX PORK CHOPS

Such a simple way of doing chops. I usually serve these with a vegetable in a sauce as there is very little gravy.

SERVES 4

Take the small Aga roasting tin and line with foil – this helps with the washing up! Spread the top of the chops with mustard and sprinkle with sugar.

Roasting Oven: with the grid shelf on the second set of runners, cook for about 20-30 minutes until when pierced in the centre the juices that run out are clear and the tops of the chops crispy and brown.

When the chops are cooked – run a little water in the cooking tin, put on the Simmering Plate and mix in the brown bits from the foil. Season and serve with the chops.

EASTERN STIR-FRY

It helps to chill the fillet before slicing into strips.

SERVES 6

Slice the fillet into fine pencil-thin strips. Shred the cabbage finely. Blend the cornflour with the sherry.

Heat the oil in a wok or large deep frying pan on the Boiling Plate until very hot. Season the pork and cook for 2 minutes, stirring all the time. Lift out with a slotted spoon and keep on one side.

Reheat the pan and add the cabbage, red pepper, bean sprouts, spring onions and garlic. Cook for about 3-4 minutes, tossing all the time. Return the pork to the pan and stir in the stock, soy sauce and sherry mixture. Cook for a further minute until the liquid has thickened slightly and the vegetables are still crisp. Taste and check seasoning. Serve at once.

TWELFTH NIGHT PORK

An easy-to-carve roast, good for entertaining. Get the butcher to bone the loin for you, also have the crackling scored and lifted off.

SERVES 6-8

Remove the skin from the kidneys and snip out the core with a pair of scissors. Mix sausagemeat with the herbs and seasoning. Turn the joint skin side down on a board and with a sharp knife remove any pieces of white tough skin from where the rib bones were. Season lightly and spread with the sausagemeat. Lay the kidneys side by side lengthways along the joint. Roll up the joint and secure with about 3 skewers, or with string. Turn over onto a piece of foil, lift into a roasting tin and lay the piece of crackling on top. Rub with oil and sprinkle with salt.

2 Roasting Oven: roast on the lowest set of runners in the oven with the cold plain shelf on the top set of runners for about 1½-2 hours.

4 Baking Oven: roast near the top of the oven for 1¾-2¼ hours.

The crackling should be crisp and when the meat is prodded with a fine skewer, the juices that run out should be clear. Serve in thin slices with a thin gravy made from the juices.

INGREDIENTS
2 pork kidneys
8oz (225g) pork sausagemeat
1 tablespoon freshly chopped parsley
1 teaspoon dried rubbed sage
salt and freshly ground black pepper
3½lb (1.5kg) joint loin of pork, boned
a little oil

PORK GUARD OF HONOUR

A showy roast. I prefer not to stuff the joint, but to make the fruit risotto and serve it with it.

SERVES 8-10

For the risotto: soften the onion in the oil for 2-3 minutes, add rice and stir well over the heat. Dissolve the stock cube in the boiling water and pour over the rice, add apricots, cover and simmer for about 15 minutes or until liquid is absorbed. Stir in pinenuts, lemon rind and juice and seasoning to taste. Set to one side and serve hot with the pork.

For the joint: wrap the trimmed bone ends with foil to prevent them from burning. Place in a small roasting tin.

2 Roasting Oven: cook in the oven for about 1½ hours, pierce with a fine
4 skewer in the middle of the thickest part, if the juices that run out are clear then the meat is cooked, if still pink, cook for a little longer.

Serve with cutlet frills on the chop bones if liked. Warm risotto, tossing well on Simmering Plate and serve with the pork.

INGREDIENTS
about 4lb (1.75kg) loin of pork in two pieces with 5 chops in each

FRUIT RISOTTO
scant tablespoon sunflower oil
1 onion, chopped
4oz (100g) brown rice
1 chicken stock cube
¾ pint (450ml) boiling water
3oz (75g) dried apricots, chopped
1oz (50g) pinenuts
grated rind and juice 1 lemon
salt and freshly ground black pepper

GRUYÈRE AND CREAM LASAGNE

A richer different lasagne dish – do not freeze because of the cream.

SERVES 6

Heat the oil in a frying pan and fry the onion and celery until golden. Add beef and fry until browned, add mushrooms and fry for a few more seconds. Pour in the wine, tomatoes and add seasoning to taste. Stir in the cream cheese. Bring to the boil, cover with a lid and simmer for 5 minutes.

2 Simmering Oven: transfer to the floor of the oven for about 30 minutes.
4

Stir the flour into the single cream. Cut the ham or sausage into thin slithers and put in the base of a large, shallow, greased ovenproof dish. Put a layer of lasagne in the dish then a layer of beef sauce, followed by cream and then cheese. Continue in layers until all the ingredients have been used, ending with a layer of cheese on top.

2 Roasting Oven: with the grid shelf on the floor of the oven bake in the
4 oven for about 30-35 minutes until golden brown.

INGREDIENTS
1 tablespoon olive oil
2 medium onions, chopped
1 stick celery, chopped
8oz (225g) raw minced beef
4oz (100g) button mushrooms, sliced
¼ pint (150ml) white wine
14oz (397g) can tomatoes
salt and freshly ground black pepper
4oz (100g) cream cheese
6oz (175g) lasagne
1 tablespoon flour
½ pint (300ml) single cream
4oz (100g) continental ham or sausage
4oz (100g) Gruyère cheese, grated

2½lb (1.25kg) knuckle veal
1½oz (40g) flour
salt and freshly ground
black pepper
3 tablespoons sunflower oil
2 cloves garlic, crushed
1 onion, sliced
3 carrots, sliced
3 sticks celery, sliced
¼ pint (150ml) white wine
¼ pint (150ml) light stock
14oz (400g) can chopped tomatoes

1½lb (675g) stewing veal
2 onions, sliced
2 carrots, sliced
1 bay leaf
juice ½ lemon
salt and freshly ground black
pepper
6oz (175g) button mushrooms,
quartered
2oz (50g) butter
2oz (50g) flour
3-4 tablespoons double cream

t o   g a r n i s h
chopped fresh parsley

2lb (900g) veal roasting joint
grated rind and juice of 1 lemon
4 sprigs thyme
3 tablespoons olive oil
ground black pepper

g r a v y
¼ pint (150ml) white wine
¼ pint (150ml) light stock
salt and freshly ground
black pepper

OSSO BUCO

A good winter casserole which needs long slow cooking. Ask your butcher to cut the veal knuckle into 2 inch (5cm) chunks.

SERVES 6

Toss the veal in the flour and seasoning until evenly coated. Heat 2 tablespoons of the oil in a heavy frying pan on the Boiling Plate and brown the meat then transfer to a large casserole. Add the remaining oil to the pan with the garlic, onion, carrots and celery, stir well then cover and leave to cook for 2 or 3 minutes. Add wine and bring to the boil and pour over the meat. Put the stock and tomatoes into the pan and also bring to the boil then pour over the meat. If the meat isn't covered then add a little extra water. Bring to the boil, cover and simmer 5 minutes.

2▉ ▉4▉ Simmering Oven: transfer the casserole to the floor of the oven and leave for 2-3 hours or until tender. Check seasoning before serving.

BLANQUETTE OF VEAL

A classic stew in a creamy mushroom sauce.

SERVES 6

Cut the veal into 1 inch (2.5cm) cubes. Place in a pan, cover with cold water and bring to the boil on the Boiling Plate, skim off the scum and drain the veal. Return the veal to the pan with the onion, carrot and bay leaf and add 1½ pints (900ml) of water; add the lemon juice, seasoning and bring to the boil. Simmer for 15 minutes. Cover.

2▉ ▉4▉ Simmering Oven: transfer to the oven for about 1 hour.

Add the mushrooms and return to the oven for a further 20 minutes or until the veal is tender. Lift out the veal and vegetables into a shallow serving dish. Discard the bay leaf. Reduce the stock to 1 pint (600ml). Melt the butter in a pan on the Simmering Plate, add the flour and cook for a minute. Blend in the warm stock, stirring until thickened. Return the meat and vegetables to the sauce and bring to the boil, stirring. Check seasoning. When ready to serve, stir in the cream and heat through. Turn into the warmed serving dish and sprinkle with parsley.

LEMON MARINATED VEAL

Veal is often dry and without flavour. The lemon marinade is a great improvement and tenderizes the meat.

SERVES 4-6

Put the veal in the piece in a polythene bag. Add remaining ingredients, put a tie twist at the end of the bag and leave in the fridge for 3 days, turning each day. Put the contents of the bag into the small roasting tin.

2▉ ▉4▉ Roasting Oven: with the grid shelf near the top of the oven, roast for 20 minutes to the lb (450g). If it is a very compact, solid joint it may take a few more minutes.

Lift joint onto an enamel plate, discard the thyme. Transfer the joint to the Simmering Oven whilst making the gravy. Skim fat off juices, add wine and stock and reduce by half. Season to taste and serve with the veal.

LAMB'S KIDNEYS IN MUSTARD CREAM SAUCE

Best with pasta, allow 3oz (75g) per head.

SERVES 4

Halve the kidneys. Heat oil and butter in a large pan on the Boiling Plate. Brown the kidneys on both sides, lift out onto a plate. Add flour, cook for a few moments, add Madeira and allow to thicken slightly, stir in cream. Reduce a little, until the sauce will coat the back of the spoon. Add seasoning and mustard. Return kidneys, include any juices on the plate, to the pan and bring to the boil. Check seasoning. Cover with a lid.

2 4 Simmering Oven: stand on the floor of the oven for about 20 minutes.

Meanwhile cook the pasta as instructed on the packet, drain and toss in a little butter and lots of parsley. Serve the kidneys with the pasta and a green salad.

INGREDIENTS

1lb (450g) lamb's kidneys,
skinned and cored
2 tablespoons sunflower oil
1oz (25g) butter
1 teaspoon flour
small wine glass Madeira
½ pint (300ml) double cream
3 good teaspoons Dijon mustard
salt and freshly ground
black pepper
12oz (350g) Penne (Quills)
pasta shapes
chopped parsley

CALVES' LIVER WITH SAGE AND LEMON

If you like your liver rare, just half a minute on each side is sufficient cooking time. Make sure that your butcher cuts the liver in thin slices whichever way you like it done.

SERVES 4

Season the liver on both sides. Melt the butter in a large frying pan, add the lemon juice and sage. On the Boiling Plate bring the butter to foaming point and drop in the slices of liver a few at a time. Fry for barely a minute on each side and serve at once with green salad and fresh bread.

INGREDIENTS

1lb (450g) fresh calves' liver,
thinly sliced
salt and freshly ground black
pepper
1oz (25g) butter
juice ½ lemon
3 sprigs sage, the leaves chopped
coarsely, or 1 tsp dried sage

OXTAIL

If you use a non-stick frying pan there is no need for any extra fat as the oxtail has plenty of its own, even when trimmed.

SERVES 6

Trim off any excess fat from the oxtail joints. Brown really well on all sides then transfer to a casserole. Fry the bacon strips in the pan for about 5 minutes then add the chopped vegetables and cook for a further 4-5 minutes, add the flour and stock, stir well and cook until beginning to thicken, pour over the meat and add remaining ingredients, bring to the boil, cover and simmer for 5 minutes.

2 4 Simmering Oven: transfer to the floor of the oven for 6-7 hours or until tender. Take care to skim off any excess fat once the oxtail is cooked, this is much more easily done if the dish is allowed to go cold and the fat sets. Check seasoning before serving.

INGREDIENTS

3lb (1.5kg) oxtail, in pieces
2 rashers streaky bacon,
cut into strips
2 onions, sliced
3 carrots, sliced
8 sticks celery, chopped
2oz (50g) flour
1½ pints (900ml) beef stock
2 bay leaves
3 sprigs parsley
salt and freshly ground
black pepper

I N G R E D I E N T S

4 lamb's hearts

s t u f f i n g
**4 rashers streaky bacon, snipped
4oz (100g) mushrooms, chopped
salt and freshly ground
black pepper**

s a u c e
**1oz (25g) butter
1 large Spanish onion, chopped
1 level tablespoon flour
¹⁄₈ pint (75ml) wine or stock
14oz (397g) can chopped tomatoes**

t o   g a r n i s h
freshly chopped parsley

I N G R E D I E N T S

2lb (900g) lamb's tongues

s t o c k
**1 onion, 2 carrots, 2 sticks celery,
bunch fresh herbs
salt and freshly ground
black pepper
4 rashers streaky bacon
10 shallots
3 carrots, sliced
4oz (100g) button mushrooms,
halved
7oz (200g) can tomatoes
1 tablespoon Worcestershire sauce
6 fl oz (175ml) cider**

c a p e r   s a u c e
**1¹⁄₂oz (40g) butter
1¹⁄₂oz (40g) flour
³⁄₄ pint (450ml) milk
2 tablespoons capers
salt and freshly ground
black pepper**

BRAISED STUFFED LAMB'S HEARTS

Lamb's hearts are inexpensive and with care they can be a good family supper. I cannot be bothered to sew up the hearts to keep them together, it is such a chore. I just put a little stuffing into the prepared heart and lift them onto a tomato and onion sauce. There is masses of sauce so serve with something to sop it up such as mashed celeriac and potato or rice.

SERVES 4

Take the lamb's hearts, wash in cold water and snip out the white tubes and the centre channel to make room for stuffing. Brown the hearts in a little fat in a frying pan and lift out onto a plate.

Add bacon and mushrooms to the pan, toss for about 5 minutes, season. Divide this mixture between the four hearts, stuffing it well down into the cavity. It will not fill the hearts to the brim.

Now make the sauce: add the butter to the pan, then the onion and fry gently on the Simmering Plate until just beginning to brown. Sprinkle in the flour. Add wine or stock, stirring until thickened. Add contents of the can of tomatoes, season well. Pour into a small deep Aga casserole. Arrange hearts on top, open side uppermost. Cover with a lid.

Roasting Oven: with the grid shelf on the floor of the oven cook for about 15 minutes.

Simmering Oven: transfer to the floor of the oven for 4-5 hours or until tender. Skim off any extra fat, taste and check seasoning and serve from the casserole, each heart sprinkled with parsley.

OLD ENGLISH LAMB'S TONGUES SERVED WITH CAPER SAUCE

A traditional recipe, easy to prepare ahead, making the caper sauce at the last minute. Also a marvellous way to get children to eat offal as the mild flavour of this dish is generally more to their taste than liver or kidneys. The size of the lamb's tongues does vary, small ones can be left whole. The larger ones need a longer time for the initial cooking and should be cut into diagonal pieces.

SERVES 6

Rinse the lamb's tongues in cold water, put into a large pan with the vegetables, herbs and seasoning, cover with water, bring to the boil, cover and simmer for 10 minutes.

Simmering Oven: transfer to the floor of the oven and cook for 2¹⁄₂ hours.

Drain the lamb's tongues and vegetables, discard the vegetables and set the tongues to one side. Reduce the stock to about two thirds. When the tongues have cooled a little, take off the skins and remove any gristly pieces.

Cut the bacon into thin strips, fry until nearly crisp, add shallots and cook until just beginning to brown, then add the carrots, mushrooms, tomatoes and lamb's tongues. Stir well and transfer to a large casserole. Add the reduced stock, Worcestershire sauce and cider to nearly cover the tongues. Bring to the boil then return to the floor of the oven for a further hour. Check the seasoning.

For the sauce: melt the butter in a pan, add the flour and cook for a minute then gradually add the milk and bring to the boil, stirring until thickened. Add capers and seasoning and serve with the tongues.

POULTRY & GAME

ROAST PHEASANT P.52 · FRIED BREADCRUMBS P.52 · DEAD EASY REDCURRANT JELLY P.131

*R*oasts, of course, are perfect in the Aga. Crisp outside and beautifully moist on the inside. Served with all the traditional accompaniments, there's nothing quite like a brace of golden Aga-roasted pheasants or a celebration turkey. Country dwellers, whose freezers tend to fill up in the winter months with gifts of game, will find lots of different ideas for casseroling and simmer-roasting. In addition, I've included some easy ways with chicken leftovers. Try Hot American Chicken Salad (P.60). I defy anyone to take longer than ten minutes to prepare it!

ROAST CHICKEN

Lightly smear chicken with soft butter or sunflower oil. Season. Put onion, whole lemon cut in halves or herbs in the cavity. Stuff the breast end, if liked. Stand on grill rack in a roasting tin. Cover breast with foil, remove to brown.

2▪ Roasting Oven: slide the tin onto the lowest set of runners.
▪4▪

2lb (900g) small chicken about 45 minutes;
3lb (1.5kg) medium chicken about 1 hour;
4lb (1.75kg) large chicken about 1½ hours.

To see if cooked, pierce the thickest part of the thigh with a small sharp knife and if the juices that run out are clear then the chicken is done, if still pink cook for a little longer.

ROAST TURKEY

There are two methods of cooking turkey in the Aga. The slow overnight method not only gives a very moist bird but leaves the oven free to cook all the other trimmings that go with the turkey. Rest the bird 15 minutes before serving covered with foil. If your Aga Simmering Oven is slow it is advisable to lightly brown the turkey in the Roasting Oven first.

Preparation of turkey for the oven: stuff the breast end with any meat stuffing and the body cavity with non-meat stuffing. Lightly butter the bird. Lift into the large roasting tin – putting on a grill rack if liked. Leave untrussed. Loosely cover with foil.

2▪ **Slow roasting:** place on the grid shelf on the floor of the Simmering
▪4▪ Oven. See column.

For a turkey over 22lb (10kg) start off in the Roasting Oven until lightly browned, about 30 minutes. Cover loosely with foil and transfer to the Simmering Oven for 11 – 16 hours.

Take the turkey out of the oven, pierce the thickest part of the thigh with a small sharp knife – if the juices that run out are clear then the turkey is done, if they are still tinged with pink then cook for a little longer. If in doubt use a meat thermometer to check.

Drain off the liquid from the tin, skim off the fat and keep the stock for gravy. Remove the foil. Transfer the bird to the Roasting Oven to brown the skin. Serve with bacon rolls, gravy, sausages, bread sauce (page 86) and cranberry sauce (page 86).

If a smaller bird is cooked too far ahead, keep covered and put in a cool place. Then uncover and transfer to the Roasting Oven half an hour before serving to crisp and reheat.

2▪ **Fast roasting:** cover with foil and cook in the large roasting tin on
▪4▪ the lowest set of runners in the Roasting Oven. See column.

Baste the bird from time to time. Remove the foil 30 minutes before the end of cooking to crisp the skin. Test that the bird is done and serve as above.

ROAST PHEASANT

Serve with game chips, bread sauce or fried breadcrumbs. To make these, fry fresh white breadcrumbs in butter and oil until golden – season well. Also serve gravy made from the stock from the giblets plus the juices and a fruit jelly, such as redcurrant or apple. Garnish with watercress. Put the birds in a roasting tin, rub with butter, season and lie the bacon over the breasts.

2▪ Roasting Oven: hang the tin on the middle set of runners. Roast, basting
▪4▪ once, for 45 – 50 minutes until golden and when the thigh is pierced with a fine skewer the juices that run out are clear.

8 – 10lb (3.6 – 4.5kg)
turkey about 8 – 10 hours;
11 – 16lb (5 – 7.25kg)
turkey about 9 – 12 hours;
17 – 22lb (7.5 – 10kg)
turkey about 10 – 14 hours.

8 – 10lb (3.6 – 4.5kg)
turkey about 1¾ – 2 hours;
11 – 16lb (5 – 7.25kg)
turkey about 2½ hours;
17 – 22lb (7.5 – 10kg)
turkey about 3 hours.

I N G R E D I E N T S
**Brace of young pheasants
knob butter
seasoning
2 rashers streaky bacon**

ROAST PARTRIDGE

Cook as for pheasant for 30 – 35 minutes as the birds are smaller.

ROAST DUCK OR GOOSE

It is better to buy two smaller geese at 10 – 12lb (4.5 – 5kg) rather than one large. Each goose serves 6 – 8. Also two smaller ducks rather than one large. Cooking times are not that much longer.

Prick the skin and place upside down on the grill rack in the roasting tin. Place on the lowest set of runners in the Roasting Oven. Roast until brown on the underside, goose about 30 minutes, duck about 20 minutes. Reverse to sit the right way up and brown the breast, the time will vary but less than the underside.

Transfer to the Simmering Oven until tender, goose about 2 hours, duck about 1 hour. Return to the Roasting Oven to crispen the skin. Serve with sage and onion stuffing, apple sauce and thick gravy.

ROAST GROUSE

A great luxury these days. Again only roast young ones – casserole older birds, using the recipe on page 56. Roast as for pheasant but for only 30 minutes or less for a small bird. Serve each bird on a disc of fried bread spread with sautéed grouse liver. Don't leave the bird to stand on the bread for too long as the juices from the bird drain out and makes it soggy. Serve with the same delicious trimmings as pheasant.

WOODCOCK, SNIPE OR QUAIL

Roast as for grouse but only 15 minutes.

JUGGED HARE

One of the recipes that the Aga is made for. Serve with forcemeat balls and a fruit jelly. The hare gravy is thickened with beurre manié, just equal quantities of butter and flour creamed together and then dropped into the hot gravy.

SERVES 6-8

The day before: combine all the ingredients for the marinade, take two large strong freezer bags, putting one inside the other and put the jointed hare and marinade into them. Seal and leave overnight in the refrigerator.

Next day: remove hare from the marinade, strain liquid and set aside. Fry bacon gently for 2 minutes, add a little butter and fry the hare joints a few at a time until browned and transfer into a casserole dish. Add the onion to the pan and fry until softened, add redcurrant jelly and stir until dissolved, then pour over the hare with the remaining ingredients and season. Measure the saved marinade and make up to 1 pint (600ml) with water, add to the casserole. Bring to the boil, cover and simmer 5 minutes.

2▮
▮4▮ Simmering Oven: transfer to the floor of the oven for about 5-7 hours until tender, according to how old the hare is.

Make the beurre manié: cream the butter with the flour. Lift the hare joints out of the casserole with a slotted spoon and add teaspoons of the beurre manié to the hot liquid in the casserole, bring to the boil and stir until thickened. Return the hare to the casserole and check seasoning.

Meanwhile prepare the forcemeat balls, snip the bacon and blend all the ingredients together and season well. Roll into about 12 balls, then fry until crisp and brown on all sides. Add to the jugged hare just before serving.

INGREDIENTS

MARINADE

½ pint (300ml) red wine
2 bay leaves
freshly ground black pepper
2 cloves garlic, split in 4
2 tablespoons sunflower oil
1 onion, sliced

JUGGED HARE

1 hare, jointed
2oz (50g) streaky bacon,
cut into strips
1oz (25g) butter
2 onions, chopped
2 tablespoons redcurrant jelly
¼ pint (150ml) inexpensive port
grated rind and juice ½ lemon
4 sticks celery, chopped
salt

BEURRE MANIÉ

2oz (50g) butter
2oz (50g) flour

FORCEMEAT BALLS

2oz (50g) cooked bacon rashers,
2oz (50g) shredded suet
grated rind 1 lemon
2 tablespoons chopped parsley
4oz (100g) white breadcrumbs
1 egg, beaten
a little butter and oil for frying

**2lb (900g) stewing venison, cut into
1 inch (2.25cm) cubes
½ pint (300ml) inexpensive
red wine
2 bay leaves
1oz (25g) butter
1 tablespoon sunflower oil
1 large onion, chopped
1oz (25g) flour
½ pint (300ml) stock
4oz (100g) German smoked sausage,
sliced
1 tablespoon redcurrant jelly
salt and freshly ground
black pepper
6oz (175g) button mushrooms,
sliced**

**2 tablespoons sunflower oil
1oz (50g) butter
1 good sized pheasant or a brace of
smaller birds
4oz (100g) streaky bacon, snipped
1½oz (40g) flour
½ pint (300ml) red wine
½ pint (300ml) stock
2 tablespoons bramble jelly
1 tablespoon Worcestershire sauce
1 teaspoon freshly chopped thyme
salt and freshly ground
black pepper
about 16 button onions
a little gravy browning**

**6oz (175g) dried chestnuts,
soaked overnight in cold water
2 tablespoons sunflower oil
1oz (25g) butter
a brace roasting pheasants
2oz (50g) flour
½ pint (300ml) inexpensive
red wine
1 pint (600ml) good stock
2 onions, quartered
thinly peeled rind and
juice 1 orange
2 teaspoons redcurrant jelly
salt and freshly ground
black pepper**

HIGHLAND VENISON

Venison for stewing is very lean, reasonable in price and so good. I find it best if marinated in the refrigerator for at least 48 hours first.

SERVES 4

Put the venison in a glass or china bowl with the red wine and bay leaves, cover and leave to marinade in the refrigerator for about 48 hours. Strain the red wine from the venison and keep. Discard the bay leaves.

Measure the butter and oil into a large pan, cook the onion gently on the Simmering Plate for about 10 minutes, then stir in the flour and cook for a minute. Gradually blend in the stock and red wine. Bring to the boil, stirring until thickened. Stir in the venison with the smoked sausage, redcurrant jelly and seasoning. Bring back to the boil and cover with a lid. Simmer 5 minutes.

2 Simmering Oven: cook on the floor of the oven for about 4 hours or
4 until the venison is tender, adding the mushrooms for the last 30 minutes or so of cooking.

Serve with creamy mashed potato and a green vegetable such as green beans or broccoli.

COUNTRY PHEASANT CASSEROLE

Cooking time will vary according to the age of the pheasant – an older bird will take longer, about 4-5 hours.

SERVES 4

Heat the oil and butter in a large pan, add the pheasant and fry quickly on the Boiling Plate to brown. Lift out onto a plate and leave on one side. Fry the bacon in the pan for about 3 minutes and then lift out with a slotted spoon and add to the pheasant. Stir the flour into the fat remaining in the pan and cook for a minute. Gradually blend in the wine and stock, bring to the boil, stirring until thickened. Add the remaining ingredients, return the pheasant to the pan with the bacon, cover with a lid and bring back to the boil. Simmer 5 minutes.

2 Simmering Oven: transfer to the floor of the oven for about 3-4 hours
4 until the pheasant is tender. Lift the pheasant out of the pan, take the meat off the bone and return the meat to the sauce. Taste and check seasoning. Reheat and serve with creamy mashed potato and a crisp green vegetable.

PHEASANT WITH ORANGE AND CHESTNUTS

The timing of this recipe is for roasting birds, but you can use old birds very satisfactorily or even ones that are old and badly shot. They may well take 4-5 hours to get really tender.

SERVES 6-8

Strain the chestnuts. Heat 1 tablespoon of the oil in a large pan with the butter and fry the pheasant on the Boiling Plate until browned all over. Lift out and put on one side. Add the remaining oil to the pan with the chestnuts and fry quickly to brown. Lift out with a slotted spoon and add to the pheasant. Add the flour to the fat remaining in the pan and cook gently for a minute. Stir in the wine and stock and bring to the boil, stirring until thickened.

Add the onions to the pan with the orange rind, juice, redcurrant jelly and seasoning, blend together then return the pheasant and chestnuts to the pan. Cover with a lid and bring back to the boil, simmer for about 10 minutes.

2 Simmering Oven: transfer the pan to the floor of the oven for about 3-4
4 hours. The timing will depend largely on the age of the birds. Taste to check seasoning and remove the rind before serving.

HIGHLAND VENISON
IN ITS MARINADE P.54
JUGGED HARE P.53

INGREDIENTS

1oz (25g) butter
1 tablespoon oil
3 old grouse
6oz (175g) streaky bacon, cut into strips
2 sticks celery, chopped
8oz (225g) button onions
1½oz (40g) flour
½ pint (300ml) chicken stock
¼ pint (150ml) inexpensive red wine
bouquet garni
1 tablespoon redcurrant jelly
salt and freshly ground black pepper

t o   g a r n i s h
chopped parsley

INGREDIENTS

2oz (50g) boiled ham, diced
1 onion, chopped
2 carrots, diced
2 sticks celery, sliced
2oz (50g) butter
1 tablespoon sunflower oil
4 pigeons
¾oz (20g) flour
½ pint (300ml) cider
salt and freshly ground black pepper
¼ pint (150ml) double cream, optional

INGREDIENTS

4 poussins
4 sprigs fresh thyme, parsley and marjoram
1 tablespoon sunflower oil
good knob butter
4 onions, sliced
4oz (100g) button mushrooms
1 heaped teaspoon flour
½ pint (300ml) cider
salt and freshly ground black pepper
a little ground mace or nutmeg

t o   g a r n i s h
freshly chopped parsley and thyme

KETTLEPOT GROUSE CASSEROLE

Of course you could use any aged game bird for this recipe. Why Kettlepot? Because the grouse used to test the recipe came from Kettlepot Moor.

SERVES 6

Heat butter and oil in a large pan. Fry the grouse quickly on the Boiling Plate to brown on all sides. Lift out and place in a casserole breast side down. Add the bacon, celery and onions to the pan and fry gently for 5 minutes. Lift out with a slotted spoon and add to the grouse in the casserole.

Stir flour into the pan and cook for a minute. Add the stock with the wine and bring to the boil, stirring until thickened. Season and add bouquet garni and redcurrant jelly. Pour over grouse. Cover with a lid.

2◼ ◼4◼ Roasting Oven: with the grid shelf on the floor of the oven cook for 20 minutes.

Simmering Oven: transfer to the floor of the oven and cook for a further 1½ hours or until the grouse are tender.

Lift out the grouse and cut in half. Remove bouquet garni, check seasoning of sauce then return grouse to casserole, sprinkle with chopped parsley to serve.

WOOD PIGEON IN CIDER

Very successful for cooking an old pheasant also. To smarten up the sauce for a dinner party, add 2 tablespoons of Calvados to the final stage.

SERVES 4

Soften the ham, onion, carrot and celery in 1oz (25g) of the butter in a large covered frying pan. Transfer with a slotted spoon into a large casserole dish. Add the remaining 1oz (25g) butter and sunflower oil and brown the pigeon on all sides. Lift the birds onto the bed of vegetables. Stir the flour into the fat remaining in the pan and cook for a minute, add the cider a little at a time and bring to the boil, stirring until thickened. Season and pour over the pigeon, bring to the boil and cover with a lid.

2◼ ◼4◼ Roasting Oven: transfer to the floor of the oven for 10 minutes.

Simmering Oven: transfer to the floor of the oven for about 4 hours. Remove birds from the sauce, arrange on a warmed serving dish, stir the cream into the sauce, bring to the boil, check seasoning and pour over the birds. Serve immediately.

HERBED POUSSIN

Also very good with pigeons, but cooking time is about 6 hours.

SERVES 4

First take the poussins and put a bunch of the three herbs inside each carcass. Heat the oil and butter in a large pan on the Boiling Plate and brown the birds on all sides, lift out with a slotted spoon and leave on one side.

Add the onions to the pan and toss in the fat to take up all the sediment, add mushrooms and cook for a minute. Stir in the flour, mix well and then add the cider. Bring to the boil and season with salt, pepper and mace. Pour this mixture into a casserole large enough to take the four birds.

Arrange the poussins on top, season the breasts with salt and pepper. Cover with a lid and bring back to the boil.

2◼ ◼4◼ Simmering Oven: transfer to the floor of the oven for about 1½ hours or until the birds are tender. Taste and check seasoning of the sauce then serve sprinkled with chopped parsley and thyme.

Duck Breast Fillets with Lemon and Honey Sauce

Duck breast fillets are becoming more available. If you like the meat still pink, roast for a shorter time.

SERVES 4

Dry the duckling fillets with kitchen paper. Place, skin side down in a frying pan on the Boiling Plate and fry quickly to brown the skin and release some of the fat. Drain well and arrange, skin side up in the small roasting tin. Pour a teaspoon of honey over each breast.

2 Roasting Oven: roast near the top of the oven for 15 – 20 minutes.
4

For the sauce, add the onion and garlic to the juices remaining in the pan and cook gently on the Simmering Plate until lightly browned. Stir in the stock, lemon rind, juice and honey. Blend the cornflour with the port and stir into the pan. Simmer, stirring for 2 minutes. Add the soy sauce and season.

Cut each breast fillet diagonally across the grain into thin slices and arrange on hot individual serving plates together with a little sauce. Garnish with watercress and lemon slices.

INGREDIENTS
**4 large duck breast fillets
1 tablespoon clear honey**

sauce
**4oz (100g) onion, finely chopped
1 clove garlic, crushed
¼ pint (150ml) stock
finely grated rind and juice 1 lemon
1 tablespoon clear honey
2 level teaspoons cornflour
2 tablespoons port
1 teaspoon soy sauce
salt and freshly ground black pepper**

to garnish
watercress and lemon slices

Duck Leg Portions in Orange Port Sauce

Duckling is now available in portions and the Aga makes them really tender.

SERVES 4

Cut any surplus fat away from the underside of the duck portions. Prick skin. Cut orange in four. Line the small Aga roasting tin with foil, arrange the joints in the tin with a slice of orange underneath each. Season.

2 Roasting Oven: hang the tin on the highest set of runners in the oven for
4 20-30 minutes to brown. Cover with foil.

Simmering Oven: transfer to the bottom set of runners in the oven for about 1½ hours until tender. Strain off all the liquid. Return to the Roasting Oven for a few minutes to crisp the duckling.

Meanwhile prepare the sauce; spoon off 2 tablespoons duck fat from the liquid into a small pan and fry the shallot until tender. Stir in the flour. Make skimmed juices up to ½ pint (300ml) with stock. Gradually stir into the shallot and flour and bring to the boil, stirring until thickened. Add the redcurrant jelly, port and seasoning and add a dash of gravy browning, if liked. Garnish with slices of orange and sprigs of watercress.

INGREDIENTS
**4 duckling leg portions, thawed
1 orange
salt and freshly ground
black pepper
2 tablespoons duck fat
1 shallot, chopped
1oz (25g) flour
about ¼ pint (150ml) stock
1 teaspoon redcurrant jelly
1 glass port
dash gravy browning**

to garnish
slices of orange and watercress

Garlic Chicken

Quick and easy. Can be prepared well ahead and cooked later.

SERVES 4

Trim off any surplus fat and skin from the breasts. Measure the butter, herbs, garlic and seasoning into a small bowl and mix well until thoroughly blended. With a sharp knife, make three deep cuts in each of the chicken breasts and spread a little garlic butter into each of the cuts. Arrange in a shallow ovenproof dish so the breasts are just touching.

2 Roasting Oven: With the grid shelf on the floor of the oven, cook the
4 chicken breasts for about 20 minutes, or until tender. Serve straight away.

INGREDIENTS
**4 boneless chicken breasts
4oz (100g) butter, softened
2 good tablespoons freshly chopped
mixed herbs
2 fat cloves garlic, crushed
salt and freshly ground black pepper**

GARLIC CHICKEN P.57
DUCKLING PORTIONS IN
ORANGE PORT SAUCE P.57
HOT AMERICAN CHICKEN SALAD P.60

COQ AU VIN

A classic French dish. Wonderful to leave in the Simmering Oven to cook. Garnish with button onions and fried croûtons of bread.

SERVES 4

Heat the butter and oil in a large pan and fry the chicken until evenly browned, lift out with a slotted spoon and leave on one side. Add the bacon to the pan with the onion and celery and fry on the Simmering Plate for about 10 minutes until soft. Add the garlic and flour and cook for a minute, then gradually blend in the stock and wine. Bring to the boil, stirring until thickened. Season to taste and return the chicken and add the mushrooms to the pan. Bring back to the boil, cover with a lid and simmer for 5 minutes.

2 **4** Simmering Oven: transfer the casserole to the floor of the oven and cook for about 1½ – 2 hours until the chicken is tender. Skim off any fat and taste and check seasoning before serving.

I N G R E D I E N T S
1oz (25g) butter
1 tablespoon sunflower oil
4 chicken joints, skinned
4oz (100g) smoked bacon rashers, snipped
1 large onion, chopped
2 sticks celery, chopped
1 fat clove garlic, crushed
1 oz (25g) flour
¾ pint (450ml) light stock
¼ pint (150ml) red wine
salt and freshly ground black pepper
4oz (100g) button mushrooms

BONED HERBED CHICKEN WITH CREAMY WINE SAUCE

A favourite for a dinner party. You'll find it a lot easier not to bone out the last bones of the limbs. The sauce is a thin cream sauce – double the amount of flour for a thicker sauce.

SERVES 6

Bone the chicken. Make a cut along the length of the back bone and with a small sharp knife cut the flesh away from the bones down each side. When you come to the wing knuckle cut it away from the carcass. Scrape the meat off the bone down to the first joint. Cut off there and then repeat with the other side.

With the leg joint, cut away again at the carcass, but scrape the meat away from the first bone of the leg, cut off there and then repeat with the other side. Carefully cut the meat away from the rest of the carcass until you can lift it out. Remove any excess lumps of fat and lay the chicken skin side down on a board, turning the legs back into shape. Use the carcass for making stock.

Mix together the stuffing ingredients in a bowl and spread this mixture down the centre of the chicken. Wrap the chicken over. Turn over and shape to resemble a chicken. I would sew up with a trussing needle and fine string, or with skewers. Lift into the small Aga roasting tin and lightly spread the breast with a little butter.

2 **4** Roasting Oven: hang the roasting tin on the second set of runners and cook in the oven for about 1¼ – 1½ hours. The chicken is cooked when the juices run clear when pierced with a fine skewer.

Make the sauce whilst the chicken is roasting. First melt the butter in a pan then add the onion and sauté on the Simmering Plate with the pan lid on. When the onion is soft add the wine and boil with the lid off until a syrupy consistency. Mix 2 tablespoons of the stock with the flour and blend well. Add the remainder of the stock to the reduced wine, bring to the boil. Add some of this hot stock to the flour mixture then return it to the pan, stir well and bring back to the boil; it will be slightly thick. Season well and just before serving stir in the cream, then keep warm.

Serve the chicken hot, carved in not too thin slices, with the sauce.

I N G R E D I E N T S
3.5lb (1.5kg) roasting chicken

s t u f f i n g

1lb (450g) pork sausagemeat
1 teaspoon dried sage
1 shallot, grated
2 fat cloves garlic, crushed
6oz (175g) chopped cooked ham
6oz (175g) chopped cooked tongue
grated rind 1 lemon
2 tablespoons chopped fresh parsley
1 teaspoon chopped fresh thyme
salt and freshly ground black pepper

s a u c e

good knob butter
1 small onion, finely chopped
1 glass white wine
1 heaped tablespoon flour
½ pint (300ml) chicken stock
¼ pint (150ml) double cream

INGREDIENTS

12oz (350g) cooked chicken, diced
4 sticks celery, finely sliced
4 spring onions, finely sliced
½ pint (300ml) mayonnaise
2 teaspoons lemon juice
salt and freshly ground black pepper
4oz (100g) well-flavoured Cheddar cheese, grated

t o p p i n g
1 packet potato crisps, crumbled
little paprika pepper.

INGREDIENTS

2 tablespoons olive oil
1 small onion, chopped
1 fat clove garlic, crushed
2 tablespoons tomato purée
6.5oz (185g) can red peppers, drained
1 tablespoon redcurrant jelly
juice ½ lemon
salt and freshly ground black pepper
¾ pint (450ml) good thick mayonnaise
1lb (450g) cooked chicken, diced

t o   g a r n i s h
watercress

INGREDIENTS

1½ inch piece fresh root ginger, peeled and chopped finely
3 fat cloves garlic, pressed
pinch chilli powder
¼ teaspoon ground cloves
¼ teaspoon ground cardamoms
2 teaspoons ground coriander
¼ teaspoon ground turmeric
2oz (50g) butter
2 onions, finely chopped
2lb (900g) chicken thighs
½ pint (300ml) natural yogurt
2 good teaspoons flour
juice of ½ lemon
salt

HOT AMERICAN CHICKEN SALAD

A very easy recipe – take great care not to cook for too long otherwise the sauce will curdle. This recipe makes the last cuts from a roast chicken into something special.

SERVES 4

Measure into a bowl all the ingredients, together with 3oz (75g) of the cheese. Season and blend together. Turn into a shallow ovenproof dish. Top with the remaining cheese, crisps and a dusting of paprika pepper.

2▪ Roasting Oven: with the grid shelf on the top or second runners cook
▪4▪ for about 10 – 15 minutes until hot. Don't cook longer otherwise the sauce will separate. Serve straight away. The cooking time is short so cook as required. Garnish with fresh tarragon or parsley.

PIMENTO CHICKEN MAYONNAISE

Essential to mix the chicken and sauce together the day before so that the flavours have time to develop.

SERVES 8

Heat the oil in a small pan on the Simmering Plate, add the onion and garlic and fry gently for about 10 minutes until the onion is tender. Add the tomato purée, all but one of the red peppers, the jelly, lemon juice and seasoning. Continue to cook until the jelly has melted. Turn the mixture into a processor or blender and reduce to a purée. Turn into a bowl and allow to cool then stir in the mayonnaise and chicken meat. Cover and leave in the refrigerator overnight.

To serve, arrange the watercress around a large flat dish and pile the chicken into the centre. Slice the reserved red pepper into thin strips and arrange in a lattice pattern over the chicken.

CHICKEN CURRY

A creamy mild curry. Take care not to overcook. Serve with brown rice with added chopped parsley and a little freshly chopped coriander.

SERVES 6

Mix together ginger, garlic and all the spices. Melt the butter in a pan on the Simmering Plate, add the onions and chicken and fry for about 5 minutes, then stir in the spice mixture with the yogurt and mix well. Cover the pan with a lid and bring to simmering point.

2▪ Simmering Oven: cook on the floor of the oven for about an hour. Stir
▪4▪ the flour into the lemon juice, add salt, and mix well into the chicken. Continue to cook for a further 30 minutes or until the chicken is tender and the sauce has thickened.

FISH & SEAFOOD

BAKED STUFFED RED MULLET P.62 · SALMON AND SCALLOP MONEYBAGS P.63

*R*ich in protein, low in fat and carbo-
hydrate, it's little wonder that fish is
becoming more and more popular
with the cholesterol-conscious.
Remember, fish takes very little
cooking, so do note that it is rarely necessary
to pre-poach fish before cooking in pastry or
baking in a sauce. Overcooked fish becomes
dry, stringy and flavourless.
Take advantage too of the seasonality of fish
and ring the changes according to the
availability and peak perfection of different
varieties.

POACHING FISH

I add salt, but the choice is yours!

SALMON

Using a fish kettle: half fill the fish kettle with boiling water, add 2 tablespoons salt, 3 bay leaves, 1 sliced onion, 12 peppercorns and the juice of 1 lemon. Bring to the boil. Put in the fish. Fish under 5lb (2.2kg) return to the boil and remove from the heat.

2▇ 5 – 7lb (2.2 – 3.2kg) return to the boil, simmer for 3 minutes.
▇4▇ 7 – 10lb (3.2 – 4.5kg) return to the boil, simmer for 4 minutes.

Remove from the heat, leave until the fish is lukewarm, lift out and skin.

2▇ **Roasting Oven method:** remove the head, season and wrap in buttered
▇4▇ foil. Lie in the large roasting tin. Pour boiling water round the fish to come half-way up the tin. Carefully slide onto the lowest set of runners. Turn fish over in foil half-way through cooking. (See opposite for timings). Leave in foil to become lukewarm, skin and decorate.

To serve fish hot, increase cooking time by one-third and leave in the hot water for 15 minutes before serving.

COD, BREAM, FRESH HADDOCK, HALIBUT, MONK FISH, TROUT:

Put the fish in 1 pint (600ml) cold water in a pan and add ½ tablespoon of salt, 1 bay leaf and the juice of half a lemon. Bring to the boil on the Boiling Plate then simmer gently for 2 minutes.

Simmering Oven: cover and transfer to the oven, allowing 10 minutes per lb (450g) and 10 minutes over. Drain thoroughly.

OVEN STEAMED FISH

COD, BREAM, HAKE, FRESH HADDOCK, HALIBUT, SMOKED FISH FILLETS, MONK FISH, PLAICE FILLETS, SOLE, TROUT:

Take a buttered ovenproof dish, arrange the fish in a single layer – or roll up the fillets. Season, add butter and a little milk or fish stock. Cover.

2▇ Roasting Oven: cook in the oven for 5 minutes then transfer to the
▇4▇ Simmering Oven for about 20 minutes or more until the fish is opaque and cooked through. Use the strained fish juices and stock for a sauce.

FRIED FISH

I prefer to fry in a little sunflower oil in the Roasting Oven, no smells!

Dry the fish after washing and coat with either: seasoned flour, fine oatmeal for herrings and mackerel, batter if you must, egg and white breadcrumbs.

2▇ Roasting Oven: use just enough oil to cover the base of the Aga roast-
▇4▇ ing tin. Preheat on the floor of the Roasting Oven until smoking, then cook the fish in the roasting tin on the floor of the oven. Start with the white side down first and then turn the fish half way through cooking so that the dark skinned side is under for serving.

BAKED RED MULLET

You can also use fresh trout instead.

SERVES 4

Trim all the fins off the fish. Mash down the cream cheese with the lemon juice. Add dill, parsley and seasoning and enough of the top of the milk to make a soft spreading consistency. Spread inside fish. Season and brush the fish with melted butter. Arrange in a shallow buttered ovenproof dish.

2▇ Roasting Oven: with the grid shelf on the second set of runners cook for
▇4▇ about 15-20 minutes. Brush again with butter half way through cooking It is done when the juices that flow from the thickest part are clear. Garnish.

TIMINGS FOR ROASTING OVEN METHOD

2lb (1kg)   about 10 minutes
3lb (1.3kg) about 15 minutes
4lb (1.8kg) about 20 minutes
6lb (2.7kg) about 25 minutes
8lb (3.6kg) about 30 minutes
10lb (4.5kg) about 35 minutes
12lb (5.4kg) about 40 minutes

INGREDIENTS

**4 cleaned fish about
12oz (350g) each
3oz (75g) rich cream cheese
juice ½ lemon
2 tablespoons chopped dill and
parsley
salt and freshly ground
black pepper
a little top of the milk
a little melted butter**

to garnish
wedges of lemon and dill

Salmon and Scallop Money Bags

A really exciting way of serving salmon, perhaps when you have a small tail end piece or odd cut left in the freezer. These are individual parcels with a filling of salmon and scallop, a little cream sauce and added fresh dill, if you have some. If scallops are unavailable then use prawns instead. I have made these and the sauce the day before, then cooked the parcels just when they are needed and reheated the sauce gently. I used PITTA strudel leaves bought from good supermarkets and delicatessens. The box contained two packs, each pack containing 4 leaves of pastry. If you buy thin sheets of pastry use 2 thicknesses of pastry to make the final 'dolly bag.' Keep well wrapped in the freezer.

SERVES 8

First make the sauce: measure the vermouth into a pan and boil rapidly until reduced to about 3 tablespoons, add the cream and transfer to the Simmering Plate. Simmer until a light coating consistency. Remove from the heat and season to taste. Add dill. Transfer $1/3$ of the sauce to a small bowl and allow to cool. Keep the remainder to reheat later.

Divide the salmon and scallops into 8 portions, season and sprinkle with a little lemon juice. Lift out 4 sheets of pastry and cover with a damp teatowel, take one sheet of the pastry and lie out flat on a work surface. Brush with a mixture of melted butter and oil then divide into 4. Put one portion of the salmon and scallop in the centre, top with $1/8$ of the sauce in the bowl. Bundle into a parcel. Do this with the remaining portions of fish, using up second sheet of pastry. Brush the remaining 2 sheets of pastry with melted butter and oil and divide each into 4. Put one of the bundles in the centre of each and draw up the sides of the pastry to form a dolly bag, squeezing the pastry at the neck. Lift the 8 dolly bags onto a greased baking sheet. Brush each with more melted butter and oil. Either cook now or keep uncovered in the fridge until required.

2 | **4** Roasting Oven: with the grid shelf on the floor of the oven, cook for about 15 minutes until pale golden brown and crisp, turn once. If the tops begin to over brown, just protect them with the cold plain shelf. Serve as soon as possible with the remaining cream sauce reheated but not boiled.

for the sauce

1/4 pint (150ml) vermouth or dry white wine
3/4 pint (450ml) double cream
1 teaspoon freshly snipped dill
salt and freshly ground black pepper

for the parcels

1½lb (675g) boned and skinned salmon
10oz (275g) scallops
4 sheets of phyllo pastry
melted butter and oil to brush

Gravadlax

A classic Scandinavian recipe for pickled fresh salmon. This speciality is appearing in top restaurants in Britain – no wonder, it tastes quite wonderful served with mustard dill sauce. Not difficult to prepare – leave to marinate for 48 hours. For larger fish increase the time eg. 12lb (5.4kg) fish for 4 days. Turn each day.

SERVES 10

Cut the fins off the fish. Lie the fish on a board. Make a long cut down the back of the salmon slightly above the bone. Slip your fingers over the bone and take off the first fillet. Then gently slip the knife under the back bone and pull it out. Pull out any tiny bones you can see.

Mix all the pickling ingredients together in a bowl. Put the two fillets, skin side down on the board. Spread with the mixture, then sandwich the two fillets together skin side outside. Wrap in a double layer of foil. Lie in a dish. Place weights on top – a couple of cans will do. Put in the fridge for 48 hours, turning every day.

To serve: freeze for 6 hours – this makes the fish firm and then easier to carve. Cut slices a little thicker than you would for smoked salmon. Cut the slices obliquely to the skin. Each slice should then have an edging of dill which looks so attractive. Serve with Mustard Dill Sauce (page 87), brown bread rolls and unsalted butter.

INGREDIENTS

3lb (1.4kg) piece fresh salmon

PICKLING INGREDIENTS

4 level tablespoons caster sugar
3 level tablespoons coarse sea salt
1 tablespoon sunflower oil
masses of freshly ground black pepper
2 tablespoons freshly chopped dill

DOUBLE FISH PIE P.65
SALMON EN CROUTE P.65
CHILLED TROUT P.65

CHILLED FRESH TROUT

I have given the recipe below for 10 trout. For 5 trout use the small roasting tin and halve the amount of liquid and shorten the cooking time by one minute.

SERVES 10

Take the large roasting tin and put a piece of foil in the bottom. Arrange the fish in two lines with their tails facing towards the sides of the tin. Measure all the remaining ingredients into a pan and bring to the boil. Pour this over the fish.

2 Roasting Oven: push the tin onto the third set of runners in the oven and **4** cook uncovered for 10 minutes. Cool in the liquid until the fish are firm enough to handle. Lift out very carefully and peel off the skin. Cut a V at the tail end of the fish. See picture on page 64. Arrange on a serving platter, cover with clearfilm and chill.

To serve: garnish each with three slices of cucumber, a little dill and a wedge of lemon. Serve with hot buttered baby new potatoes, a green salad and creamy dill sauce.

INGREDIENTS

**10 x 12oz (350g) pink trout, gutted and heads removed
1 pint (600ml) white wine
3 pints (1.75lt) water
2 teaspoons salt
1 teaspoon ground black pepper
2 bay leaves
fresh dill stalks
sprig lemon thyme
1 onion, thinly sliced**

t o g a r n i s h
**½ cucumber, sliced
fresh dill
10 wedges of lemon**

SALMON EN CROUTE

Serve hot with Fresh Herb Sauce (see page 87)

SERVES 8

First bone the salmon; fillet the fish by slipping the knife on top of the backbone. Take off the first fillet. Turn the fish over and do the same on the other side and take off the second fillet.

Remove the skin, lay each fillet skin side down on a chopping board and using a sawing action with a sharp knife work along the fillet from the tail, pressing the knife down on to the fish skin at an angle until the skin is removed. Pull out any small bones in the fillets.

Squeeze the lemon juice over the fish and season well. Dot with a little butter and sprinkle with dill. Put the other fillet on top. Dot with a little more butter.

Roll out the pastry thinly, lift pastry onto a baking tray, and use to wrap the fish in, sealing the pastry very thoroughly with beaten egg. Keep the fold of pastry on top fluting the edges. Glaze with egg.

2 Roasting Oven: with the grid shelf on the third set of runners cook **4** for about 30 minutes until the pastry is risen and golden brown.

INGREDIENTS

**3lb (1.5kg) tail piece Scottish salmon
juice ½ lemon
salt and freshly ground black pepper
a little soft butter
1 teaspoon snipped fresh dill
14oz (397g) pkt frozen puff pastry
1 beaten egg**

DOUBLE FISH PIE

A wonderful dish to prepare ahead for Friday night supper if you have a crowd, you only need to serve fresh spinach or peas with it.

SERVES 6

Put the fish in the small Aga roasting tin with the milk and cook in the Roasting Oven on the second set of runners for about 15 minutes or until the fish can be flaked with a fork. Strain the milk from the fish, then skin the fish and flake, removing any bones.

Heat the butter in a pan on the Simmering Plate and stir in the flour, cook for a minute, then gradually blend in the milk from the fish and bring to the boil, stirring until thickened. Add seasoning, parsley, nutmeg and the flaked fish, mix lightly. Taste and check seasoning then stir in the eggs.

Turn into a shallow 3 pint (1.5 litre) ovenproof dish and leave to cool. Mash the potatoes, with the milk and butter, season to taste. Spread over the fish.

2 Roasting Oven: with the grid shelf on the second set of runners cook the **4** pie for about 30 minutes or until heated through and the potatoes on top are beginning to brown.

INGREDIENTS

**8oz (225g) boneless smoked haddock
1lb (450g) cod
1 pint (600ml) milk
2oz (50g) butter
2oz (50g) flour
salt and freshly ground black pepper
2 good tablespoons freshly chopped parsley
good pinch freshly ground nutmeg
4 hard-boiled eggs, quartered
2lb (900g) potatoes, boiled
milk and butter**

INGREDIENTS

**6 frozen haddock or cod portions,
thawed
juice 1 large lemon
salt and freshly ground
black pepper**

s a u c e

**2½oz (60g) butter
2oz (50g) flour
1 pint (600ml) milk
salt and freshly ground
black pepper
1 teaspoon Dijon mustard
a little freshly ground nutmeg
1½lb (675g) frozen leaf spinach,
thawed and well drained
6oz (175g) well-flavoured
Cheddar cheese, grated**

INGREDIENTS

**2 large lemon sole,
filleted and skinned
salt and freshly ground
black pepper
1 tablespoon sunflower oil
good knob butter
1 onion, finely chopped
2 tomatoes, skinned and chopped
¼ pint (150ml) white wine
or vermouth
5oz (150g) carton soured cream**

t o   g a r n i s h

freshly chopped parsley

INGREDIENTS

**2 hard-boiled eggs
12oz (350g) skinless cod fillets
½ pint (300ml) milk
1oz (25g) butter
1oz (25g) flour
4 tablespoons single cream
4oz (100g) shelled prawns**

t o p p i n g

**1oz (25g) butter
3oz (75g) wholemeal breadcrumbs
3oz (75g) mild Cheddar cheese,
grated**

HADDOCK FLORENTINE MORNAY

*Make ahead and cook later. For more special occasions use fillet of sole,
soak in lemon juice, season then roll up into neat rolls.*

SERVES 6

Put the fish on a deep plate, pour over the lemon juice, season and leave for about 30 minutes, turning occasionally in the juice.

Heat the butter in a pan on the Simmering Plate, add the flour and cook for a minute then gradually blend in the milk. Bring to the boil, stirring until thickened. Remove from the heat, season to taste and add mustard and nutmeg. Add ¼ of this sauce to the spinach, season and spread in a shallow ovenproof dish. Lift the fish onto the spinach and add the lemon juice to the remaining white sauce with half of the cheese. Pour over the fish and sprinkle with the remaining cheese.

2 ▪ Roasting Oven: with the grid shelf on the third set of runners, cook
▪4▪ in the oven for about 30 minutes until the top is golden brown and bubbling.

LEMON SOLE IN SOURED CREAM

*A light and refreshing way to serve sole. Do take care not to boil the sauce once
the cream has been added as it may separate if heated too fiercely.*

SERVES 4

Lay the fillets of fish out flat, season and roll up neatly. Heat the oil and butter in a pan and gently fry the onion for about 5 minutes on the Simmering Plate until beginning to soften. Add the tomatoes and vermouth and cook quickly on the Boiling Plate until the liquid has reduced by half. Pour into an ovenproof dish and arrange the rolls of fish on top. Cover with a lid or piece of foil.

2 ▪ Roasting Oven: with the grid shelf on the third set of runners, cook the
▪4▪ fish for about 20 minutes or until just tender.

Carefully lift the fish onto a warmed serving dish and keep warm. Stir the soured cream into the tomato mixture and reheat gently, taking care not to boil the sauce. Taste and check seasoning then pour over the fish and serve sprinkled with the parsley.

BENTLEY'S FISH CRUMBLE

*This dish has a fairly substantial topping and can be easily served with just a
salad or crisp green vegetable.*

SERVES 4

Chop eggs coarsely. Put cod into a pan with the milk, bring to the boil and allow to simmer for 1 minute. Remove from the heat and leave for 5 minutes. Strain off and reserve the liquid. Heat the butter in a pan on the Simmering Plate, add flour and cook for a minute then gradually blend in the reserved liquid and bring to the boil, stirring until thickened. Add cream and season to taste. Flake and remove any bones from the fish and add fish to the sauce with the chopped eggs and prawns. Turn into a shallow ovenproof dish.

For the topping: melt the butter in a pan and fry the breadcrumbs for 2 minutes on the Boiling Plate then transfer to the Simmering Plate for a further 5 minutes. Leave to cool. Mix together the cheese and the crumbs and sprinkle over the fish mixture.

2 ▪ Roasting Oven: with the grid shelf on the third set of runners bake in the
▪4▪ oven for about 20 minutes until hot and bubbling.

VEGETABLES

TABOULEH P.77 · RATATOUILLE P.77 · STUFFED PEPPERS P.77

*T*he wonder of the Aga! Just think, baked potatoes for one, two or twenty-two, the heat is always there – use it.

Vegetables are so versatile. A nutritious meal in themselves or a delicious accompaniment to a main course, they add enormously to the presentation of food with such a rich choice of colours and varieties so readily available. I have also included some mouth watering vegetarian dishes such as my crispy topped Thatched Beanbake and easy Wholewheat Asparagus Flan (P. 76).

ARTICHOKES

Globe: an attractive leafy globe shaped vegetable. Choose large fresh green ones.

Cut off the stalks, wash well, trim tops off outer leaves, then immerse in boiling water and cook until tender – about 40 minutes on the Simmering Plate. Drain upside down and serve hot or cold.

To eat: pull off each leaf one by one and dip the fleshy end into melted butter, mayonnaise or French dressing then with the teeth scrape off the fleshy part and enjoy it. Discard the leaves when they have all been removed, then take out the "choke" (the hairy bit) and you are left with the "fond" (fleshy base). This is the best part – eat with a knife and fork with more of the chosen sauce.

Jerusalem: these are small off-white knobbly root vegetables, the flavour is subtle and they are reasonably priced. Buy clean fleshy-looking ones.

Scrub them clean, then cook in their skins. They are extremely difficult to peel raw because of their shape. Cook in boiling salted water, covered with a lid, on the Simmering Plate for about 8 minutes until the skins peel away easily. Lift out with a slotted spoon, place in a colander and run under cold water for a moment until cool enough to handle. Peel off the skins, slice the artichokes thickly and return to the pan with 3 tablespoons fresh water, cover with the lid and bring to the boil. Transfer the pan to the floor of the Simmering Oven for a further 10 minutes to cook until just tender.

To eat: serve with parsley sauce or just melted butter.

ASPARAGUS

A luxury vegetable best very simply served so as not to impair the superb flavour. Select straight, even stalks with compact closed tips. The thicker the stems the better the quality; they should look fresh and the tips should be bright green. Best eaten fresh.

Wash asparagus and trim off the woody ends, scrape down the stalks. Bring a pan of salted water to the boil on the Boiling Plate and cook the asparagus immersed in the water until just tender. An old coffee pot is ideal. Cook stalk end down. This will take 12-20 minutes according to the thickness. Drain well.

To eat: dip each tip into melted butter; if the stalks are very young almost all of these may be eaten too.

AUBERGINES

These now come in various colours, the best known is a glossy purple, though they can be mottled purple and white, or be smaller and completely white – this is why they are also known as "eggplants."

Slice and fry gently in a little oil on the Simmering Plate or use for made up dishes, such as Moussaka or Ratatouille. No need to peel them. Halved aubergines may be scooped out and stuffed with minced meat or chopped vegetables.

BEANS AND PEAS

Green beans, runner beans, broad beans and peas add variety at different times of the year. Choose firm bright, stiff looking beans and, in the case of broad beans and peas, those that look well-filled in the pod.

Top and tail green and runner beans; remove the strings. Either leave the green beans whole or cut into 1 inch (2.5cm) slices. Slice runner beans diagonally. Shell broad beans and peas. Bring a pan of salted water to the boil on the Boiling Plate and cook until just tender. Green beans take about 6-8 minutes if whole, 3-5 minutes if cut; runner beans about 3-5 minutes; broad beans about 5-6 minutes; fresh peas 5-8 minutes, depending on size. They may all be drained and served with a little butter and freshly ground black pepper. Broad beans are traditionally served with parsley sauce.

BEAN SPROUTS

Small fleshy white shoots with green hoods.

Rinse in cold water and use in salads or stir-fry. If you do this the cooking time is just one minute.

BEETROOT

At its best pulled young.

Wash well to remove soil and cut off the stalks to within about 1 inch (2.5cm) of the root. Be careful when washing not to damage the skin otherwise the beetroot will "bleed." Boil for 10 minutes on the Boiling Plate and transfer to the Simmering Oven in the water for about 2-3 hours, depending on size. Remove the skin after cooking. Serve hot with a white sauce or cold, sliced in vinegar, or in a salad.

BROCCOLI

There are three main kinds of broccoli. The most well-known purple sprouting broccoli has several heads of purple/green flower buds and leaves on one stem. Calabrese has a large head, usually on one stem. Cape broccoli is similar to cauliflower except that the colour is purple and the head more open.

Trim off the ends of the stalks or stalk, and wash. Slice the thick stalk of broccoli or calabrese. Bring a pan of salted water to the boil on the Boiling Plate, add the stalks and cook covered with a lid for 2 minutes, add rest of broccoli and continue to cook until just tender. Purple sprouting broccoli takes about 5 minutes; calabrese about 6 minutes; cape broccoli about 7 minutes. Drain well, toss in a little butter and serve seasoned with freshly ground black pepper.

BRUSSELS SPROUTS

Good not only cooked but finely shredded raw in salads.

Trim the ends of the sprouts and remove any tatty outside leaves. Cut a cross in the base of the stalk of large sprouts with a sharp knife; this helps them to cook more quickly. Bring a pan of salted water to the boil on the Boiling Plate, just enough to almost cover the sprouts, add the vegetables and cook for about 6-8 minutes until just tender – have the lid just half on. Drain well and serve tossed in a little melted butter and freshly ground black pepper. Add fried chestnuts or fried almonds to buttered sprouts for a special occasion.

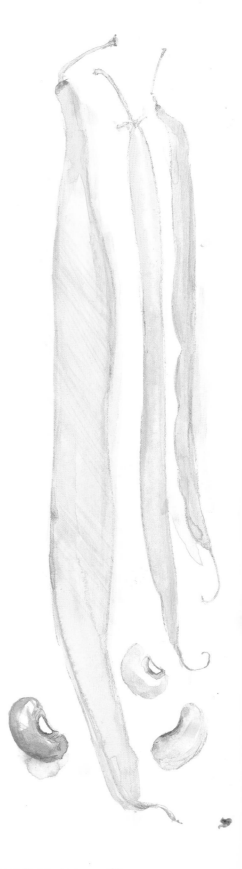

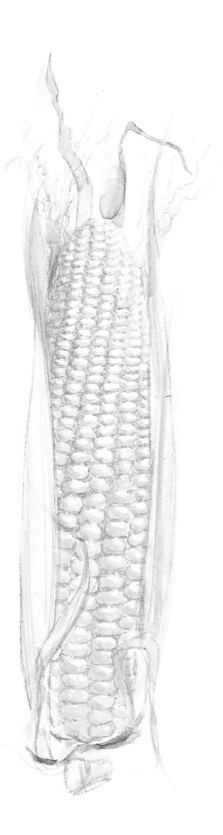

CABBAGE

Red, green and white, curly kale and greens. Cabbage is usually the cheapest vegetable and I think one of the best. There are many different varieties, one of the most popular being the crisp, dark green, crinkle-leaved winter savoy cabbage.

First, with green or white cabbage remove any limp, damaged or coarse outer leaves, then quarter and remove the thick stalk. Shred, wash and cook. Bring a large pan with a little salted water to the boil on the Boiling Plate, add the cabbage and cook uncovered for a few minutes, then partially cover the pan for the last few minutes. The total cooking time will be 5-6 minutes according to the age of the cabbage. When cooked, it should still be crisp. Drain well, toss in butter and lots of freshly ground black pepper.

Cook kale and greens in the same way, but just shred the leaves and remove any coarse ribs or stems.

CAULIFLOWER

So often cauliflower is overcooked; it is so much more delicious and nutritious when slightly underdone.

Trim off all but a few green leafy branches at the stem. I favour dividing the cauliflower into large florets with a little leaf attached to some. In this way they cook fast and serving is easy. Cook in boiling salted water barely covering the cauliflower, on the Boiling Plate with a tight fitting lid on the pan. Serve with butter and black pepper, or with a good sauce made with half milk and half cauliflower water.

CELERIAC

An off-white knobbly looking turnip shape, this is root celery. Choose fleshy looking celeriac which is heavy for its size.

Peel off the brown skin just before cooking; doing it too soon means it will discolour. This can be prevented by adding a couple of tablespoonfuls of lemon juice to the cooking water. Cube and cook in a pan of boiling salted water on the Simmering Plate, covered with a lid for about 15 minutes until tender, then toss in butter, or cook a little longer, transferring to the Simmering Oven and mash to a purée. If liked it may be mixed with equal quantity of mashed potato, adding salt and black pepper. For salads: cut into julienne strips, blanch for a few moments, allow to cool then toss in mayonnaise.

CHICORY

Use when the chicory are young and firm, before the leaves yellow.

Remove outside leaves if necessary, trim the root end and wash. Place in a buttered Aga casserole and cover with a good chicken stock and the juice of half a lemon, season. Bring to the boil and simmer on the Simmering Plate for 10 minutes, transfer to the Simmering Oven for about 45 minutes to 1 hour.

CORN ON THE COB

A beautiful looking vegetable with a subtle flavour. Choose ears of corn that are well filled and pale yellow – the deep golden ones are over-ripe.

Remove any leaves and threads, trim the stalk. Cook in boiling water on the Boiling Plate until tender for about 10 minutes. Drain, toss in butter and eat in the fingers, or speared on corn picks.

COURGETTES (ZUCCHINI)

Very delicious, they should be bright green, shiny and heavy for their size.

Wipe, slice if liked or leave whole, trimming away each end. Cook in boiling salted water on the Boiling Plate until just tender. Whole about 5 minutes; sliced about 2 minutes. Drain well, return to the pan and toss in butter with black pepper. They can also be sliced and fried gently on the Simmering Plate in a little butter for about 15 minutes until tender.

FLORENCE FENNEL

Can be served raw in salad but is more often cooked. It has an aniseed flavour.

Trim any leafy stems and the root. Cut into quarters, boil in salted water, with a little lemon juice, on the Boiling Plate for 5 minutes. Drain and replace lid then transfer to the Simmering Oven for 45 minutes. Serve covered with white sauce or au gratin.

LEEKS

Useful to serve in winter soups, casseroles or for adding to meat pies.

First with a sharp knife, remove just the very end of the root, the tops of the leaves and any damaged leaves. If serving them sliced, wash in several lots of water and drain. If cooking them whole, cut through to within 2 inches (5cm) of the base three times and soak in warm water for 10 minutes, then rub the leeks with the hands under running cold water until all the earth is washed away.

The cooking time very much depends on the thickness of the stalk. Boil in salted water on the Boiling Plate until tender. Sliced leeks should take about 5 minutes; whole leeks about 10 minutes. Drain very well and serve with a little white sauce or just butter and freshly ground black pepper.

MANGETOUT

Choose crisp flat pods.

Top and tail, string if necessary. Boil rapidly on the Boiling Plate in 1 inch (2.5cm) salted water until tender, about 3-5 minutes. Drain and serve with a knob of butter and freshly ground black pepper.

MARROW

Choose younger smaller marrows if cooking as a vegetable. The larger ones are good when stuffed and baked.

To cook as a vegetable – peel, cut in half and remove seeds. Cut in slices or cubes, cook in boiling salted water on the Boiling Plate for 3-5 minutes until just tender, drain thoroughly. Serve in a white sauce or with butter and black pepper.

MUSHROOMS

Do not peel, wash if large, wipe if small, dry on kitchen paper, trim stalks. Fry gently in butter on the Simmering Plate or use in stews, casseroles and sauces.

OKRA (LADIES FINGERS)

A green podded vegetable which looks like a pointed ridged bean. Choose firm, plump green pods.

Cook in a little boiling salted water on the Boiling Plate for about 5 minutes until just tender, then drain and toss in butter. If over-cooked they tend to turn slimy. They are also good stir-fried.

PEPPERS

These now come in multi-colours – green, red, yellow, purple and white. The paler colours have a slightly milder flavour.

Remove stalk and scoop out core and seeds. Use cooked in savoury dishes, stuffed whole, or sliced in salads.

PULSES

Dried seeds of plants such as beans and peas.

Generally these should be left to soak overnight before cooking. To cook pour off the water and cover with fresh water, add a bouquet garni for extra flavour. Bring to the boil, simmer for 10 minutes and then transfer to the Simmering Oven until tender, about 1-3 hours, depending on the type.

N.B. Boil red kidney beans for 15 minutes before simmering.

AGA OVEN RICE

As an alternative to cooking on the hotplate, this absorption method works well.

SERVES 4

Wash rice and place in a 2 litre Agaluxe pan with the water and salt, bring to the boil, stir, replace the lid and place on the floor of the Simmering Oven.

RICE	RAW WEIGHT	WATER	SALT	TIMING
Basmati	8oz (225g)	12 fl oz (360ml)	½-1 tsp	15-20 mins
Brown	8oz (225g)	14 fl oz (420ml)	½-1 tsp	40-45 mins
Long Grain (Easy cook/ par boiled)	8oz (225g)	12 fl oz (360ml)	½-1 tsp	15-20 mins

UNDERGROUND VEGETABLES

The well-known ones – potatoes, carrots, parsnips, kohlrabi, turnips and swedes. Wonderful cooked in the Simmering Oven – no steam in the kitchen.

For old potatoes, carrots, parsnips and turnips; use a potato peeler and remove any eyes or small blemishes. The first new potatoes, or small ones, I think are best just scrubbed. All can be kept, peeled in cold water until needed (the convenience may outweigh the loss of vitamins). If they are needed for the weekend, do them on Friday, change the water on Saturday and keep them very cold. Swedes need peeling with a vegetable knife.

Bring a pan of salted water to the boil on the Boiling Plate. I use about 2 teaspoons salt to each pint (600ml) water. Add vegetables and cook with the lid on for about 5 minutes. Drain off all the water, replace lid and transfer to the floor of the Simmering Oven for about 30 minutes to 1 hour or until just tender. Root vegetables will keep beautifully in the Simmering Oven like this for up to 2 hours. To serve, add butter and season with freshly ground black pepper. For mashed potatoes, add milk too. NB. The cooking time in the Simmering Oven depends on the size of vegetable.

SCALLOPED POTATOES

This is a tasty way to serve potatoes and can be assembled very quickly.

SERVES 6

Melt a small knob of butter in a small casserole dish and arrange a layer of potatoes in the bottom. Arrange some onion on top and season. Add another layer of potatoes. Repeat this layering process until all the potatoes and onion are used up. Dot a little more butter on top and pour the stock over.

2 4 Roasting Oven: with the grid shelf on the bottom set of runners, cook uncovered in the oven for about an hour until golden brown and the potatoes are tender.

INGREDIENTS
butter
2lb (900g) potatoes, sliced
1 large onion, finely sliced
salt and freshly ground
black pepper
1/4 pint (150ml) stock

BAKED POTATOES

We all love these and they are a great welcome on a cold day. If you are in a great hurry simply cut the potatoes in half before baking. It cuts down the baking time by at least one-third and the cut side has a crisp brown appearance.

Scrub the potatoes thoroughly and prick with a fork. Brush with oil, if liked.

2 4 Roasting Oven: with the grid shelf on the third set of runners bake the potatoes in the oven for about 1¼ hours. The time will vary depending on the size of the potatoes. Cut each potato in half, fork up the inside slightly and serve dotted with butter.

INGREDIENTS
4 large potatoes
oil
1-2oz (25-50g) butter, for serving

ROAST POTATOES

Serve with roasts of all kinds: beef, lamb, pork, chicken, duck, turkey, goose and veal. If you need to roast the potatoes quickly just cut them into smaller pieces.

SERVES 4

Peel the potatoes and cut into even-sized pieces. Parboil in water for 3 minutes on the Boiling Plate then drain well. Place a good knob of fat or a little oil in a small roasting tin.

2 4 Roasting Oven: place the tin on the floor of the oven until the fat or oil is sizzling. Add the potatoes and roast, turning occasionally, for about 1¼ hours or until the potatoes are crisp and golden brown.

INGREDIENTS
1½lb (675g) medium sized
old potatoes
lard, oil or dripping

CARROT AND SWEDE PURÉE

A colourful vegetable dish, so easily cooked in the Simmering Oven.

SERVES 6

Put swede and carrot into a large pan, cover with salted water and bring to the boil. Cover and simmer 5 minutes. Drain.

2 4 Simmering Oven: stand the pan on the floor of the oven and leave for about an hour or until tender. Drain again and mash with a generous amount of butter, or reduce to a purée in a processor. Turn into a warm serving dish to serve.

INGREDIENTS
1lb (450g) swede, peeled and sliced
1lb (450g) carrots, peeled and sliced
generous knob butter
salt and freshly ground
black pepper

BARRIE'S MASH P.75
RÖSTI P.75
GARLIC CREAM POTATOES P.75
JACKET POTATOES P.91

BARRIE'S MASH

A wonderfully individual potato dish as indeed was the dear man who invented it. A processor helps chop the skins and herbs.

SERVES 4

2/4 Roasting Oven: with the grid shelf on the floor of the oven cook the potatoes for about 45 minutes.

When cooked, allow to cool a little then cut in half, scoop out the potato and keep the skins. Mash the potato with the milk, butter and seasoning. Put into a buttered shallow ovenproof serving dish.

Chop the potato skins finely with a little butter, seasoning and the herbs. Spoon on top of the potato and spread roughly with a fork.

Roasting Oven: with the grid shelf on the second set of runners cook for about 20 minutes until golden brown.

INGREDIENTS

**2lb (900g) old potatoes, scrubbed and pricked
3 tablespoons hot milk
butter
salt and freshly ground
black pepper
2 tablespoons leafy herbs such as chives, basil and marjoram or spring onion tops**

AGA GARLIC CREAM POTATOES

Potatoes served this way are wonderful, especially with something without sauce or gravy such as lamb chops or perhaps steaks.

SERVES 4-6

Well butter a 3 pint (1.8 litre) shallow ovenproof dish. Slice the potatoes into slices about the thickness of 2 x 10p coins. Arrange half the potatoes over the bottom of the dish and season well with salt and pepper. Crush the garlic into the carton of cream, stir well then pour half over the potatoes in the dish. Cover with the remaining slices of potato. Season with salt and pepper and pour over the remaining cream. Cover with foil.

2/4 Roasting Oven: with the grid shelf on the second set of runners, cook in the oven for about 1 hour 10 minutes, removing the foil after 30 minutes. The top should be just beginning to brown. Ideally serve straight away or they can be kept warm safely in the Simmering Oven for about 30 minutes or so.

INGREDIENTS

**2lb (900g) potatoes
2 fat cloves garlic, crushed
½ pint (300ml) double cream
salt and freshly ground
black pepper**

RÖSTI-OVEN BAKED

Take care not to overcook the potatoes; they should still be very firm which makes the grating easier. In Switzerland bacon and onion are often added.

SERVES 4-6

Scrub the potatoes and boil in salted water on the Simmering Plate for 10 minutes or until the point of a knife can be inserted into the potato for about 1 inch (2.5cm) before meeting resistance. Drain and cool, then peel and leave in a cool place overnight. Grate the potatoes coarsely into a bowl, add seasoning and mix well.

2/4 Roasting Oven: with the grid shelf on the floor of the oven. Melt half the dripping or butter in a small roasting tin or shallow dish. Add the grated potato, flattening it with a fish slice. Dot with the remaining dripping or butter. Return the tin to the oven for about 25 minutes until golden brown. Turn out onto a warm dish and serve.

INGREDIENTS

**2lb (900g) large potatoes
salt and freshly ground
black pepper
2oz (50g) pork dripping or butter**

2 onions, chopped
2 tablespoons olive oil
14oz (397g) can chopped tomatoes
1lb (450g) cooked pulse beans, any colour or shape
1 tablespoon chopped marjoram seasoning
4oz (100g) well flavoured Cheddar cheese, grated
3oz (75g) brown breadcrumbs
1 egg, beaten
¼ pint (150ml) milk
good knob butter

pastry

3oz (75g) wholemeal flour
1oz (25g) plain flour
2oz (50g) margarine
about 2½ tablespoons cold water

filling

2oz (50g) butter
1 onion, chopped
1oz (25g) flour
14oz (397g) can asparagus pieces
¼ pint (150ml) double cream
1 tablespoon chopped parsley
1 egg, beaten
salt and freshly ground black pepper
1½oz (40g) Cheddar cheese, grated

6 medium sized onions with the skin left on

THATCHED BEANBAKE

Cook in a shallow ovenproof dish so that there is plenty of crisp thatched topping. Serve hot with salad.

SERVES 4

Fry onions in oil until soft, add tomatoes and mix well. Mash 8oz (225g) of the beans and leave the rest whole, add to the pan with the marjoram and seasoning. Stir in ¾ of the cheese and 2oz (50g) of the breadcrumbs. Stir in milk and egg and heat through. Turn into a lightly greased ovenproof dish. Mix cheese and breadcrumbs together and sprinkle over bean mixture, dot with butter.

2 / 4 Roasting Oven: with the grid shelf on the middle set of runners cook in the oven for 15 minutes until golden brown on top.

WHOLEWHEAT ASPARAGUS FLAN

Crisp pastry with a creamy aparagus filling. Can be served hot or cold. Using a mixture of white and wholemeal flour gives a lighter texture and makes the handling of the pastry much easier.

SERVES 6

Measure the flours into a bowl and rub in the fat until the mixture resembles fine breadcrumbs, add sufficient water to form a soft dough. Roll out and use to line an 8 inch (20cm) loose bottomed flan tin. Line with foil then leave in the fridge for 15 minutes.

2 / 4 Roasting Oven: bake the pastry case on the floor of the oven for 15 minutes, removing the foil for the last 5 minutes. Cool before filling.

Heat the butter in a pan and cook the onion until soft, add the flour and cook for a minute. Gradually add the liquid from the can of asparagus and bring to the boil, stirring until thickened. Stir in the remaining ingredients, except the cheese and mix well. Pour into the cooled pastry case and sprinkle with cheese. With the grid shelf on the highest set of runners return to the Roasting Oven for about 6-8 minutes until pale golden on top.

BAKED ONIONS

A simple and simply delicious recipe which comes originally from France via Elizabeth David – and it was in fact passed on to me by a great friend and Aga owner. The flavour retained by cooking the onions in their skins is quite wonderful.

SERVES 6

Wipe the onions and put into the small roasting tin.

2 / 4 Roasting Oven: with the grid shelf on the floor of the oven cook for about an hour.

Simmering Oven: transfer to the oven until you are ready to serve them. If the onions are small reduce the cooking time to 45 minutes.

Serve with roast and grilled meat and just scoop the onion out of its skin as you would a baked potato.

SPECIAL STUFFED PEPPERS

Use red, green or yellow peppers, or a mixture, but choose even-sized ones.

SERVES 4

Slice each pepper in half, lengthways, remove the seeds and white pith. *Make the filling:* cook the pasta in boiling salted water then drain and rinse well. Melt the butter in a large frying pan and fry the onion and bacon on the Simmering Plate for about 5 minutes or until the onion is golden brown. Add the mushrooms and fry for a further minute or so. Remove from the heat and stir in the pasta, parsley and egg, mix well to bind the mixture together. Season.

Spoon the filling into the peppers, then stand them upright in an ovenproof dish so they are just touching.

Prepare the cheese sauce: melt the butter in a pan on the Simmering Plate, stir in the flour and cook for a minute then gradually blend in the milk and bring to the boil, stirring until thickened. Remove from the heat and stir in two thirds of the cheese with the mustard, nutmeg and seasoning. Pour the sauce around the peppers in the dish. Sprinkle the remaining cheese over the top of the peppers. Garnish with strips of pepper before serving.

2 Roasting Oven: with the grid shelf on the bottom set of runners and the cold plain shelf on the second set of runners, cook the peppers for about 45 minutes to an hour. Turn dish once if need be.

4 Baking Oven: with the grid shelf on the second runners, cook the peppers for 45 minutes to an hour. Turn dish once if need be.

It's ready when the peppers are tender and the topping is golden brown.

INGREDIENTS

4 large even-sized peppers
3oz (75g) small pasta shells
1oz (25g) butter
1 small onion, chopped
3oz (75g) streaky bacon, snipped
4oz (100g) button mushrooms, sliced
1 tablespoon finely chopped parsley
1 egg, beaten
salt and freshly ground black pepper

for the sauce

1oz (25g) butter
1oz (25g) flour
½ pint (300ml) milk
4oz (100g) well-flavoured Cheddar cheese, grated
1 teaspoon Dijon mustard
a little freshly ground nutmeg

TABOULEH

This dish uses bulgar or burghul wheat as a main ingredient. It is partially cooked cracked wheat and only needs soaking for about an hour before it is ready to serve.

SERVES 6

Mix the wheat with a little salt in a bowl, pour over the boiling water and leave to soak for about an hour. Sauté the onion in 2 tablespoons of the oil until soft. Leave to cool. Mix remaining dressing ingredients and pour over the wheat at the end of the soaking time. Stir in the cooked onion. Cover and leave overnight in a cool place. The following day: mix in the remaining ingredients and check seasoning.

INGREDIENTS

8oz (225g) Bulgar wheat
¾ pint (450ml) boiling water
1 onion, finely chopped

dressing

4 tablespoons walnut oil
juice 1 lemon
8 tablespoons chopped mint
2 fat cloves garlic, crushed
3 tablespoons chopped parsley
1lb (450g) tomatoes, skinned, seeded and chopped
½ cucumber, seeded and diced
ground black pepper

NOUVELLE RATATOUILLE

The vegetables are still slightly crispy and bright in colour. The peppers can easily be skinned after being roasted in the Roasting Oven.

SERVES 6

2 *Oil the peppers* and put in the small roasting tin towards the top of the
4 Roasting Oven. Roast for about 15 minutes until the skins are scorched. When cool enough to handle peel off the skins. Cut in half and remove the stalk and seeds then slice the flesh thinly. Cut the stalk from the aubergine and cut into small discs. Blanch in boiling water for 2 minutes then drain well.

Measure the oil into a fairly large pan. Sauté the onion and garlic with the lid on until onion is transparent but not soft, add aubergine and cook for 5 minutes, stir in peppers and tomatoes. Season. Lastly add the courgettes tossing well and cooking fast until courgettes are just becoming tender.

INGREDIENTS

2 red peppers
1 yellow pepper
1lb (450g) aubergines
5 tablespoons olive oil
2 medium onions, chopped
2 cloves garlic, crushed
1½lb (675g) canned tomatoes
salt and freshly ground black pepper
12oz (350g) small courgettes, thinly sliced

BROCCOLI POLONAISE P.79
SPINACH SAMOSAS P.79
SPINACH ROULADE P.79

BROCCOLI POLONAISE

This is a good way of cooking cauliflower too; top this with chopped parsley as the white cauliflower needs brightening up.

SERVES 4

Cook the calabrese or broccoli spears on the Boiling Plate in boiling salted water for about 6 minutes until just tender, drain well. Keep warm in a serving dish in the Simmering Oven. Shell and finely chop the egg.

Heat the butter in a small pan and stir in the breadcrumbs, fry until golden, add chopped egg, season well. Spoon over the cooked broccoli and serve.

INGREDIENTS

**1lb (450g) fresh calabrese or broccoli spears
1 hard-boiled egg
1oz (25g) butter
3 tablespoons fresh white breadcrumbs
salt and freshly ground black pepper**

SPINACH AND CHEESE SAMOSAS

The wafer thin sheets of pastry make very crisp triangular parcels. Keep pastry covered with a damp clean teacloth. Quickly re-freeze any unused pastry.

MAKES ABOUT 30

Heat the butter in a pan and add the flour and cook for a minute, then gradually blend in the milk and bring to the boil, stirring until thickened, remove from the heat and stir in the seasoning, nutmeg, cheeses and spinach. Leave to cool.

Unwrap the thawed pastry and carefully separate the sheets. Brush a sheet of pastry with a mixture of the melted butter and oil. Cut into 2½ inch (6cm) strips. Put a teaspoon of the spinach mixture into one corner of the pastry strip and fold this over to form a triangle, keep folding the triangle over until you reach the end of the strip. Repeat until all the filling has been used. Arrange the triangles on a baking sheet and brush again with butter and oil.

2 | **4** Roasting Oven: with the grid shelf on the lowest set of runners cook for about 8-10 minutes until crisp and golden brown. Turn once. Serve warm.

INGREDIENTS

**1lb (450g) packet phyllo pastry, thawed
4oz (100g) butter, melted
2 tablespoons oil**

filling

**2oz (50g) butter
2oz (50g) flour
½ pint (300ml) milk
salt and freshly ground black pepper
little grated nutmeg
3oz (75g) Cheddar cheese, grated
3oz (75g) full fat cream cheese
4oz (100g) cooked finely chopped spinach**

SPINACH ROULADE

Start by making the filling as the roulade must be rolled as soon as it leaves the oven.

SERVES 3

Grease and line an 8 x 12 inches (20 x 30cm) swiss roll tin with greased greaseproof paper.

Start by making the sauce filling: melt the butter in a pan on the Simmering Plate, stir in the flour and cook for a minute then gradually blend in the milk and bring to the boil, stirring until thickened. Add nutmeg and seasoning. Roughly chop the spinach and stir into the sauce. Taste and check seasoning.

Whisk the egg whites until stiff. Gently fold in the egg yolks and seasoning. Carefully turn into the prepared tin and level out evenly.

2 | **4** Roasting Oven: with the grid shelf on the bottom set of runners, cook the roulade for about 8 minutes until soft to the touch and pale golden brown.

Turn out of the tin onto a sheet of greaseproof paper sprinkled with Parmesan. Quickly and carefully loosen the paper on the bottom of the roulade and peel off. Spread evenly with warm spinach mixture. Roll up, like a swiss roll, using the greaseproof paper beneath for support to keep a firm roll. Serve at once with any left-over spinach filling.

INGREDIENTS

filling

**2oz (50g) butter
2oz (50g) flour
½ pint (300ml) milk
a little freshly ground nutmeg
salt and freshly ground black pepper
8oz (225g) frozen leaf spinach, thawed and well-drained
1oz (25g) grated Parmesan cheese**

roulade

**4 large eggs, separated
salt and freshly ground black pepper**

3 tablespoons good olive oil
1 large onion, finely sliced
6 sticks celery, chopped diagonally
1 small white cabbage, finely sliced
2 red peppers, deseeded and cut
into strips
1 yellow pepper, deseeded and cut
into strips
6oz (175g) large button mushrooms,
quartered

1 medium red cabbage
1lb (450g) windfall apples,
weight after peeling
6 tablespoons water
1½oz (40g) sugar
salt
6 tablespoons vinegar
2oz (50g) butter
1 tablespoon redcurrant jelly

3oz (75g) brown rice
1oz (25g) butter
1 tablespoon oil
1 onion, chopped
8oz (225g) button mushrooms,
sliced
6oz (175g) white cabbage, shredded
3 hard boiled eggs, chopped
1 tablespoon chopped parsley
salt and freshly ground
black pepper
14oz (397g) packet frozen puff
pastry, thawed
beaten egg

t o   s e r v e
¼ pint (150ml) soured cream
juice 1 lemon
¼ pint (150ml) natural yogurt
2oz (50g) butter, melted

CABBAGE AND PEPPER STIR FRY

Good to serve as a different vegetable when entertaining. You can do the final cooking in 3 minutes.

SERVES 6-8

Measure a tablespoon of the oil into a flat-based wok or large deep pan on the Boiling Plate and stir fry the onion for 2 minutes. Add the celery, stir for 1 more minute then transfer to the Simmering Plate for 2 minutes. Add 1 more tablespoon of oil and cabbage and stir well for 2 minutes. Add the red and yellow peppers, mushrooms and the last tablespoon oil and stir well. Set on one side with the lid on.

When ready to serve, lift off the lid and put onto the Boiling Plate and, stirring continuously, fry for 3 minutes.

RED CABBAGE

One of the best and most warming vegetables, it also reheats well, should some be left.

SERVES 4

Trim and clean cabbage. Shred finely. Core and slice apples. Place cabbage and apples in a pan with the water, sugar and salt. Cover and bring to the boil.

2▋ Simmering Oven: transfer to the floor of the oven for about an hour.
▋4▋ Add the vinegar, butter and jelly. Blend well on the Simmering Plate. Check seasoning and serve hot with meat dishes.

MUSHROOM KOULIBIAC

A large posh pasty to serve six.

SERVES 6

Cook the rice as directed on the packet then drain (or use the Aga oven method page 72) and leave to cool. Heat the butter and oil and sauté the onion until soft, add the mushrooms and cook until just beginning to soften. Blanch the cabbage in boiling salted water for 1 minute, drain and leave to cool. In a bowl, combine the rice, onion and mushrooms, cabbage, eggs, parsley and seasoning.

Roll out the pastry to an oblong 11 x 16 inches (28 x 40cm). Trim off a little of the pastry to decorate. Lift the pastry onto a large baking sheet. Pile the rice mixture down the centre of the pastry. Fold over both long sides of pastry so they overlap and tuck the ends under. Score across the top 2 or 3 times with a knife. Roll out the trimmings and use to make a lattice pattern on top. Brush with beaten egg.

2▋ Roasting Oven: with the grid shelf on the bottom set of runners cook
▋4▋ for about 20-25 minutes until golden brown. Turn once.

Mix the sour cream, yogurt and lemon juice together and serve with the koulibiac. Pour the melted butter into the scored cuts.

SAVOURIES & SAUCES

PHYLLO SAVOURIES P.82 · SESAME CHEESE SABLÉS P.82 · DEVILS ON HORSEBACK P.83 · FLAKY CHEESE CRISPS P.83
SALTED ALMONDS P.83

*T*his could be one of the most-used chapters in the book. I've crammed it with all those basic recipes like gravies, Horseradish sauce and real Bread sauce. Then there are cooler complements such as Creamy Dill sauce and Cucumber sauce. And on the sweeter side some wicked treats like Butter Caramel Fudge sauce and Dark Chocolate sauce. Try out my savoury nibbles – tempting little mouthfuls to serve with drinks. Keep the hot ones in the Simmering Oven until you're ready to serve them – they're delicious.

I N G R E D I E N T S
½ **packet phyllo pastry**
8oz (225g) pork sausage meat
1 tablespoon freshly chopped mixed herbs
salt and freshly ground black pepper
melted butter

Mini Phyllo Sausage Rolls

Delicious tiny savouries to serve with drinks.

MAKES ABOUT 30

Unroll the pastry and cover with a clean damp tea cloth to prevent the pastry from drying out. Re-wrap and freeze any remaining pastry. Soften the sausage meat in a bowl and stir in the herbs and seasoning until blended. Turn into a piping bag fitted with a ½ inch plain icing nozzle.

Peel off one of the sheets of pastry and flatten out. Brush evenly with melted butter. Pipe a line of sausage meat along the longest side of the pastry and then roll the pastry over and over until the sausage meat is secured in the middle, with the sheet of pastry wrapped round it. Brush again with melted butter. With a sharp pair of scissors, cut the roll at an angle to give lots of small diagonally shaped sausage rolls. Repeat until all the sausage meat and pastry have been used. Lift onto a lightly greased baking tray.

2▮ ▮4▮ Roasting Oven: with the grid shelf on the second set of runners, cook the sausage rolls in the oven for about 10-15 minutes, turning from time to time until crisp and golden brown.

Serve warm with drinks.

I N G R E D I E N T S
½ **packet phyllo pastry**
4oz (100g) Stilton cheese, crumbled
salt and freshly ground black pepper
1 teaspoon Dijon mustard
a little freshly ground nutmeg
½ **pint (300ml) cold thick white sauce**
melted butter

Stilton Phyllo Savouries

Wafer thin phyllo pastry can be bought from Greek shops, good delicatessens and supermarkets.

MAKES ABOUT 30

Carefully unroll the phyllo pastry and lay out flat on the work surface. Cover with a clean damp cloth to prevent the pastry from drying out. Stir the cheese, seasoning, mustard and nutmeg into the sauce until thoroughly mixed.

Peel off one of the sheets of pastry and flatten out. Brush evenly with melted butter then divide into 2 inch wide strips. Spoon a small blob of the mixture onto one corner of the strips of the pastry and fold this corner over to form a triangle. Keep folding the triangle over until you reach the end of the strip of pastry and the filling is secured in the middle. Repeat this until all the pastry and cheese mixture have been used. Arrange on lightly greased baking sheets and brush with more melted butter.

Cook as for Mini Phyllo Sausage Rolls.

I N G R E D I E N T S
4oz (100g) plain flour
salt and freshly ground black pepper
½ **teaspoon dried mustard**
3oz (75g) butter, diced
3oz (75g) well-flavoured Cheddar cheese, finely grated
1oz (25g) sesame seeds, toasted
a little beaten egg

Sesame Cheese Sablés

Cheesy biscuits which are very moreish.

MAKES ABOUT 50

Measure the flour and seasonings into a processor. Add diced butter and process until the mixture resembles fine breadcrumbs. Add cheese and half the sesame seeds. Process until just together. Do not overwork. Wrap in clearfilm and chill for 30 minutes.

Roll out the pastry on a lightly floured surface to an oblong ¼ inch (½cm) in thickness. Cut into strips 2 inches wide, glaze with a little beaten egg, sprinkle with remaining sesame seeds. Then cut these strips into triangles or other shapes.

2▮ Roasting Oven: with the grid shelf on the floor of the oven cook for 7-8 minutes, turning the tray once until a pale biscuit colour.

▮4▮ Baking Oven: with the grid shelf on the second runners cook for 8-10 minutes, turning tray once until pale biscuit colour.

Serve warm or cold.

FLAKY CHEESE CRISPS

This is a really easy way to make those crisp flaky Dutch biscuits. It is well worth using silicone paper to prevent them from sticking to the baking tray.

MAKES ABOUT 100

Line a baking tray with silicone paper. Mix the cheese with the mustard and cayenne.

Roll out the pastry to an oblong on a lightly floured surface and sprinkle ⅔ of the pastry with ⅓ of the cheese. Fold over the uncovered third and then fold over again. Chill for 15 minutes in the fridge. Repeat this process twice more to use the remaining cheese. Chill again.

Take the block of cheese pastry and cut ¼ inch (½cm) slices from the block across the grain. Divide each strip into three then lay on the silicone paper well spaced apart.

2 4 Roasting Oven: with the grid shelf on the first set of runners cook for about 10 minutes until golden and crisp. Turn once if you want them exactly the same each side – usually I don't bother! Serve as they are or garnish with sliced peppers or anchovies.

INGREDIENTS

8oz (225g) well flavoured dryish Cheddar cheese, grated
½ teaspoon dry mustard
generous pinch cayenne pepper
1lb (450g) ready-made or frozen puff pastry, thawed

CHEESE AIGRETTES

Good to serve with drinks. Make ahead and reheat.

MAKES ABOUT 36 AIGRETTES

Put the butter and water in a small pan and bring to the boil. Remove from the heat and add the flour all at once. Beat well until the mixture is smooth and glossy and leaves the sides of the pan. Cool slightly.

Lightly mix the yolks and eggs together and beat into the mixture a little at a time. Stir in the cheese and seasoning. Drop the mixture in teaspoonfuls into hot deep fat and fry gently until golden brown. Lift out and drain on kitchen paper. Serve warm.

2 4 Roasting Oven: arrange the aigrettes on the cold shelf and heat at the top of the oven for about 12 minutes until heated through and crispy.

INGREDIENTS

2oz (50g) butter
½ pint (300ml) water
4oz (100g) self-raising flour
2 egg yolks
2 eggs
4oz (100g) Emmental cheese, grated
salt and freshly ground black pepper

DEVILS ON HORSEBACK

To serve as a savoury or with drinks. If liked use canned prunes.

SERVES 4 AS A SAVOURY

Spread the bacon rashers out on a chopping board and with a blunt knife stretch the bacon until it is about half as long again.

Cut the rashers in half, wrap around a prune and secure with a cocktail stick. Put in the small roasting tin.

2 4 Roasting Oven: hang on the second set of runners and cook for about 10 minutes until the bacon is crisp and the prunes heated through.

Alternatively place on the grill rack in the small roasting tin. Garnish with whole almonds and serve on a small croûton.

INGREDIENTS

6 long rashers streaky bacon, derinded
12 prunes, cooked and stoned
12 cocktail sticks

t o   g a r n i s h
12 skinned almonds
12 small croûtons

SALTED ALMONDS

To serve with drinks. Almonds easily burn when cooking so do watch them carefully.

Put nuts and oil or butter in ovenproof dish.

2 4 Roasting Oven: place dish on grid shelf set on floor of oven and cook for about 10-15 minutes. Shake dish from time to time to ensure even browning of nuts. Drain on kitchen paper and sprinkle with sea salt.

INGREDIENTS

whole or split almonds
1 teaspoon vegetable oil or small knob of butter
salt to taste

I N G R E D I E N T S

4oz (100g) streaky bacon, snipped
1 large onion, chopped
1lb (450g) frozen chestnuts, thawed
and chopped
2 good tablespoons freshly chopped
parsley
3oz (75g) fresh brown breadcrumbs
1 egg, beaten
salt and freshly ground black
pepper

I N G R E D I E N T S

1lb (450g) onions, roughly chopped
½ pint (300ml) water
3oz (75g) butter
1 level teaspoon dried sage
8oz (225g) fresh white breadcrumbs
salt and freshly ground black
pepper

I N G R E D I E N T S

1lb (450g) pork sausagemeat
4oz (100g) fresh white breadcrumbs
4 level tablespoons fresh
chopped parsley
1 level teaspoon fresh thyme leaves
finely grated rind and juice
of 2 lemons
salt and freshly ground
black pepper
1 egg, beaten

I N G R E D I E N T S

4oz (100g) plain flour
salt
2 eggs
8fl.oz (225ml) milk
a little fat or dripping

A RATHER GOOD CHESTNUT STUFFING

If you can't get frozen chestnuts, use dried chestnuts bought from a good delicatessen. Dried chestnuts can be soaked overnight to become plump. 8oz (225g) dried reconstitutes to about 1lb (450g) chestnuts.

SUFFICIENT TO STUFF A 16lb (7.25kg) TURKEY

Put the bacon into a large pan and fry slowly on the Simmering Plate to draw out the fat, then transfer to the Boiling Plate and fry until crisp. Lift out with a slotted spoon and keep on one side. Add the onion to the fat left in the pan, fry until almost soft then toss in the raw chopped chestnuts, continue to cook for a further 5 minutes. Remove from the heat, return bacon to the pan and add the parsley and breadcrumbs and bind together with the egg. Season with salt and pepper. Use to stuff the body cavity of the bird.

SAGE AND ONION STUFFING

A dish of stuffing reheats surprisingly well. Do so on the grid shelf near the top of the Roasting Oven for about 10 minutes.

SERVES 6

Place the onions and water in a pan and bring to the boil, transfer to the Simmering Plate and simmer for about 15 minutes, then drain well. Stir in the remaining ingredients and mix well. Use as a stuffing for goose or pork.

2 / 4 Roasting Oven: We prefer to serve the stuffing separately. Turn into a well buttered dish, dot with a little more butter then cook in the Roasting Oven with the joint or bird for about 25 minutes or until the top is golden brown and crisp. Keep warm on the floor of the Simmering Oven until required.

PARSLEY AND THYME STUFFING

Use for stuffing veal, chicken or turkey. It may be shaped into small balls and used as savoury forcemeat balls, fried in butter and oil on all sides until golden, keep hot.
Mix all the ingredients together.

YORKSHIRE PUDDING

Serve with roast beef.

SERVES 4-6

Measure the flour and salt into a bowl. Make a well in the centre of the flour and blend in the eggs with a little of the milk, with a whisk to make a smooth paste. Blend in the remaining liquid to make a batter. Beat really well. Place a little fat or dripping in the bottom of two 4-pan Yorkshire pudding tins, a 12-pan deep patty tin or the small Aga roasting tin.

2 / 4 Roasting Oven: with the grid shelf on the third set of runners, heat the tin in the oven until the fat has melted and is very hot. Remove the tin from the oven and pour in the batter. Return to the oven and cook the 4-pan tin for about 20-30 minutes or until well risen, crisp and golden brown, or for about 15 minutes if making small puddings, or 30-40 minutes in the Aga roasting tin. *Serve* at once. *Can be reheated (Page 14).*

THIN GRAVY

A little sherry and redcurrant jelly can be added to a thin gravy for game birds.
Add red wine for red meats and white wine for lighter meats.

SERVES 4

Pour all the fat from the roasting tin, leaving only the pan sediment. Add ½ pint (300ml) good stock. Stir well and simmer for 2-3 minutes on the Simmering Plate to reduce it slightly. Season and add a little gravy browning if liked. Serve hot with a roast.

THICK GRAVY

SERVES 4

Pour off most of the fat from the roasting tin, leaving about 2 tablespoons of the sediment. Stir in 1 tablespoon flour and blend thoroughly with the fat. Cook on the Simmering Plate until beginning to brown. Gradually blend in ½ pint (300ml) good stock and bring to the boil, stirring until thickened. Add a little gravy browning, if liked. Season to taste, strain and serve hot with a roast.

BASIC SAUCES

Proportions: For a pouring sauce: 1½oz (40g) flour and 1½oz (40g) butter to 1 pint (600ml) liquid. For a coating sauce: 2oz (50g) flour and 2oz (50g) butter to 1 pint (600ml) liquid.

Melt the butter in a thick bottomed pan on the Simmering Plate, add the flour and stir with a wooden spoon or metal whisk. Cook for about a minute. Gradually add the milk stirring continuously until it is all added and the sauce is smooth. Cook for a minute or two, stirring. Season to taste.

PARSLEY SAUCE
Add 2 tablespoons freshly chopped parsley when all the liquid has been added.

MUSTARD SAUCE
Add 1 tablespoon dry mustard mixed with good teaspoon sugar and tablespoon vinegar. Add to the sauce when made.

INGREDIENTS

WHITE SAUCE
1½ (40g) butter
1½oz (40g) flour
1 pint (600ml) milk
salt and pepper

APPLE SAUCE

Serve with duck, goose or pork.

SERVES 4-6

Peel, core and slice the apples. Put in a pan with the water and lemon juice. Cover and cook gently on the Simmering Plate or bring to the boil and transfer to the Simmering Oven and cook until the apples are soft, stirring occasionally. Beat well with a wooden spoon until smooth. Add the butter, and sugar to taste.

INGREDIENTS

1lb (450g) cooking apples
5 tablespoons water
juice ½ lemon
1oz (25g) butter
sugar, to taste

CUMBERLAND SAUCE

This sauce improves with keeping, make ahead and store in the fridge.

MAKES 1 PINT (600ML)

Remove zest from oranges and lemons with a zester or peel with a potato peeler and cut into fine julienne strips. Blanch shallots in boiling water for 2 minutes, add zest of oranges and lemons and boil for a further 2 minutes, drain and set aside. Melt redcurrant jelly, taking care not to let it burn. Slake the cornflour with orange juice. Add mustard, vinegar and port to the redcurrant jelly and bring to the boil, pour a little of the liquid over the orange and cornflour mixture and return to the pan. Add shallot and orange and lemon zest. Bring to the boil and simmer for 1 minute, stirring well. Leave to cool. Keeps in the fridge for up to 3 weeks.

INGREDIENTS

zest and juice 2 oranges
zest 2 lemons
2 shallots, finely chopped
1lb (450g) redcurrant jelly
1 teaspoon cornflour
1 dessertspoon Dijon mustard
2 tablespoons wine vinegar
¼ pint (150ml) port

2 cloves
1 onion
½ pint (300ml) milk
about 4oz (100g) white breadcrumbs
salt and freshly ground black pepper
a knob of butter

¼ pint (150ml) double cream
2 level tablespoons grated horseradish
1 teaspoon white wine vinegar
salt and freshly ground black pepper
a little caster sugar

6oz (175g) caster sugar
¼ pint (150ml) water
8oz (225g) cranberries

1lb (450g) lean minced beef
4 rashers streaky bacon, snipped
1 tablespoon flour
1 large onion, chopped
2 large carrots, diced
½ pint (300ml) beef stock
1 clove garlic, crushed
salt and freshly ground black pepper
¼ teaspoon mixed dried herbs
3oz (75g) can tomato purée

1 rasher streaky bacon, snipped
1 onion, chopped
1oz (25g) flour
14oz (397g) can tomatoes
¼ pint (150ml) stock
salt and freshly ground black pepper
1 tablespoon Worcestershire sauce
1 level teaspoon sugar
1 bay leaf
1 fat clove garlic, crushed

BREAD SAUCE

Serve with chicken, turkey or goose.

SERVES 4-6

Stick the cloves into the onion, then put in a pan with the milk. Bring to the boil slowly on the Simmering Plate then remove from the heat and leave to stand for about 30 minutes. Lift out the onion and stir in the breadcrumbs, seasoning and butter. Reheat the sauce and keep warm in the Simmering Oven until required.

HORSERADISH SAUCE

Serve this sauce with roast beef or grilled steaks.

SERVES 4

Lightly whip the cream and add the horseradish. Stir in the vinegar, salt and pepper. Add a little sugar to taste and blend thoroughly. Turn into a small serving dish, cover and chill well before serving.

CRANBERRY SAUCE

Serve with roast turkey, pheasant or goose, or with roast pork.

SERVES ABOUT 6

Put the sugar in a small pan with the water and heat gently on the Simmering Plate until the sugar has dissolved. Meanwhile, wash the cranberries. Add to the sugar syrup and slowly bring to the boil. Simmer gently for about 10 minutes or until the berries are tender, stirring occasionally. Remove from the heat, turn into a small serving dish and serve warm.

BOLOGNAISE SAUCE

A rich meaty sauce to accompany spaghetti. If I have some left-over red wine I use it to replace some of the stock.

SERVES 4

Measure the meat and bacon into a large pan and heat gently on the Simmering Plate to allow the fat to run out. Transfer to the Boiling Plate and fry quickly to brown. Stir in the flour and then the remaining ingredients. Bring to the boil, stirring occasionally. Simmer 5 minutes then cover with a lid.

Simmering Oven: transfer to the floor of the oven for about 1 hour or until the meat is tender. Taste and check seasoning before serving.

TOMATO SAUCE

This is a good sauce to serve with simple meat dishes.

SERVES 4

Heat the bacon gently in a small pan on the Simmering Plate until the fat begins to run out, add the onion and cook gently for about 5 minutes. Stir in the flour and cook for a minute, add tomatoes and stock and bring to the boil, stirring until thickened. Stir in the remaining ingredients and cover with the lid.

Simmering Oven: transfer to the floor of the oven for about 45 minutes.

Remove the bayleaf and turn the sauce into a processor or blender and reduce to a purée. Return the sauce to the pan, reheat and taste and check seasoning before serving.

FRESH HERB SAUCE

Especially good to serve with fish dishes. May be made a day ahead, refrigerated and reheated in the Simmering Oven for 2 hours, stirring from time to time.

SERVES 6

Measure all the ingredients, except the dill or chives, into a processor or blender and blend until smooth. Transfer to a bowl and stand over a pan of simmering water for about 10 minutes, stirring from time to time. Season to taste and stir in the dill or chives, transfer to a serving dish and serve hot.

INGREDIENTS

3oz (75g) butter, melted
juice 1 lemon
rounded teaspoon flour
½ pint (300ml) single cream
1 egg yolk
1 tablespoon freshly snipped dill or chives

CUCUMBER SAUCE

A light refreshing sauce, excellent to serve with fish dishes. If preferred use Greek yogurt or the Aga yogurt (see page 139) instead of cream.

SERVES 6

Put the diced cucumber onto a plate and sprinkle with the salt. Leave to stand for 30 minutes, rinse thoroughly and drain well on kitchen paper. Blend the mayonnaise and cream together then gently stir in the lemon juice, seasoning, cucumber and dill. Turn into a serving bowl and serve well chilled with salmon or trout.

INGREDIENTS

½ cucumber, diced
2 teaspoons salt
¼ pint (150ml) mayonnaise
¼ pint (150ml) whipping cream, whipped
juice ½ lemon
salt and freshly ground black pepper
2 tablespoons freshly snipped dill

MUSTARD DILL SAUCE

So quick to make – just takes 5 minutes. This sweet dill sauce goes well with Gravadlax (see page 65) and goes well with cured herrings and ham too.

SERVES 10

Whisk mustard, sugar, vinegar and egg yolk together in a bowl. A little balloon whisk is ideal. Then incorporate the oil, whisking well. The result will be the consistency of mayonnaise. Season with salt and pepper and stir in the dill.

INGREDIENTS

3 tablespoons Dijon mustard
2 tablespoons golden granulated sugar
1 tablespoon white wine vinegar
1 egg yolk
¼ pint (150ml) sunflower oil
salt and freshly ground black pepper
2 tablespoons freshly chopped dill or 1 tablespoon dried dill weed

HOLLANDAISE SAUCE

Serve with all the luxuries of summer – asparagus, salmon and other fish.

TO MAKE IN A PROCESSOR:

Place the blade in position. Heat the bowl by pouring in about 1 pint boiling water, switch on briefly then throw away the water. Add the lemon juice and vinegar, switch on then add the egg yolks through the funnel and slowly add the boiling melted butter. Process until thick, season and serve at once.

HAND METHOD:

Measure the vinegar and lemon juice into a bowl and add the egg yolks. Whisk with a wire balloon whisk until well mixed. Place the bowl over a pan of hot water and whisk. Gradually add the just warm, not melted, butter, whisking after each addition until the sauce thickens and all the butter has been used. Season.

INGREDIENTS

2 teaspoons lemon juice
2 teaspoons wine vinegar
3 egg yolks, at room temperature
4oz (100g) unsalted butter, melted or just boiled
salt and freshly ground black pepper

CREAMY DILL SAUCE

Delicious served with chilled fresh trout.

SERVES 8

Whip the cream and place into a basin, squeeze the shallot through a garlic press and add to the cream with the rest of the ingredients.
Mix lightly together until blended. Taste and check seasoning. Serve cold.

INGREDIENTS

½ pint (300ml) mayonnaise
¼ pint (150ml) whipping cream,
juice 1 lemon, small shallot
2 teaspoons freshly snipped dill
1 teaspoon freshly chopped lemon thyme
1 teaspoon chopped parsley
1 teaspoon chopped chives
salt and freshly ground black pepper

INGREDIENTS

about 8 large sprigs mint
2 level teaspoons caster sugar
1 tablespoon water boiled with
2 tablespoons vinegar

INGREDIENTS

½ pint (300ml) mayonnaise
1 good tablespoon chopped
gherkins
1 good tablespoon chopped capers
1 good tablespoon chopped parsley

INGREDIENTS

½ pint (300ml) milk
3 egg yolks or 2 whole eggs
1 level tablespoon vanilla caster
sugar
1 level teaspoon cornflour

INGREDIENTS

1oz (25g) butter
1½oz (40g) cocoa, sieved
4 fl oz (120ml) boiling water
5oz (150g) granulated sugar
a few drops vanilla essence

INGREDIENTS

3oz (75g) butter
5oz (150g) granulated sugar
6oz (175g) can evaporated milk

MINT SAUCE

Serve with roast lamb or grilled lamb chops.

SERVES 4

Wash and dry the mint well, strip the leaves from the stems and chop very finely. Place the sugar in a sauce boat with the boiling water and vinegar and stir until the sugar has dissolved. Add the chopped mint and a little extra sugar if necessary.

TARTARE SAUCE

Serve with fish or veal.

SERVES 4-6

Measure all the ingredients into a bowl and mix well until thoroughly blended. Turn into a serving bowl and serve.

PROPER CUSTARD

I always add a teaspoon of cornflour; it prevents the custard curdling. If you are brave leave it out. Add a few drops of vanilla essence if you have no vanilla sugar. For a richer custard use single cream instead of milk.

MAKES A GOOD ½ PINT (300ML)

Heat the milk in a small pan until it almost boils. Beat egg yolks (or whole eggs), sugar and cornflour together in a small bowl, pour on the hot milk stirring thoroughly the whole time. Return the sauce to the pan and heat gently until it puckers for about a minute or two, until it thinly coats the back of a spoon. Strain if liked.
Can be served hot, warm or cold.

DARK CHOCOLATE SAUCE

Cocoa burns very easily so add to butter with the pan to one side.

MAKES JUST UNDER 1/2 PINT (300ML)

Heat the butter in a pan on the Simmering Plate, remove from heat and add cocoa, mix well and gradually add the boiling water. Stir in the sugar, bring to the boil and simmer for about 5 minutes WITHOUT stirring. This does need watching as it can boil over very easily. Remove from the heat and stir in the vanilla essence.
Serve with vanilla or coffee ice cream, or leave to cool and use in meringue and cream puddings. Reheats well, store in fridge for up to 2 weeks.

BUTTER CARAMEL FUDGE SAUCE

Deliciously wicked, but very good over vanilla ice cream.

Measure all the ingredients into a pan, and heat gently on the Simmering Plate until the sugar has completely dissolved. Bring to the boil for about 5 minutes until pale golden and still runny. Allow to cool. It will then be a coating consistency and keep in the fridge for up to 4 weeks.

LUNCHES & SUPPERS

SMOKED SALMON TAGLIATELLE P.90 · PRAWNS A LA PLANCHA P.90

*A*ll my favourite lighter meals have been included in this chapter. The beauty of most of them is that they can be made ahead then chilled.

So convenient if you're expecting a crowd for an informal supper, because the Aga reheats food so beautifully.

A quick note on pasta. All my pasta recipes give cooking times for dried pasta. If you're using fresh pasta, the cooking time is much shorter.

**12 large Mediterranean prawns
(uncooked)
olive oil
1 fat clove of garlic, finely chopped
½ pint (300ml) dry white wine
a generous handful of chopped
fresh parsley
freshly ground black pepper
salt**

**3 rashers streaky bacon, cut into
thin strips
3oz (75g) onion, chopped
a little olive oil
6oz (175g) wholegrain rice
¾ pint (450ml) hot stock
1oz (25g) raisins
2 tablespoons soy sauce
freshly ground black pepper**

FOR THE SALAD

**½ bunch watercress
about 8 leaves of a red lettuce such
as oak leaf or radicchio
1 crisp lettuce heart
4-6 tablespoons French dressing**

FOR THE CHICKEN

**4oz (100g) thinly sliced streaky
bacon, snipped into strips
3oz (75g) flaked almonds
salt and ground black pepper
3 boneless chicken breasts, skinned**

to garnish
chopped parsley

**8oz (225g) tagliatelle
good knob of butter
¼ pint (150ml) double cream
4oz (100g) smoked salmon, cut into
fine strips
juice ½ lemon
salt and freshly ground black
pepper**

to garnish
freshly chopped parsley

PRAWNS A LA PLANCHA

A speedy starter or serve more for a terrace lunch with salad.

SERVES 4

Heat a large cast iron dry pan on the Boiling Plate – a frypan is ideal. Meanwhile dry the prawns and brush with olive oil. Put them into the hot pan and keep turning for a couple of minutes until they turn pink. Add the garlic then immediately drizzle in half of the white wine so that it bubbles fiercely, then add half the parsley.

Move the pan to the Simmering Plate and allow the wine to reduce slightly. Add plenty of black pepper, a little salt, then the remaining wine. Leave to simmer gently for about 5 minutes. By then, the prawns will release a rich coral juice which mixes with the wine to give a wonderful sauce. Quickly stir in the remaining parsley and serve.

PORTUGUESE RICE

I used Uncle Ben's wholegrain rice. Do not be tempted to overcook it.

SERVES 6

Put the bacon in a pan, heat until just beginning to sizzle on the Boiling Plate, add the onion and oil and when really hot, cover and transfer to the floor of the Simmering Oven for about 10 minutes. Return pan to Boiling Plate, add rice and stir until combined with onion and bacon. Add the stock, bring to the boil and cover with a lid.

2∎
∎4∎ Simmering Oven: transfer to the floor of the oven for about 20 minutes until all the liquid has been absorbed. Stir in raisins, soy sauce and pepper.

WARM CHICKEN AND ALMOND SALAD

Stir frying is very quick on the Aga using a wok or large shallow pan.

SERVES 4

Prepare the salad, trimming off the stalks of the watercress. Oil the base of the pan then fry the bacon on the Simmering Plate until the fat runs out. Move over to the Boiling Plate then add the almonds allowing both the bacon and almonds to become light golden. Lift out of the pan with a slotted spoon and keep warm in the Simmering Oven. Cut chicken into pencil strips and season. Quickly cook in the same pan, tossing all the time on the Boiling Plate for a couple of minutes. Return bacon and almonds to the pan for a moment. Toss salad in dressing and arrange on four plates. Top with the chicken, almonds and bacon. Sprinkle with parsley.

SMOKED SALMON TAGLIATELLE

Smoked salmon has a strong flavour so very little is needed.

SERVES 3 AS A MAIN COURSE OR 6 AS A FIRST COURSE

Cook the pasta until just tender. Drain well. Add the butter to the pan and allow to melt. Return the pasta to the pan with half the cream, the smoked salmon, lemon juice and seasoning to taste. Heat gently on the Simmering Plate until warmed through. Serve on plates topped with the remaining cream and a generous sprinkling of parsley.

CAULIFLOWER CHEESE

The same recipe can be made with broccoli spears if you have a glut of them.

SERVES 4

Divide the cauliflower into florets, discarding any leaves and very thick stalk. Cook in boiling salted water on the Boiling Plate for about 5 minutes, drain well and reserve ¼ pint (150ml) of the cooking water.

Heat the butter in a pan, stir in the flour and cook for a minute then gradually blend in the milk and bring to the boil, stirring until thickened and stir in the reserved cooking liquid. Add 3oz (75g) of the cheese and season with pepper and mustard. Arrange the florets in a shallow ovenproof dish and pour over the sauce. Sprinkle over the remaining cheese.

2▪ / ▪4▪ Roasting Oven: with the grid shelf on the second set of runners cook for about 15 minutes until the cheese has melted and browned.

INGREDIENTS

1 large cauliflower
salt
2oz (50g) butter
1½oz (40g) flour
½ pint (300ml) milk
4oz (100g) well-flavoured Cheddar cheese, grated
freshly ground black pepper
½ teaspoon made mustard

STUFFED JACKET POTATOES

More substantial snacks!

SERVES 4

Drain chicken livers and wrap 8 of the livers each with half a rasher of bacon. Chop the remaining chicken livers and bacon. Fry the bacon and bacon rolls until crisp, lift out the rolls and set on one side. Add the chopped chicken livers to the bacon in the pan with the spring onions and cook until just done. The livers should still be just a little pink in the middle.

Split the cooked potatoes in half, scoop out the middles, leaving a thin layer of potato inside the skin so they keep shape. Mash the potato with the warm milk, butter and seasoning, add the liver and bacon mixture then spoon back into the potato shells. Sprinkle with grated cheese and arrange on a baking sheet.

2▪ / ▪4▪ Roasting Oven: with the grid shelf on the second set of runners cook for about 15 minutes, until the cheese is golden brown and bubbling.

Top each of the potato halves with one of the bacon and liver rolls 5 minutes before the end of the cooking time.

VARIATIONS:

BAKED BEAN AND SAUSAGE: omit liver, bacon and spring onion. Top with baked beans and cooked sausages.

BACON AND ONION: omit liver and use a medium chopped onion instead of the spring onion.

CHEESE AND CHIVE: omit liver, bacon and spring onion and add 2oz (50g) grated well-flavoured Cheddar cheese and 1 tablespoon chives to the mashed potato. Sprinkle with more cheese before baking.

INGREDIENTS

4 large potatoes, scrubbed and cooked
2 tablespoons milk, warmed
1oz (25g) butter
salt and freshly ground black pepper
2oz (50g) well-flavoured Cheddar cheese, grated

CHICKEN LIVER AND BACON TOPPING

8 rindless rashers streaky bacon
8oz (225g) chicken livers
4 spring onions, chopped

TOAD IN THE HOLE

The secret behind a really good Toad in the Hole is to ensure that the Aga is right up to temperature. This way the batter mixture will rise beautifully.

SERVES 4-5

Lightly grease the small roasting tin and arrange the sausages in the bottom.

2▪ / ▪4▪ Roasting Oven: hang the tin on the second set of runners in the oven and cook for about 10 minutes. Turn the sausages over.

Meanwhile prepare the batter: measure the flour into a bowl, add a little salt and stir in the beaten egg and milk to give a smooth batter. Pour the batter over the sausages and return to the oven for a further 20-25 minutes until the batter is well risen, crisp and golden brown.

INGREDIENTS

4oz (100g) flour
salt
2 eggs, lightly beaten
8fl.oz (225ml) milk

SEAFOOD PAELLA P.93

SEAFOOD PAELLA

If you can get uncooked mussels add these after the squid and cook with the rice.
For a variation substitute the squid, mussels and shelled prawns with
1lb (450g) raw skinned chicken and 8oz (225g) thick sliced streaky bacon
cut into strips – add these to the oil, onion and garlic and cook for about
8 minutes before adding the rice. Use chicken stock and finish with a red pepper
and whole prawns

SERVES 10

Put the saffron strands into a small bowl. Bring to the boil ¼ pint (150ml) of the stock, pour over the saffron and set aside. Heat the oil in a large pan on the Simmering Plate, add the onion and garlic and cook for 5 minutes, move to the Boiling Plate, add the squid and tomatoes, cook for 2 minutes and add the rice. When the rice and oil are combined add the stock, saffron water and seasoning. Bring to the boil and cover.

2 Simmering Oven: transfer to the floor of the oven and cook for about
4 30-40 minutes or until the rice is tender and the liquid absorbed.

Return to the Simmering Plate and add the scallops and red pepper. Stir well until the scallops are cooked, this will only take 2-3 minutes, then add the prawns and mussels and heat through. Garnish with the whole prawns and serve.

INGREDIENTS

about 1 teaspoon saffron strands
1½ pints (900ml) fish stock
(see page 18)
6 tablespoons olive oil
1 large onion, chopped
3 cloves garlic, crushed
4oz (100g) squid, cleaned and sliced
8oz (225g) tomatoes, skinned and seeded
1lb (450g) Spanish rice
salt and freshly ground black pepper
4oz (100g) scallops, if using queen scallops leave whole, for large scallops slice across in three
1 red pepper, thinly sliced
4 oz (100g) peeled prawns
4oz (100g) mussels, cooked

to garnish
12 whole prawns in shell

TOASTED SANDWICHES

There are so many types of bread to choose from. We like using French bread
sometimes, you can then do them as open toasted sandwiches.

Begin by cooking the streaky bacon in the Aga roasting tin near the top of the Roasting Oven until crisp.

Meanwhile butter one side of each of the slices of bread. Place the bacon on one unbuttered piece, top with as much cheese as you like and place on top a second slice of bread, buttered side up. Place on a baking sheet, butter side down. Keep repeating this process until you have the number of sandwiches you need.

2 Roasting Oven: place the baking sheet on the grid shelf on the highest
4 set of runners for about 10 minutes, turning the sandwiches over after 5 minutes until nicely browned and crisp.

For French stick toasties, split the bread and prepare as open sandwiches.

VARIATIONS:

TUNA AND MAYONNAISE: combine the tuna with the mayonnaise, season with pepper and pile onto the bread.

BAKED BEANS AND CHEESE: spoon some baked beans onto the bread and top with cheese.

HAM AND MUSHROOM: place a slice of ham on the bread and sprinkle over some mushrooms.

INGREDIENTS

rashers streaky bacon
slices of brown or white bread
butter
cheese, cut into slices

VARIATIONS

TUNA AND MAYONNAISE

7oz (198g) can tuna fish
1½ tablespoons mayonnaise
ground black pepper

BAKED BEANS AND CHEESE

small can baked beans, drained
slices of cheese

HAM AND MUSHROOM

slices of ham
mushrooms, thickly sliced and cooked in butter

TUNA AGA STANDBY

A great family standby from store cupboard ingredients.

SERVES 4

Boil noodles and onion together in a pan of salted water on the Boiling Plate for about 12 minutes until the pasta is "al dente". Drain well and set to one side. Melt the butter in a pan, add flour and cook for a minute, gradually add the milk and bring to the boil, stirring until thickened. Stir in the noodles, tuna, eggs, seasoning and cheese and turn into a 3½ pint (2 litre) shallow dish. *Fry the breadcrumbs* in the butter until crisp then sprinkle over the noodles.

2 Roasting Oven: with the grid shelf on the lowest set of runners. Bake
4 in the oven for about 20-25 minutes until hot and bubbling.

INGREDIENTS

6oz (175g) noodles or penne
1 onion, finely sliced
2oz (50g) butter
2oz (50g) flour
1 pint (600ml) milk
7oz (198g) can tuna, drained
3 hard-boiled eggs, coarsely chopped
salt and freshly ground black pepper
4oz (100g) Cheddar cheese, grated
3oz (75g) wholemeal breadcrumbs
1½oz (40g) butter

6oz (175g) flour
3oz (75g) butter, chilled
water, to mix

filling

12oz (350g) lean bacon pieces,
chopped
a little butter, if needed
1 large onion, chopped
6 eggs
½ pint (300ml) double cream
½ pint (300ml) milk
salt and freshly ground black
pepper
6oz (175g) Lancashire cheese,
grated

1 pkt white bread mix

BASIC TOMATO TOPPING

2 tablespoons oil
2 large onions, chopped
2 x 14oz (397g) can peeled tomatoes
8oz (225g) tomato purée
2 fat cloves garlic
2 teaspoons sugar
salt and freshly ground black
pepper
chopped fresh herbs

LANCASHIRE DEEP CHEESE TART

Made in the small roasting tin – masses of filling with little pastry.
Our local supermarket sells 12oz (350g) packs of bacon pieces. You may find
them on the delicatessen counter. For a party, double the ingredients and
make in the large roasting tin. The cooking time will be a little longer and it
will then serve 16.

SERVES 8

For the pastry, measure the flour into a bowl and rub in the butter until the mixture resembles fine breadcrumbs, mix to a dough with the water. Knead lightly and roll out on a lightly floured surface. Use to line the small roasting tin, trim then flute the top edge. Chill in the fridge.

Put the bacon pieces in a pan on the Simmering Plate and allow the fat to run out – if very lean add a little butter. Add onion and cook for about 20 minutes, turning until pale golden. Meanwhile whisk the eggs, add cream, milk and seasoning, go easy on the salt if the bacon is salty. Scatter the bacon and onion over the base of the pastry case, pour over the egg mixture and sprinkle with the cheese.

2 / 4 Roasting Oven: cook on the floor of the Roasting Oven for about 25-35 minutes turning after 15 minutes, until the pastry is pale golden brown and the filling is just set and golden all over. Don't be tempted to cook for too long as the filling will puff up and overcook.

PIZZAS

This recipe is for two large pizzas, it always seems sensible to me to make one to
eat now and one for the freezer. The one I freeze, I cook for half the cooking time,
then cool and freeze. I then thaw and cook it for half the cooking time.

MAKES 2

Mix the dough base according to the instructions on the packet. Cover and leave near the Aga until doubled in size for about ½ hour. Meanwhile prepare the tomato base: heat the oil in a large pan on the Simmering Plate, add the onion and fry until soft. Add all the ingredients except herbs, transfer to Boiling Plate and cook without lid until thick. Taste and check seasoning.

Divide the dough in half and roll out to two circles about 10 inch (25cm) in diameter. Lift onto lightly greased baking trays. Spread the tomato mixture onto the bases, sprinkle with chopped fresh herbs.

Select your topping from the following:

SAUSAGE TOPPING FOR ONE PIZZA:

Make 1lb (450g) sausagemeat into a large flat round about the same size as the pizza and fry on both sides in a frying pan, cooking the second side a little less. Transfer the sausagemeat "pancake" onto the pizza, well-cooked side downwards.

BACON AND MUSHROOM TOPPING FOR ONE PIZZA:

Sprinkle 2oz (50g) grated cheese over tomato mixture. Then lightly fry 8oz (225g) sliced button mushrooms in 3 tablespoons oil and spread on top of the pizza. Arrange 16 thin rindless rashers streaky bacon in a cartwheel pattern on top of the mushrooms and season.

TRADITIONAL TOPPING FOR ONE PIZZA:

Layer the pizza base with slices of Mozarella cheese. Lattice with washed, drained, halved anchovies. Garnish with whole black olives.

2 / 4 Roasting Oven: cook on the floor of the oven for 15 minutes, then with the grid shelf on the highest set of runners, transfer to the top of the oven for about a further 15 minutes until the dough is golden and risen.

I N G R E D I E N T S

1 small onion, quartered
6oz (175g) pig's liver
8oz (225g) pork sausagemeat
8oz (225g) best raw minced beef
1 good tablespoon chopped fresh thyme or 1 teaspoon dried thyme
salt and freshly ground black pepper

t o   g a r n i s h
6 level tablespoons chopped fresh parsley to cover

I N G R E D I E N T S

1½oz (40g) butter
1½oz (40g) flour
½ pint (300ml) milk
salt and freshly ground black pepper
1 teaspoon Dijon mustard
4oz (100g) well-flavoured Cheddar cheese, grated
4 eggs

I N G R E D I E N T S

8oz (225g) plain flour
5oz (150g) hard block margarine
2 good tablespoons water

f i l l i n g
4oz (100g) bacon, snipped
1 large onion, chopped
4oz (100g) mushrooms, sliced
4 eggs, beaten
¾ pint (450ml) single cream
salt and freshly ground black pepper
4oz (100g) well-flavoured Cheddar cheese, grated

MEATLOAF

It looks wonderful in its coat of parsley and it slices without crumbling.

SERVES 4-6

Line a 1lb (450g) loaf tin with foil and grease well.

Put the onion through a processor with the liver until finely chopped then turn into a large bowl. Add the remaining ingredients and mix thoroughly. Turn the mixture into the prepared tin, level out evenly and cover with foil. Stand in the small roasting tin, half filled with boiling water.

2▮ ▮4▮ Roasting Oven: with the grid shelf on the floor of the oven, cook for 1 hour. Lift out of the oven and leave to cool in the tin. Chill then turn out and press the chopped parsley over the top and the sides of the meatloaf.

CHEESE SOUFFLÉ

This makes a delicious light lunch or Sunday night supper dish

SERVES 3-4

Heat the butter in a pan on the Simmering Plate, add the flour and cook for a minute. Gradually blend in the milk and bring to the boil, stirring until thickened. Stir in the seasoning, mustard and cheese. Separate the eggs and beat the yolks into the cheese sauce, one at a time. Whisk the whites until stiff. Stir one good tablespoon into the cheese sauce and then carefully fold in the remainder. Carefully turn into a buttered 2 pint (1.2 litre) soufflé dish.

2▮ Roasting Oven: with the grid shelf on the floor of the oven and a cold plain shelf on the second set of runners, cook the soufflé in the oven for about 20-25 minutes until well risen and golden brown. Serve at once.

▮4▮ Baking Oven: with the grid shelf on the fourth set of runners, cook for 20-25 minutes until well risen and golden brown.

VARIATIONS: Choose any flavouring and add to the mixture before the egg yolks.

HAM: add 4oz (100g) finely chopped ham or boiled bacon.

FISH: add 4oz (100g) finely flaked smoked salmon.

SHELLFISH: add 4oz (100g) peeled prawns or shrimps.

MUSHROOM: add 6oz (175g) finely chopped sautéed mushrooms.

SPINACH: add 12oz (350g) cooked finely chopped spinach with nutmeg.

WONDERFUL QUICHE

No pre-baking is needed because the floor of the Roasting Oven is hot enough to make the pastry crisp and cook the filling too.

SERVES 6

First make the pastry: rub the fat into the flour until the mixture resembles fine breadcrumbs, add water and work to a firm dough. This can also be done in a processor. Line a 10 inch (25cm) deepish flan tin. Leave to rest in the fridge while preparing the filling.

Put the bacon into a pan and cook gently on the Simmering Plate to draw out the fat, then transfer to the Boiling Plate and fry until crisp, lift out with a slotted spoon and keep on one side. Add onion to the pan, adding a little extra fat if needed. Cover with a lid and cook until just tender, adding the mushrooms for the last five minutes, stir in the bacon.

Whisk the eggs lightly to blend, add cream and seasoning. Spoon the mixture over base of pastry and pour over the egg mixture. Sprinkle with cheese.

2▮ ▮4▮ Roasting Oven: place tin on floor of oven and cook for about 30 minutes until golden brown. If necessary turn once to ensure even browning.

HOME BAKING

DUNDEE MINCEMEAT CAKE P.98 · ALMOND CAKE P.99 · SIMNEL CAKE P.99

*I*t's safe to say that you can trust your Aga with any kind of cake. Simple baking like my favourite Traybakes (P. 103), to large fruit cakes and celebration cakes (P. 100).
I find bread-making therapeutic, especially on a wild, wet day when the Aga beckons. However if you don't have the time or the inclination to bake your own bread, just try 'refreshing' bought bread in the Roasting Oven for a few minutes – you get all the smell of home-baked bread with minimum effort.

CAKE BAKING

THE AGA CAKE BAKER

Large round cakes requiring more than 45 minutes cooking are baked in the Roasting Oven of the two oven Aga, using the special Aga cake baker. Other foods, which need a high temperature such as scones or bread rolls can be cooked at the same time.

BAKING CAKES WITHOUT THE CAKE BAKER IN A 2 OVEN AGA

i.e. for Cherry, Almond and Family Fruit Cake. These cakes can be made without a cake baker but need more attention, as follows:

Put grill rack into the large roasting tin, place the cake on the rack and slide the tin into the Roasting Oven, on the lowest set of runners. Put the cold plain shelf on the second set of runners. Bake until the cake is an even, golden brown on top usually in about 20-30 minutes. Check just before 20 minutes.

Then first transfer the exceedingly hot plain shelf from the Roasting Oven to the centre of the Simmering Oven, then very carefully lift the cake onto the hot plain shelf and continue to bake until cooked – usually about 1 hour 30 minutes. To test when the cake is done, take a fine skewer and insert it into the centre of the cake and if it comes out clean then the cake is cooked.

N.B. If the Aga is not up to full temperature, say after a long cooking session, leave the cake longer in the Roasting Oven until it is golden, then transfer the now very hot plain shelf to the centre of the Simmering Oven. Place the cake on top and cook for less time just until a skewer comes out clean when pierced into the centre of the cake and the cake is shrinking away slightly from the sides of the tin.

DUNDEE MINCEMEAT CAKE

Very moist lightly fruited cake with a distinct flavour of spices and apple.

For the two oven Aga pre-heat the empty Aga cake baker – place it on the floor of the Roasting Oven whilst preparing the cake or see note above.

Grease and line an 8inch (20cm) cake tin with greased greaseproof paper.

Measure all the ingredients, except the almonds into a large bowl and beat well until thoroughly blended. Turn into the prepared tin and level out evenly, arrange the almonds on top.

2▬ Roasting Oven: place cake tin into the rack and lower into the cake baker, replace lid. Return to the floor of the oven. Cook in the pre-heated cake baker for about 1 to 1½ hours, or until a warm skewer inserted into the centre of the cake comes out clean.

▬**4**▬ Baking Oven: put the cake tin on the grid shelf on the floor of the oven, cook for about 1 to 1½ hours, or until a warm skewer inserted into the centre of the cake comes out clean. Protect the top of the cake with folded greaseproof paper if browned to your liking, but not quite cooked.

Leave to cool in the tin for a few minutes then turn out and finish cooling on a wire rack.

INGREDIENTS

5oz (150g) soft margarine
5oz (150g) light muscovado sugar
2 eggs
8oz (225g) self-raising flour
8oz (225g) mincemeat
4oz (100g) currants
4oz (100g) sultanas
2oz (50g) blanched split almonds

EASTER SIMNEL CAKE

This has become the traditional Easter Cake but originally it was given by servant girls to their mothers when they went home on Mothering Sunday.

Grease and line the base and sides of an 8 inch (20cm) deep round cake tin with greased greaseproof paper.

Measure all the cake ingredients into a large mixing bowl and beat well until thoroughly blended. Place half of the mixture into the prepared tin and level the surface.

Take one-third of the almond paste and roll it out to a circle, the size of the tin and then place on top of the cake mixture. Spoon the remaining cake mixture on top and level the surface.

Bake on the grid shelf in the centre of the Simmering Oven for 5-10 hours, or until a warm skewer comes out clean from the centre and the cake is pale golden. Should the cake top be getting brown and is not done, cover with a piece of foil. Allow the cake to cool in the tin for about 30 minutes before turning out and cooling on a wire rack.

When the cake is cool, brush the top with a little warmed apricot jam and roll out the remaining almond paste to fit the top. Press firmly on the top and crimp the edges to decorate. Mark a criss-cross pattern on the almond paste with a sharp knife. Form the remaining almond paste into eleven balls to represent the Apostles. Brush the almond paste with the beaten egg and arrange the almond paste balls around the outside. Brush the tops of the balls with beaten egg too, and then wrap all but the top of the cake in foil. Stand in roasting tin and slide the tin in the centre of the Roasting Oven. Brown for a few minutes until the balls are golden.

To decorate fill the centre of the top of the cake with a little lemon icing and decorate with crystallised primroses or small foil eggs.

INGREDIENTS

8oz (225g) soft margarine
8oz (225g) light soft brown sugar
4 eggs
8oz (225g) self-raising flour
8oz (225g) sultanas
4oz (100g) currants
4oz (100g) glace cherries, washed and quartered
2oz (50g) candied peel chopped
grated rind of 2 lemons
2 level teaspoons mixed spice

for the filling and topping
1lb (450g) almond paste
about 2 tablespoons apricot jam
1 egg, beaten, to glaze
crystallized primroses or small eggs

ALMOND CAKE

A lovely light cake, perfect for coffee mornings. Well worth trying.

For the two oven Aga pre-heat the empty Aga cake baker on the floor of the Roasting Oven whilst preparing the cake.

Grease and line an 8 inch (20cm) cake tin with greaseproof paper.

Measure the butter and sugar into a bowl and beat well until light and fluffy. Beat in the eggs a little at a time with half the flour. Gently fold in the ground almonds, remaining flour and almond essence until thoroughly blended. Turn into the prepared tin and level out evenly. Sprinkle the flaked almonds on top.

2▪ Roasting Oven: place the cake into the rack and lower into the cake baker, replace lid. Return to the floor of the oven, cook in the cake baker for about 1 hour 10 minutes, until well risen and golden brown. A warm skewer should come out clean when inserted into the centre of the cake.

▪4▪ Baking Oven: put the cake tin on the grid shelf on the floor of the oven cook the cake for around 1 hour 15 minutes, until well risen and golden brown. A warm skewer should come out clean when inserted into the centre of the cake.

Leave to cool in the tin for a few minutes, then turn out and finish cooling on a wire rack.

INGREDIENTS

6oz (175g) butter, softened
6oz (175g) caster sugar
4 eggs, beaten
7oz (200g) self-raising flour
4oz (100g) ground almonds
1 teaspoon almond essence
1oz (25g) flaked almonds

AGA CELEBRATION FRUIT CAKE

*Baking the cake slowly in the Simmering Oven gives excellent results.
Bake two tiers of a wedding cake at one time but check first that the tins
will go in the oven!*

First prepare the fruit. Chop the raisins with a damp knife and quarter the cherries. Put the fruit in a container and pour over the sherry and stir in grated rind. Cover with a lid and leave to soak for 3 days, stirring daily.

Measure the margarine, sugar, eggs, treacle and chopped almonds into a large bowl and beat well. Add the flours and spice and mix thoroughly until blended. Stir in the soaked fruit and sherry.

Grease and line the appropriate sized tin with greased greaseproof paper. Spoon the mixture into the tin and level out evenly.

2 Simmering Oven: place the cake tin on the grid shelf (or a rack) on **4** the floor of the oven. The cooking time required will be between the minimum and maximum times shown below.

The times do vary as sometimes older Aga cookers have slower Simmering Ovens, look at the cake after the minimum time shown to gauge further cooking time.

ROUND TIN	SQUARE TIN	COOKING TIME
7 inch (18cm)	6 inch (15cm)	4-8 hours
8 inch (20cm)	7 inch (18cm)	4-10 hours
9 inch (23cm)	8 inch (20cm)	4½-11 hours
10 inch (25cm)	9 inch (23cm)	4½-12 hours
11 inch (28cm)	10 inch (25cm)	5-13 hours
12 inch (30cm)	11 inch (28cm)	5½-14 hours
13 inch (33cm)	12 inch (30cm)	5½-15 hours

To check when the cake is done: pierce through the centre of the cake with a warm skewer. If it comes out clean, then cake is cooked. If not, cook for a further 30 minutes or so. Leave to cool in the tin. This is a very moist cake.

CHERRY CAKE

*A classic cake. It is important to cut the cherries up and then wash and dry them
thoroughly so that all the moisture is removed.*

For two oven Aga pre-heat the empty Aga cake baker, place it on the floor of the Roasting Oven.

Grease and line a 7 inch (18cm) cake tin with greased greaseproof paper.

Cut each cherry into quarters and rinse in a sieve under running water. Drain well and dry thoroughly on absorbent kitchen paper.

Place all the remaining ingredients in a large bowl and beat well for 1 minute, then lightly fold in the cherries. The mixture will be fairly stiff, which will help keep the cherries evenly suspended in the cake whilst it is baking.

2 Roasting Oven: place cake tin into the rack and lower into the cake baker, replace lid. Return to the floor of the oven, bake in the pre-heated cake baker for about 1 to 1¼ hours, or until a warm skewer inserted into the centre comes out clean.

4 Baking Oven: put the cake tin on the grid shelf on the floor of the oven cook for about 1¼ hours, or until a warm skewer inserted into the centre of the cake comes out clean.

Leave to cool in the tin for 10 minutes then turn out and finish cooling on a wire rack. Store in an airtight tin.

INGREDIENT QUANTITIES FOR CELEBRATION CAKE
(Imperial)

Round tin	Square tin	Currants	Sultanas	Raisins	Glacé cherries	Orange rind	Sherry	Soft marg.
7"	6"	6oz	4oz	2oz	4oz	1	2.5fl oz	4oz
8"	7"	12oz	8oz	4oz	8oz	1	¼pt	6oz
9"	8"	1lb 2oz	12oz	6oz	12oz	2	¼pt	9oz
10"	9"	1lb 8oz	1lb	8oz	1lb	2	½pt	12oz
11"	10"	1lb 14oz	1lb 4oz	10oz	1lb 4oz	2	½pt	15oz
12"	11"	2lb 4oz	1lb 8oz	12oz	1lb 8oz	3	¾pt	1lb 2oz
13"	12"	2lb 10oz	1lb 12oz	14oz	1lb 12oz	3	¾pt	1lb 5oz

Round tin	Square tin	Dark brown sugar	Eggs	Self-raising flour	Plain flour	Blanched chopped almonds	Black treacle	Ground mixed spice
7"	6"	4oz	2	2oz	2oz	1oz	½tblsp	½tsp
8"	7"	6oz	3	2oz	4oz	2oz	1tblsp	1tsp
9"	8"	9oz	5	3oz	6oz	3oz	1tblsp	1½tsp
10"	9"	12oz	6	4oz	8oz	4oz	2tblsp	2tsp
11"	10"	15oz	7	5oz	10oz	5oz	2tblsp	2½tsp
12"	11"	1lb 2oz	9	6oz	12oz	6oz	3tblsp	3tsp
13"	12"	1lb 5oz	10	7oz	14oz	7oz	3tblsp	3½tsp

INGREDIENT QUANTITIES FOR CELEBRATION CAKE
(Metric)

Round tin	Square tin	Currants	Sultanas	Raisins	Glacé cherries	Orange rind	Sherry	Soft marg.
17cm	15cm	175g	100g	50g	100g	1	65ml	100g
20cm	17cm	350g	225g	100g	225g	1	150ml	175g
23cm	20cm	500g	350g	175g	350g	2	150ml	250g
25cm	23cm	675g	450g	225g	450g	2	300ml	350g
28cm	25cm	850g	550g	275g	550g	2	300ml	425g
30cm	28cm	900g	675g	350g	675g	3	450ml	500g
32cm	30cm	1.25kg	675g	400g	675g	3	450ml	575g

Round tin	Square tin	Dark brown sugar	Eggs	Self-raising flour	Plain flour	Blanched chopped almonds	Black treacle	Ground mixed spice
17cm	15cm	100g	2	50g	50g	25g	½tblsp	½tsp
20cm	17cm	175g	3	50g	100g	50g	1tblsp	1tsp
23cm	20cm	250g	5	75g	175g	75g	1tblsp	1½tsp
25cm	23cm	350g	6	100g	225g	100g	2tblsp	2tsp
28cm	25cm	425g	7	150g	275g	150g	2tblsp	2½tsp
30cm	28cm	500g	9	175g	350g	175g	3tblsp	3tsp
32cm	30cm	575g	10	200g	400g	200g	2tblsp	3½tsp

TRAYBAKES
CHOCOLATE FUDGY SLICES P.103
FRUITY TRAYBAKES P.103
SHARP LEMON SLICES P.103

Traybakes

Definitely the quickest and easiest way to cook a quantity of cakes for a party. These recipes fit the large roasting tin, halve the quantities for the small roasting tin.

Chocolate Fudgy Slices

MAKES 30 PIECES

Turn the tin you have chosen upside down and mould a piece of foil over the top to make a foil case of the same size. Use this to line the roasting tin and grease well. Measure the cocoa into a bowl, mix with the boiling water to give a smooth paste. Add the remaining ingredients, except the jam and beat well until smooth. Spread evenly in the tin.

2∎ Roasting Oven: hang the tin on the lowest set of runners a ..c cold plain shelf on the second set of runners. Bake for about 30 minu ᵣ the large tin or 20 minutes for the smaller tin, turning once during cooking.
∎4∎ Baking Oven: hang the tin on the lowest set of runners and bake for about 30 minutes for the large tin or 20 minutes for the smaller tin, turning once during cooking.
The sides of the cake should be shrinking away from the sides of the tin, and the top of the cake spring back when lightly pressed with a finger. Leave in the tin to cool. Lift out of the tin, keeping the foil intact and spread with warm apricot jam.
For the icing: melt the margarine gently in a pan, add the cocoa, stir well and cook for a minute. Remove from the heat and stir in the icing sugar and milk. Mix well until smooth, cool to a soft spreading consistency, then pour over the cake and spread out evenly. When set, the large cake will cut into 30 pieces and the smaller cake into 16.

Fruity Traybake

Add no extra baking powder to this recipe as the fruit might sink.

Measure all the ingredients, except the demerara sugar into a bowl and beat well for about 2 minutes. Line the tin and bake as for the Chocolate Fudgy Slices traybakes. Before serving sprinkle with demerara sugar.

Sharp Lemon Slices

For a crunchy topping use granulated or caster instead of icing sugar.

Measure all the ingredients into a bowl and beat well for 2 minutes until smooth. Line tin and bake as for the Chocolate Fudgy Slices. For the icing: warm the lemon juice, mix in the icing sugar and beat until smooth. Add a little more lemon juice if necessary, to give a runny consistency. Spread out evenly over the cake and leave to set. Decorate with lemon and orange sugar slices if liked.

INGREDIENTS

large roasting tin
2oz (50g) cocoa
6 tablespoons boiling water
5 eggs
9oz (250g) soft margarine
9oz (250g) caster sugar
10oz (275g) self-raising flour
3 level teaspoons baking powder
3 tablespoons milk
8oz (225g) apricot jam

icing
2oz (50g) margarine
2oz (50g) cocoa, sieved
12oz (350g) icing sugar, sieved
about 3 tablespoons milk

INGREDIENTS

large roasting tin
4 eggs
9oz (250g) soft margarine
9oz (250g) caster sugar
12oz (350g) self-raising flour/
4 tablespoons milk
12oz (350g) mixed dried fruit
a little demerara sugar

INGREDIENTS

large roasting tin
4 eggs
9oz (250g) soft margarine
9oz (250g) caster sugar
12oz (350g) self-raising flour
3 level teaspoons baking powder
6 tablespoons milk
grated rind 2 lemons

icing
about 5 tablespoons lemon juice
12oz (350g) icing sugar, sieved

I N G R E D I E N T S

6oz (175g) soft margarine
6oz (175g) caster sugar
6oz (175g) sultanas
6oz (175g) currants
3 large eggs
9oz (250g) self-raising flour
2oz (50g) glace cherries, quartered
1 level tablespoon marmalade

I N G R E D I E N T S

6oz (175g) soft margarine
6oz (175g) caster sugar
3 eggs, beaten
6oz (175g) self-raising
wholewheat flour
1 level teaspoon baking powder
grated rind of 1 orange

filling and
topping

3oz (75g) soft margarine
8oz (225g) icing sugar, sieved
3 tablespoons orange juice

FAMILY FRUIT CAKE

A good sound fruit cake. If you are too generous with the marmalade the fruit will sink to the bottom.

For a two oven Aga pre-heat the empty Aga cake baker on the floor of the Roasting Oven whilst preparing the cake.

Grease and line an 8 inch (20cm) cake tin with greased greaseproof paper.

Measure all the ingredients into a bowl and beat well until blended. Spread the mixture into the prepared tin and level the surface.

2▦ Roasting Oven: place the cake tin into the rack and lower into the pre-heated cake baker, replace lid. Return to the floor of the oven, bake in the cake baker for about 1 hour 25 minutes.

▦4▦ Baking Oven: put the cake tin on the grid shelf on the floor of the oven, cook the cake for about 1 hour 30 minutes.

The cake should be shrinking away from the sides of the tin and be pale golden in colour. A warm skewer should come out clean when pierced into the centre of the cake.

Cool in the tin for about 10 minutes, then turn out, peel off the paper and finish cooling on a wire rack.

VARIATION:

For a plainer fruit cake use only 7oz (200g) mixed dried fruit in total, 3 eggs plus 2 tablespoons milk and omit the marmalade and cherries. Make in the same sized tin and bake for about 1 hour 15 minutes.

ORANGE WHOLEWHEAT CAKE

A cake which uses wholewheat flour and is absolutely delicious.

Grease and line the base of two 7 inch (18cm) sandwich tins with greased greaseproof paper.

Measure the margarine, sugar, eggs, flour, baking powder and orange rind into a bowl and beat well for about 2 minutes until smooth and blended. Divide between the tins and level out evenly.

2▦ Roasting Oven: with the grid shelf on the floor of the oven and a cold plain shelf on the second set of runners, bake the cakes for about 20 minutes.

▦4▦ Baking Oven: with the grid shelf on the floor of the oven, bake the cakes for about 20 minutes.

When the cakes are cooked they should be shrinking away slightly from the sides of the tin and spring back when lightly pressed with a finger. Turn the sponges out onto a wire rack to cool and remove the paper.

For the filling and topping: measure all the ingredients into a bowl and beat well until smooth. Use half to sandwich the cakes together and spread the remainder evenly on top of the cake, then mark decoratively with a fork and leave to set.

QUEEN CAKES

Quick to make and to cook.

MAKES 24

Place all the ingredients into a bowl and beat well together. Put heaped teaspoonsful into traditional paper cases or greased bun tins.

2▤ Roasting Oven: cook in two batches. Place the cake cases or bun tin into the large meat tin and hang on the lowest set of runners. Bake for 8-10 minutes, turning once, until risen and browned.

▤4▤ *Baking Oven:* cook in two batches. Bake at the top of the oven for 8-10 minutes, turning tin once, until risen and browned.
Cool on a wire rack.

INGREDIENTS

4oz (100g) soft margarine
4oz (100g) caster sugar
2 eggs
6oz (175g) self-raising flour
1 level teaspoon baking powder
2oz (50g) sultanas
2oz (50g) glacé cherries, washed and chopped

OLD-FASHIONED ROCK CAKES

No time at all to prepare, they are best eaten when freshly made.

MAKES ABOUT 15 CAKES

Lightly grease the cold plain shelf.
Measure the flour, baking powder and mixed spice into a bowl and rub in the margarine until the mixture resembles fine breadcrumbs. Add the sugar and fruit and mix to a stiff dough with the egg and milk, adding a little extra milk if the dough is too dry. If using a mixer, then put everything in the bowl together.
Spoon the mixture in rough mounds on the plain shelf using two teaspoons, sprinkle with a little demerara sugar.

2▤
▤4▤ Roasting Oven: slide the shelf onto the second set of runners in the oven and cook for about 10 minutes, turning once, until just beginning to turn golden brown. Carefully lift off the shelf and leave to cool on a wire rack.

INGREDIENTS

8oz (225g) self-raising flour
1 good teaspoon baking powder
½ level teaspoon ground mixed spice (optional)
4oz (100g) soft margarine
2oz (50g) demerara sugar
4oz (100g) mixed dried fruit
1 egg, beaten
about 1 tablespoon milk

t o p p i n g
a little extra demerara sugar

GINGERBREAD

This gingerbread is wonderful eaten on the day it is made but is equally as good a few days later with a lemon-flavoured icing on top.

Line the small roasting tin with foil and grease well.
Measure the flour and spices into a bowl. Put the sugar, margarine, syrup and treacle in a pan and heat gently on the Simmering Plate until melted. Allow to cool slightly. Beat the egg into the milk. Add the treacle mixture and milk to the flour gradually and beat well. Pour into the prepared tin.

2▤ Roasting Oven: with the grid shelf on the floor of the oven and the cold plain shelf on the second set of runners cook for about 30 minutes until well risen and springy to the touch and beginning to shrink away from the sides of the tin.

▤4▤ Baking Oven: hang the tin on the fourth set of runners and cook for about 30 minutes, turning the tin once, until well risen and springy to the touch and beginning to shrink away from the sides of the tin.
Allow to cool then cut into squares to serve.

INGREDIENTS

8oz (225g) self-raising flour
1½ teaspoons ground ginger
½ teaspoon mixed spice
4oz (100g) soft brown sugar
4oz (100g) margarine
4oz (100g) golden syrup
4oz (100g) treacle
1 egg
¼ pint (150ml) milk

INGREDIENTS

6oz (175g) soft margarine
6oz (175g) caster sugar
6oz (175g) self-raising flour
1 rounded teaspoon baking powder
3 large eggs
4 tablespoons raspberry jam
extra caster sugar for dusting

INGREDIENTS

4oz (100g) self-raising flour
1oz (25g) caster sugar
1 egg
¼ pint (150ml) milk

VICTORIA SANDWICH

With the all-in-one method the whole process takes under half an hour.

Lightly grease two 7inch (18cm) sandwich tins and line the bases with greased greaseproof paper.

Measure the margarine, sugar, flour, baking powder and eggs into a large bowl. Beat well for 2 minutes until smooth and blended. Divide the mixture between the two tins and level the tops.

2■ Roasting Oven: with the grid shelf on the floor of the oven and the cold plain shelf on the second set of runners bake in the oven for about 20 minutes until well risen and golden brown.

■4■ Baking Oven: with the grid shelf on the floor of the oven cook for about 20 minutes, until well risen and golden brown.

Remove from the tins, peel off the paper and leave to cool on a wire rack.

When cool, spread one cake with raspberry jam then put the other cake on top. Dust with caster sugar to serve.

VARIATIONS:

ORANGE AND LEMON SANDWICH: add the finely grated rind 1 orange or 1 lemon to the cake mixture. Fill with lemon curd mixed with equal quantity of whipped cream or if preferred, just orange or lemon flavoured buttercream.

CHOCOLATE SANDWICH: blend 2 rounded tablespoons cocoa with 4 tablespoons hot water in the bowl then add the remaining ingredients. Fill inside and decorate top with white buttercream – blend 4oz (100g) soft margarine with 8oz (225g) sieved icing sugar, decorate with grated chocolate.

COFFEE SANDWICH: dissolve 2 heaped teaspoons instant coffee in the beaten eggs. Fill with coffee buttercream – add 1 tablespoon coffee essence to the white buttercream above – and dredge with icing sugar.

SCOTCH PANCAKES

These are simple to make and a great standby for unexpected guests.

MAKES ABOUT 20 PANCAKES

Put the flour and sugar in a bowl, make a well in the centre and add the egg and half the milk and beat to a thick batter. Stir in the remaining milk.

Grease the Simmering Plate lightly with lard or oil. Use a pad of kitchen paper for this. When ready to cook the pancakes, the fat should be just hazy, wipe off any surplus fat with more kitchen paper. If your Aga is particularly hot, it may be necessary to lift the lid of the Simmering Plate for a few minutes to reduce the heat of the plate a little before cooking.

Spoon the mixture onto the plate in tablespoonfuls, spacing them well apart. When bubbles rise to the surface, turn the pancakes over with a palette knife and cook on the other side for a further 30 seconds or so until golden brown. Lift off and keep wrapped in a clean tea towel to keep them soft. Continue cooking until all the batter has been used and then serve them warm with butter and strawberry jam.

SPECIAL SCONES

The secret of good scones is not to have the mixture too dry – it should feel a bit sticky. Don't handle the dough too much, cut out quickly and bake. Use self-raising wholewheat flour if you prefer, you will find that you need a little more milk.

MAKES 8-10 SCONES

Lightly grease the cold plain shelf.

Measure the flour and baking powder into a bowl, add the butter and rub in until the mixture resembles fine breadcrumbs. Stir in the sugar. Break the egg into a measuring jug, whisk lightly and add the milk. Stir into the flour and mix to a soft dough. Turn onto a lightly floured surface and knead gently. Roll out to ¾ inch (2cm) thick. Cut into rounds with a 2 inch (5cm) fluted cutter.

Arrange on the greased plain shelf, brush the tops with a little milk.

2▮ ▮4▮ Roasting Oven: slide the shelf on the third set of runners, cook the scones in the oven for about 10 minutes or until pale golden brown. Lift off the shelf and leave to cool on a wire rack.

INGREDIENTS

8oz (225g) self-raising flour
1 level teaspoon baking powder
1½oz (40g) butter, softened
1oz (25g) caster sugar
1 egg
about ¼ pint (150ml) milk

CHOCOLATE ECLAIRS

Fill them with cream just before serving.

MAKES ABOUT 12

Grease two baking sheets.

Melt the butter in a pan with the water and slowly bring to the boil, making sure all the butter has melted. Remove from the heat and quickly add the flour all at once and beat with a wooden spoon until it forms a ball and looks all shiny. Gradually beat in the eggs a little at a time to give a smooth paste.

Put the mixture into a piping bag fitted with a ½ inch (1cm) nozzle and pipe into 4 inch (8cm) lengths on the baking trays leaving room in between for them to expand.

2▮ ▮4▮ Roasting Oven: with the grid shelf on the lowest set of runners cook in the oven for about 20 minutes until light golden brown. When cool enough to handle split the eclairs down one side with a sharp knife to let the steam escape.

Simmering Oven: transfer to the Simmering Oven for about 20 minutes until they are completely dry inside.

For the filling, pipe or spoon whipped cream into the middle of the eclairs.

For the icing, heat the butter in a pan, stir in the cocoa and cook gently for 1 minute. Remove from the heat and stir in the sugar and milk, beat well until starting to thicken. Spear each eclair with a fork and dip into the icing to just cover the tops.

Leave to set on a wire tray.

INGREDIENTS

choux pastry
2oz (50g) butter
¼ pint (150ml) water
2½oz (60g) flour
2 eggs, beaten

filling
½ pint (300ml) whipping cream

icing
1oz (25g) butter
1oz (25g) cocoa
4oz (100g) icing sugar, sieved
3-4 tablespoons milk

Lemon Biscuits

These are lovely, crisp little biscuits with a refreshing lemon tang. They do need watching whilst baking as they can easily become too dark and then taste bitter.

MAKES ABOUT 50 BISCUITS

Measure the butter and sugar into a large bowl and cream together. Add the flour, lemon rind and mix well to form a firm dough. Roll the mixture into a long sausage shape 1½ inches (4cm) in diameter, wrap with clearfilm and chill in the refrigerator for about an hour. Unwrap and roll the sausage in granulated sugar then slice off rounds ¼ inch (0.75cm) thick. Arrange on greased baking sheets.

2 Roasting Oven: with the grid shelf on the bottom set of runners and a cold plain shelf on the second set of runners, cook the biscuits in batches for about 10 minutes until very pale golden brown.

4 Baking Oven: place on the greased plain shelf and slide into the oven on the fourth set of runners. Cook for 12-15 minutes, turning once, until very pale golden brown.

Allow to cool for a few moments then lift off with a palette knife and finish cooling on a wire rack.

Swiss Roll

I use self-raising flour, although I was taught to use plain. I find I get success every time with no effort. Essential to weigh the ingredients accurately for this recipe. Warm the sugar in the Simmering Oven.

Grease and line with greased greaseproof paper a 13 x 9 inch (33 x 23cm) Swiss roll tin. Secure the corners with four paper clips, or staple each corner. Loosen the lid of the jam and place in the Simmering Oven to warm.

Whisk the eggs and sugar together in a large bowl until the mixture is light and creamy and the whisk will leave a trail when lifted out. Sieve the flour and carefully fold it into the mixture, using a metal spoon.

Turn the mixture into the tin and give it a gentle shake, or smooth level with the back of a spoon, so that the mixture finds its own level and it is spread evenly into the corners.

2 4 Roasting Oven: with the grid on the floor of the oven, cook for about 8 minutes. The sponge should be golden brown and shrinking away slightly from the sides of the tin.

While the cake is cooking, cut out a piece of greaseproof paper a little bigger than the tin and sprinkle it with caster sugar.

Invert the cake onto the sugared paper. Quickly loosen the paper on the bottom of the cake and peel it off. To make rolling easier, make a score mark 1 inch (2.5cm) in from one short edge, being careful not to cut right through. Spread the cake with jam, taking it almost to the edges. Fold the narrow strip created by the score mark down on to the jam and begin rolling, using the paper to keep a firm roll.

Leave for a few minutes with the paper still around it, to settle. Lift the Swiss roll on to a wire rack, remove the paper, sprinkle with more sugar and leave to cool.

Ingredients:
4oz (100g) butter, softened
3oz (75g) caster sugar
6oz (175g) plain flour
grated rind 1 lemon
1oz (25g) granulated sugar

3 large eggs, at room temperature
3oz (75g) caster sugar, warmed
3oz (75g) self-raising flour

filling
caster sugar
about 4 tablespoons raspberry jam

Ingredients

12oz (350g) butter
12oz (350g) plain flour
6oz (175g) ground rice, cornflour or semolina
6oz (175g) caster sugar
a little demerara sugar

Ingredients

1 rounded tablespoon golden syrup
2oz (50g) cocoa, sieved
2oz (50g) butter
2 tablespoons double cream
4 tablespoons rum
12oz (350g) icing sugar, sieved
chocolate vermicelli, cocoa or drinking chocolate

Ingredients

8oz (225g) digestive biscuits
1 teaspoon golden syrup
4oz (100g) margarine
6oz (175g) snipped dried apricots, sultanas and raisins mixed
1oz (25g) glace cherries, chopped
6oz (175g) plain chocolate

BUTTER SHORTBREAD

This quantity is made in the large Aga roasting tin. Half this quantity fits into the small roasting tin and cooks for 15 minutes in the Roasting Oven, turning once, in the suggested position, and then in the Simmering Oven for 35 minutes, or for about 30 minutes in the Baking Oven of the four oven Aga.

MAKES 40 PIECES

To make in the processor: simply cut up the butter and put everything in together, process until the mixture just holds together. In a small processor this will need to be done in two batches.

To make in a mixer: put everything in together and mix with the dough hook until all is combined.

To make by hand: rub the butter into the flour until the mixture resembles fine breadcrumbs, add remaining ingredients then work together.

Lightly grease the large Aga roasting tin, press mixture into the bottom of the tin and level out with a damp palette knife. Prick all over with a fork and sprinkle with sugar.

2 Roasting Oven: with the cold plain shelf on the second set of runners, hang the roasting tin on the lowest set of runners. Cook for about 15-20 minutes, turning the tin once half way through, until very pale golden at the edges.

Simmering Oven: transfer the shortbread to the third set of runners for a further 30-40 minutes until a pale biscuit colour.

4 Baking Oven: slide the tin onto the fourth set of runners, cook for about 35-45 minutes until a pale biscuit colour, turning the tin once half way through cooking. If getting too brown, slide in the cold plain shelf.

Divide into 40 pieces, lift out and cool.

VARIATIONS:

WHOLEWHEAT: use 8oz (225g) wholewheat flour instead of half the plain flour.
LEMON: add grated rind of 2 lemons.
GINGER: take out 1 tablespoon of flour and add 1 level tablespoon of ground ginger to the mixture.

FRESH CREAM RUM TRUFFLES

Wonderful with coffee after a special meal.

MAKES ABOUT 60 TRUFFLES

Measure syrup, cocoa, butter and cream into a pan. Stir at first on the Simmering Plate until well blended then bring to the boil. Remove from the heat, add rum and stir in the icing sugar. Beat until smooth. Chill well. Roll into balls and toss in vermicelli, cocoa or drinking chocolate. Place each one in a paper case and store in the refrigerator.

AUNTY MOLL'S PRALINES

My aunt is a wonderfully inventive cook, this recipe is a great standby for her bridge parties.

MAKES 32 PIECES

Grease an 8 inch (20cm) square tin and line the base with a piece of greaseproof paper. Crush digestive biscuits, in a polythene bag with a rolling pin. Melt syrup and margarine in a pan on the Simmering Plate, add dried fruits and biscuits, mix well. Tip into the prepared tin, level out and leave to set. Melt the chocolate in a bowl over a pan of simmering water and pour over the biscuit mixture. Leave to set. When completely cold, cut into small pieces and store in the refrigerator.

AGA FUDGE

There is always a tendency to cook it too quickly, over too intense a heat and then it catches on the bottom of the pan. Make it on the Simmering Plate and it is so easy. To test I simply take a glass of cold water and after 10 minutes or so drop a small amount of the mixture into the water. If it goes cloudy, continue to cook the fudge. If the mixture forms tiny blobs of toffee, remove from the heat.

MAKES 36 SQUARES

Butter a 7 inch (18cm) shallow square tin. Measure the evaporated milk, water, butter and sugar into a heavy saucepan and heat through slowly until the sugar has dissolved, without boiling, on the Simmering Plate. Then boil steadily, on the Boiling Plate if necessary, for about 10-15 minutes, stirring constantly so that the fudge does not stick. Test the fudge as described above with a glass of water. Remove the pan from the heat and add the vanilla essence. Cool slightly then beat until the mixture starts to thicken and crystallise. Pour into the tin and leave to set. When firm mark into 36 squares and store in an airtight tin until required.

CREAMY FUDGE: for a more creamy fudge, use ½ pint (300ml) evaporated milk instead of evaporated milk and water.

CHOCOLATE FUDGE: measure 1oz (25g) cocoa into the pan and blend to a smooth paste with the evaporated milk, then add the remaining ingredients (except vanilla essence) and make as above.

RAISIN FUDGE: add 3oz (75g) raisins to the fudge whilst thickening.

CHERRY AND WALNUT FUDGE: add about 2oz (50g) chopped glace cherries and 2oz (50g) roughly chopped walnuts to the pan whilst thickening.

GINGER FUDGE: add 1oz (25g) finely chopped stem ginger – take care to drain off all the syrup first. Add to the pan whilst thickening.

RUM FUDGE: add 2 tablespoons rum instead of vanilla essence whilst thickening.

INGREDIENTS

¼ pint (150ml) evaporated milk, roughly a small can
¼ pint (150ml) water
3oz (75g) butter
1lb (450g) granulated sugar
about ¼ teaspoon vanilla essence

CARAMEL CRUNCH BARS

Children love these chewy bars, they are also popular served with ice cream.

MAKES ABOUT 20

Grease the small Aga roasting tin.

Melt the margarine, marshmallows and caramels in a pan, on the Simmering Plate stir gently until the mixture is melted and smooth. This takes about 5 minutes. Meanwhile put the krispies into a large bowl. Remove the pan from the heat and pour all at once onto the krispies and stir very thoroughly until they are well coated. Spoon into the prepared tin and press flat. Leave in a cool place until set and quite firm then cut into bars.

INGREDIENTS

4oz (100g) hard margarine
4oz (100g) marshmallows
4oz (100g) caramels
7oz (200g) rice krispies

MINCE PIES

I make these ahead, freeze them uncooked, then cook from frozen when needed.

MAKES 12

Rub the fat into the flour until it is like fine breadcrumbs (or use processor). Add the water to mix and firm into stiff dough. Leave to rest in fridge for about 20 minutes.

Roll pastry out thinly and with 3 inch (7cm) cutter make 12 rounds. Press gently into pie tins. Place 1 teaspoon mincemeat into centre of pastry. Cut 12 lids using smaller cutter. Damp edges of top and place damp side down on top of mincemeat, pressing gently to seal top and bottom pastry together.

2▪ / ▪4▪ Roasting Oven: place pie tin on grid shelf set on floor of Roasting Oven. Cook for about 15 minutes until pale golden brown. Cool on wire tray and dust with icing sugar to serve.

INGREDIENTS

8oz (225g) plain flour
2oz (50g) white vegetable fat
2oz (50g) butter
about 2 tablespoons cold water
mincemeat
1oz (25g) icing sugar

A SELECTION OF BREADS PP.113-114
INCLUDING GRANARY LOAF,
DEVON FLAT BAPS,
CHEESE TOPPED ROLLS, SEEDED ROLLS
AND CROWN LOAF.
CROISSANTS P.139

BREADMAKING

Before writing and testing this breadmaking section I decided to seek advice from Tom Jaine of The Carved Angel in Dartmouth fame. Tom bakes for a few local delicatessens and favoured friends, when he is not writing! I needed to update my knowledge and improve my technique. I had a blissful two days in deepest Devon with his family, goats, ducks, sheep and all!

Proving and rising: stand dough away from draughts, preferably at a temperature of 70°-80°F (20°-30°C); a work surface beside the Aga is ideal.

COVER DOUGH: when leaving to prove always cover loosely with oiled clear-film or an oiled polythene bag.

PRE-WARM TINS AND BOWLS: for best results always put greased bread tins to warm on the hob of the Aga. The same applies to bowls and flour to a slightly lesser degree.

AMOUNT OF LIQUID: brown flour generally absorbs a little more water than white flour.

MIXERS AND PROCESSORS: rubbing in and kneading can be done perfectly successfully in a food mixer – see its instruction book for timing. Brown bread requires less kneading. You can also make your bread using a processor, follow the instructions being very careful not to over-process.

DRIED YEAST: there are two main types of dried yeast: Fermipan sold under various trade names contains no artificial bread improvers and Fast Action dried yeast which contains vitamin C (ascorbic acid). Follow instructions carefully on the packet.

STICKY DOUGH: if dough is a bit wet and sticky put your hand in a polythene bag and knead using the bag as a glove.

GLAZING: for a shiny top, glaze with egg wash (beaten egg with a little water).

WHITE, BROWN OR GRANARY BREAD

The constant warmth of the Aga is ideal for rising and proving and the perfect oven for the actual baking. To make a lighter wholemeal or granary loaf substitute half the quantity of flour with strong white flour – this also makes the dough easier to handle. Brown flour absorbs more liquid so increase the water accordingly.

MAKES 2 x 1LB (450G) OR 1 x 2LB (900G) LOAF

INGREDIENTS
1½lb (675g) strong white, granary or wholemeal flour
2 teaspoons salt
¾oz (20g) butter
¾oz (20g) fresh yeast
(or dried yeast – see notes)
¾ pint (450ml) water, hand hot

Grease the loaf tins or tin. Measure the flour into a large bowl, add the salt and rub in the butter until the mixture resembles fine breadcrumbs. Make a well in the centre, crumble in the yeast and then pour in the water. Mix by hand and knead into a ball in the bowl. Turn out onto a clean dry surface and knead for about 4 minutes (brown bread will not require as long). Return the dough to the bowl, cover with clearfilm and leave to rise near the Aga for 1-1½ hours until double in size.

Put the greased tins near the Aga to warm, knock back the dough and knead again for 2-3 minutes then divide in half if making two loaves. Slightly flatten the ball of dough with the heel of your hand and fold in two opposite sides, slightly overlapping, roll up like a Swiss roll. With the fold underneath put in the loaf tin, or tins, cover with oiled clearfilm and leave to prove for about ½ hour. (With brown bread as soon as a few "pin" holes begin to appear the loaf is ready to bake). Remove clearfilm.

2▮ ▮4▮ Roasting Oven: with grid shelf on the floor of the oven bake for about 20-30 minutes for two tins, 35-40 minutes for a 2lb loaf until evenly browned and when the loaf is turned out a hollow noise is made when the loaf is knocked on the base.

For a crown loaf, use half the quantity of dough to make 12 equal sized balls. Place in a greased 8 inch (20cm) shallow cake tin and bake for 25 minutes.

I N G R E D I E N T S

6oz (175g) currants
6oz (175g) sultanas
8oz (225g) dark soft brown sugar
½ pint (300ml) hot tea
10oz (275g) self-raising flour
1 egg, beaten

I N G R E D I E N T S

1lb 1oz (475g) strong plain flour
1 teaspoon salt
1½oz (40g) butter
¾oz (20g) fresh yeast
(or dried yeast – see notes)
¼ pint (150ml) water, hand hot
¼ pint (150ml) milk, hand hot
1 teaspoon runny honey or syrup

SMASHING BARA BRITH

Very moist and fruity and doesn't crumble when sliced.

MAKES 2 x 1LB (450G) LOAVES

Measure the fruit and sugar into a bowl and pour over the hot tea, stir well, cover and leave to stand overnight. Grease and line with greased greaseproof paper 2 x 1lb (450g) loaf tins. Stir the flour and egg into the fruit mixture, mix thoroughly and divide between the tins.

2▪ Roasting Oven: with the grid shelf on the floor of the oven and the cold plain shelf on the second set of runners, cook the loaves for about 30 minutes until set and just beginning to brown. Then:
Simmering Oven: transfer the now hot plain shelf to the centre of the Simmering Oven, very carefully transfer the loaves on to the shelf for a further 30 minutes or until cooked through.

▪4▪ Baking Oven: place grid shelf on the fourth set of runners, and put the loaf tins one in front of the other. Cook for about 1 hour.
A skewer should come out clean when pierced into the centre of the loaves. Turn out and leave to cool on wire racks. Serve sliced with a little butter.

DEVON FLAT BAPS

For Cheese Topped Baps, instead of dusting with flour, sprinkle with coarsely grated mature Cheddar cheese before baking.

MAKES 16

Grease two baking trays. Measure the flour and salt into a large mixing bowl, rub in the butter until the mixture resembles fine breadcrumbs. Make a well in the centre of the mixture, crumble in the fresh yeast then pour in the liquid and the honey. Mix by hand and knead well in the bowl. Turn out onto a clean surface and knead for a further minute or two. Return the dough to the bowl, cover with oiled clearfilm and leave near the Aga for about ¾ hour until doubled in size. Knock back and shape into 16 pieces, knead and roll each piece and put onto the baking trays leaving a generous space between each. Flatten with the heel of your hand to 2-3 inch (5-7.5cm) rounds or ovals. Cover loosely with oiled clearfilm and leave to prove for about 1 hour or until doubled in size. Remove clearfilm then dust with flour using a small sieve.

2▪ Roasting Oven: put one tray on the floor of the oven and the other
▪4▪ on the grid shelf hung on the lowest set of runners. Bake for 12 minutes changing the trays over after 6 minutes.

PUDDINGS

RASPBERRY PAVLOVA P.116 · MERINGUES P.116

*I*t's a comforting feeling to know that the Aga ovens are always at the ready to poach some fruit, reheat a treacle tart, or cook a proper robust pudding without too much effort on my part.
But, I never cease to be amazed at the Aga's ability to cope with the lighter delights such as soufflés, meringues and pavlovas, or even a crème brulée.

p a v l o v a
3 egg whites
6oz (175g) caster sugar
1 teaspoon vinegar
1 level teaspoon cornflour

f i l l i n g
**½ pint (300ml) whipping cream,
whipped
8oz (225g) fresh raspberries**

3 egg whites
6oz (175g) caster sugar
a little demerara sugar
¼ pint (150ml) whipping cream

4 eggs
2 large lemons
8oz (225g) caster sugar
1oz (25g) butter
2oz (50g) flour
16 fl oz (475ml) milk

RASPBERRY CREAM PAV

The Aga makes a good Pavlova. Take special note of the coo. ....
Silicone paper, available from all good stationers, can be used a, *l again.*

SERVES 6

Lay a sheet of silicone paper on the cold plain shelf and   18 inch (20cm) circle on it.

Whisk the egg whites until they are stiff, then whisk in the sugar a teaspoonful at a time until all added. Blend the vinegar with the cornflour and whisk in.

Spread the mixture out to cover the circle on the silicone paper – building up the sides so they are higher than the centre.

2 4 Roasting Oven: Slide the baking sheet onto the grid shelf on the floor of the oven for about 3-4 minutes until lightly coloured.
Then transfer to the Simmering Oven for 1-1½ hours until firm but still gooey in the centre.

N.B. If the Pavlova is not cooked it may be necessary to turn it over and leave upside down in the Simmering Oven to dry out the underneath. Allow to cool, peel away paper and place on a serving plate.

Fold together the cream and raspberries and pile into the centre of the Pavlova. Leave to stand in the refrigerator for about an hour before serving.

MERINGUES

Aga meringues are quite wonderful – a beautiful creamy colour. If you like more toffee-flavoured ones, use half caster and half light muscovado sugar.

MAKES 8 MERINGUES WHEN FILLED WITH CREAM

Line the cold plain shelf with a sheet of silicone paper.

Whisk the egg whites until they form soft peaks. Add the caster sugar, a teaspoonful at a time, whisking well. Using   dessertspoons, spoon the meringue out onto the silicone paper. Dust with   ara sugar.

2 4 Simmering Oven: slide onto the lowest runners in the oven for 1-2½ hours until the meringues are firm and dry and will lift easily from the silicone paper. If you like them very dry in the middle, after 1½ hours turn the meringues on their sides. (They will be pale off-white, or slightly darker if you have used muscovado sugar). Cool. Whip the cream until it is thick and use to sandwich the meringues together, or store until required in an air-tight tin.

If the meringues are coloured to your liking they can be dried out on the top of the Simmering Plate lid – protect it with a tea towel.

LEMON SOUFFLÉ CUSTARD

A delicious light and easy pudding, much more special than it sounds. The top of the pudding is a hot spongy mousse and the underneath a sharp lemon sauce.

SERVES 8

Separate the eggs. Put the egg yolks, grated rind and juice of the lemons, sugar, butter and flour into a processor and process to blend. Add milk through the funnel. If without a processor rub the butter into the flour. Add the sugar and the yolks and mix together with a little of the milk until smooth then add the remaining milk. Beat the egg whites until firm and fold into the liquid. Pour into a 2½ pint (1.4 litre) greased ovenproof dish.

2 Roasting Oven: place dish in the small Aga roasting tin, pour boiling water to surround dish, hang on lowest set of runners and bake for about 35 minutes. If browned to your liking, protect with the solid plain shelf.
4 Baking Oven: place dish in the small Aga roasting tin, surround with boiling water and place in the centre of the oven for about 35 minutes.
Serve hot or cold with cream.

CRÈME CARAMEL

Make th... ...ard the day before so it comes out complete with the caramel.

SERVES 4-6

...re the sugar into a small pan, add all but a tablespoon of the water. D...s...e sugar then boil rapidly until the caramel is a deep golden colour then at once remove from the heat and carefully add the tablespoon of water to stop the caramel from cooking further. Take great care as it bubbles and spits fiercely at this point. Pour at once into a 2 pint (1 litre) soufflé dish.

Lightly whisk eggs in a bowl with the sugar. Heat the milk until hand hot then pour onto the eggs, stirring constantly. Butter the sides of the dish above the caramel and strain the custard into the dish. Place the dish in the small roasting tin half filled with boiling water. Cover the top with a piece of foil.

2▉
▉4▉ Roasting Oven: hang the tin on the lowest set of runners in the oven for 25 minutes.

Simmering Oven: transfer the tin to the floor of the Simmering Oven for about 1 hour or until the custard is set. Leave to get completely cold before turning out, preferably overnight in the fridge.

caramel
4oz (100g) granulated sugar
¼ pint (150ml) water

custard
4 eggs
2oz (50g) vanilla sugar
(or caster sugar and vanilla essence)
1 pint (600ml) milk

CRÈME BRULÉE

The brulée part can be a simple caramel poured over the top of the rich set custard. If you prefer the oven method, it is very quick but needs watching.

SERVES 6

Lightly butter 6 ramekin dishes. Beat the egg yolks with the sugar until smooth. Heat the cream in a pan to a hot bath temperature and gradually beat onto the egg yolk mixture.

Stand the dishes in the sm... Aga roasting tin then pour the egg yolk mixture through a sieve into the dish... Pour boiling water into the tin to come half way up the sides of the dish.

2▉
▉4▉ Roasting Oven: carefully push the tin onto the third set of runners. Cook for about 10 minutes.

Simmering Oven: carefully transfer the tin to the bottom set of runners and cook for about 45 minutes until set. Lift out, leave to cool, then chill.

For the brulée: measure the sugar and water into a heavy pan and heat on the Simmering Plate until the sugar has dissolved. Transfer to the Boiling Plate and bring to the boil. Allow to boil steadily until the syrup is pale golden brown. Remove from the heat and allow to cool slightly, then pour over the top of the set custard and allow to set. Chill again for a couple of hours before serving.

OVEN METHOD OF MAKING BRULÉE:

Slide the plain shelf onto the second set of runners in the Roasting Oven. Draw, on a sheet of silicone paper, a circle about ½ inch (1cm) smaller than the dish in which you have made the custard. Sprinkle sugar evenly over circle. Lift shelf onto Simmering Plate for a moment. Very carefully lift silicone paper with sugar onto the shelf. Return to the oven on the second set of runners for about 5 minutes until sugar has just melted. Lift out of oven. Cool, then peel off paper and slip on top of the custard. Chill for a couple of hours before serving.

4 egg yolks
1oz (25g) vanilla sugar
1 pint (600ml) single cream

brulée
4oz (100g) granulated sugar
4 tablespoons water

oven method of making brulée
about 2-3 tablespoons demerara sugar
sheet of silicone paper

PANCAKES

SERVES 4

Use the batter from the Yorkshire Pudding recipe (page 84). Heat oil in the small omelette pan until very hot. Pour in a thin film of batter, cook until golden, flip and cook other side. Serve immediately with sugar and lemon juice.

4oz (100g) flour
1 egg
½ pint (300ml) milk
oil for cooking

TARTE TATIN

Louis XIV's personal baker Monsieur Tatin had two daughters who made their father a caramelised upside down apple pie using dessert apples. The King was so impressed with the tart that he always had it on his menu.

SERVES 6

For the topping, measure the butter and sugar into a heavy pan. Gently melt together without boiling on the Simmering Plate, until the sugar has dissolved, stirring occasionally.

Peel, core and thickly slice the apples. Add the apples, lemon juice and rind to the sugar mixture, stir well until all the apples are coated. Tip or arrange the apples and juices into a lightly greased 8 inch (20cm) sandwich tin and leave to cool.

Make a rich shortcrust pastry and roll it out onto a lightly floured surface and use to cover the apples, trim off any surplus pastry.

2▪ Roasting Oven: with the grid shelf on the floor of the oven and the cold plain shelf on the second set of runners bake for about 20-25 minutes until the pastry is crisp and golden brown.

▪4▪ Baking Oven: with the grid shelf on the second set of runners cook for about 30 minutes, until the pastry is crisp and golden brown.

When cooked lift out of the oven, the pastry will have shrunk a little and tip all of the juices from the tin into a small pan. Turn the tart out onto a plate, with the pastry on the bottom.

Reduce the juices to a caramelised sauce on the Boiling Plate for 3-4 minutes, pour over the apples. Serve warm or cold with lightly whipped cream.

INGREDIENTS

topping
2oz (50g) butter
2oz (50g) light muscovado sugar
2lb (900g) Cox's dessert apples
finely grated rind and juice 1 lemon

pastry
4oz (100g) flour
3oz (75g) butter
1 egg yolk
scant tablespoon water
½oz (15g) icing sugar

OLD FASHIONED TREACLE TART

For a more substantial pudding use the pastry trimmings to make pattern on top.

SERVES 6

Measure the flour into a bowl, add the margarine cut into small pieces and rub in until the mixture resembles fine breadcrumbs. Add sufficient cold water to mix to a firm dough. Roll out the pastry and use to line an 8 inch (20cm) shallow flan tin or deep ovenproof plate or dish. Chill in the refrigerator for about 15 minutes then prick the bottom with a fork.

Meanwhile mix together all the ingredients for the filling. Put the bowl in the Simmering Oven for the crumbs to swell for about 10 minutes. Pour into the pastry case and level out. Decorate with pastry trimmings.

2▪
▪4▪ Roasting Oven: with the grid shelf on the floor of the oven, bake for about 25 minutes or until the pastry is golden brown. Don't worry if the filling is still runny, it will solidify as it cools.

INGREDIENTS

pastry
6oz (175g) flour
3oz (75g) butter or margarine
about 2 good tablespoons cold water

filling
14oz (400g) golden syrup
4oz (100g) fresh white breadcrumbs
grated rind and juice 1 lemon

DOUBLE CRUST FRUIT PIE

The Aga cooks plate pies well getting the pastry crisp top and bottom.

SERVES 6

Make shortcrust pastry as the recipe above and use half to line a plate. Toss fruit in the sugar and pile into the centre of the plate. Damp the edge of the pastry then top with a circle of pastry. Use any trimmings to decorate. Brush with a little milk to glaze. Sprinkle with a little sugar – demerara looks best. Stand pie in the large roasting tin.

2▪
▪4▪ Roasting Oven: stand the tin on the floor of the oven for about 20-25 minutes until the pastry is golden brown. Turn the pie round in the tin once during cooking, if necessary. Transfer the tin to the top of the Simmering Oven and cook for a further 20 minutes to cook the fruit through.

INGREDIENTS

pastry
8oz (225g) flour
4oz (100g) butter or margarine
about 3 tablespoons cold water

fruit
1-1½lb (450-675g) prepared fruit
3-4oz (75-100g) granulated sugar
9 inch (23cm) deep enamel pie plate

SUMMER PUDDING P.121
POACHED FRUITS P.121
WILD BRAMBLE MOUSSE P.121

An Exceedingly Good Summer Pudding

I often double the recipe and then freeze one pudding.

SERVES 8

Put two slices of bread on one side for the middle and top, and use the remainder to line the base and sides of a 2 pint (1 litre) basin, or round fairly shallow dish.

Put the rhubarb, cut in ½ inch (1cm) slices, blackcurrants, blackberries and redcurrants into a pan, and add the sugar and water. Bring to the boil on the Boiling Plate.

2 **4** Simmering Oven: transfer to the floor of the oven for about 30 minutes until barely tender. Add the strawberries and raspberries.

Turn just under half the fruit into the dish, put a layer of bread then the remaining fruit. Keeping a little back to serve on top of the turned out pudding. Place the last slice of bread on top and bend over the tops of the slices of bread at the sides towards the centre. Place a saucer on top, pressing down a little until the juices rise to the top. Leave to cool then put in the refrigerator overnight. Turn out and serve with lots of thick cream.

INGREDIENTS
6 to 8 large, fairly thin slices white bread with crusts removed
8oz (225g) rhubarb
4oz (100g) blackcurrants
8oz (225g) blackberries
8oz (225g) redcurrants
8oz (225g) granulated sugar
6 tablespoons water
8oz (225g) small strawberries
8oz (225g) raspberries

To Poach Fresh Fruit

Bring prepared fruit, sugar and water to the boil on the Simmering Plate, when it comes just to the boil, stir then cover and transfer to the grid shelf on the floor of the Simmering Oven for ½-1 hour according to the type of fruit. If liked, honey or syrup may be used as the sweetener instead of sugar.

Wild Bramble Mousse

These very attractive mousses make a special end to a dinner party menu. They can be assembled ahead of time and left until required, add cream just before serving. Although I do like to make these as individual mousses, if preferred make in one large dish.

SERVES 6

Put the blackberries in a pan with the sugar and lemon juice. Cover and cook gently on the Simmering Plate for about 10 minutes until soft and the juice is beginning to run out. Reduce to a purée in a processor or blender and sieve to remove the seeds. Decant off and reserve one third of the purée to decorate.

Measure the water into a small bowl and sprinkle the gelatine on top, leave to stand for about 3 minutes to form a sponge. Stand the bowl in the Simmering Oven for about 10 minutes until clear and runny. Allow to cool slightly, then stir into the remaining fruit purée. Leave on one side until cold and just beginning to thicken.

Lightly whisk the cream until it forms soft peaks, and whisk the egg whites until it forms peaks. Fold whipped cream and egg whites into fruit purée until blended. Divide between six individual ramekin dishes and leave in a cool place to set.

To serve: turn the mousses out onto flat serving plates. Pour a little of the reserved purée around each mousse. Pour the cream into a greaseproof paper piping bag, snip the end and trail three rings of cream around each mousse on top of the purée. Drag a skewer carefully in lines, from the mousse to the edge of the purée, then in between these, drag the skewer in the opposite direction from the edge of the purée to the mousse to give a "feathering" effect. Serve as soon as possible.

INGREDIENTS
1½lb (675g) blackberries
6oz (175g) caster sugar
juice ½ lemon
3 tablespoons cold water
¾oz (20g) powdered gelatine
¼ pint (150ml) double cream
2 egg whites

to decorate
¼ pint (150ml) double pouring cream

FRUIT CRUMBLE P.123
TREACLE SUET PUDDING P.123
BREAD & BUTTER PUDDING P.124
PROPER CUSTARD P.88

TRADITIONAL CHRISTMAS PUDDING

A rich dark Christmas pudding which has been in my sister-in-law's family for years. Two hours in the Simmering Oven on Christmas Day. There is no sugar in this recipe as I find it just sweet enough. Do add sugar if you prefer.

SERVES 10-12

Grease a 2 pint (1 litre) pudding basin.

Place all the ingredients in a large bowl and mix together very thoroughly. Turn into the prepared basin, cover with greased greaseproof paper and a foil lid and lift into a pan, pour water half way up the side of the basin. Cover and bring to the boil then simmer on the Simmering Plate for 30 minutes.

2 Simmering Oven: with the grid shelf on the floor of the oven, transfer **4** the pan with the water and the pudding to the oven for 12 hours or overnight. Next day, remove from the pan, cool and cover with fresh foil to store.

On Christmas Day: stand in a pan, pour water half way up the side of the basin. Bring to the boil, cover and simmer for 30 minutes on the Simmering Plate, then transfer to the back of the Simmering Oven for 2 hours. Turn out and serve with a Brandy Butter or Sauce.

INGREDIENTS

6oz (175g) raisins
3oz (75g) currants
3oz (75g) sultanas
2oz (50g) candied peel, chopped
2oz (50g) blanched almonds, chopped
3oz (75g) self-raising flour
2 eggs
4oz (100g) fresh white breadcrumbs
4oz (100g) shredded suet
¼ pint (125ml) Guinness
1 cooking apple, peeled, cored and diced
grated rind and juice 1 orange
grated rind and juice 1 lemon
2 tablespoons black treacle
½ teaspoon ground nutmeg
½ teaspoon ground mixed spice

TREACLE SUET PUDDING

An old fashioned favourite.
The Cake Baker can be used as a saucepan for steaming this.

SERVES 6

Grease a 2 pint (1 litre) pudding basin and measure syrup into bottom of basin.

Mix together flour, sugar and suet. Add enough milk to bind together in a soft dough and put in basin. Cover with greaseproof paper and seal top with a foil lid.

Put the basin in a heavy bottomed pan with a tight fitting lid. Fill with enough water to come half way up the basin and bring to the boil on the Boiling Plate. Move to the Simmering Plate and simmer for 35 minutes.

2 Simmering Oven: transfer pan, water and basin to the floor of the oven **4** for about 3 hours until the pudding is nicely risen.

Turn the pudding out of the basin so that all the syrup runs down the sides and serve warm with custard.

INGREDIENTS

4 good tablespoons golden syrup
6oz (175g) self-raising flour
3oz (75g) prepared shredded suet
2oz (50g) caster sugar
aboout ¼ pint (150ml) milk

FRUIT CRUMBLE

For most Aga owners Crumble is one of the great Sunday lunch puddings. So quick to make and quite wonderful to eat. Vary the fruit as the seasons come round: rhubarb, gooseberries, blackcurrants, plums, apples etc. If using frozen fruit, measure out the amount that you need then put in a dish at the back of the Aga until just thawed and omit the water from the recipe. If you are in a hurry thaw the fruit in the Simmering Oven for about ½ hour – do keep an eye on it!

SERVES 8

Measure the flour into a bowl, add the butter and rub in until the mixture resembles breadcrumbs, stir in the sugar. Tip the prepared fruit into the dish and level out. Sprinkle over the crumble.

2 Roasting Oven: stand the dish in an Aga roasting tin and hang on the fourth set of runners, cook for about 20-25 minutes. Then, transfer it to the top of the Simmering Oven for a further 20-25 minutes, until the crumble is cooked through and the fruit tender.

4 Baking Oven: stand the dish in an Aga roasting tin and hang on the third set of runners, cook for 35-40 minutes, until the crumble is cooked through and the fruit tender.

Serve with cream or custard.

INGREDIENTS

crumble
8oz (225g) flour
4oz (100g) butter
2oz (50g) demerara sugar

fruit
2lb (900g) prepared fruit
6oz (175g) sugar
6 tablespoons water
4 pint (2.5 lt) dish

I N G R E D I E N T S

1¹/₂oz (40g) butter
1¹/₂oz (40g) flour
¹/₂ pint (300ml) milk – less
3 tablespoons
grated rind and juice 2 lemons
2oz (50g) caster sugar
4 large eggs

HOT LEMON SOUFFLÉ

*A simple sauce to go with this pudding is made from natural yoghurt with
2 tablespoons lemon curd stirred in and sharpened with a little lemon juice.*

SERVES 6

Thoroughly grease a 2 pint (1.2 litre) soufflé dish.

Melt the butter in a pan, add the flour and cook for a minute then gradually blend in the milk and bring to the boil, stirring until thickened. Stir in the grated lemon rind and juice and leave to cool.

Separate the eggs and beat the yolks one at a time into the lemon sauce. Add the sugar. Whisk the egg whites until they are stiff but not dry. Stir 1 tablespoon into the lemon mixture then carefully fold in the remainder. Pour into the prepared dish.

2 Roasting Oven: with the grid shelf on the floor of the oven and the cold plain shelf on second set of runners bake the soufflé for about 25 minutes until well risen and golden brown.

4 Baking Oven: with the grid shelf on the fourth set of runners bake for 30 minutes until well risen and golden brown.

The very middle of the soufflé will still be a little runny. If you like it firm cook for a little longer.

I N G R E D I E N T S

2oz (50g) pudding rice
1 pint (600ml) milk
1oz (25g) sugar
¹/₂oz (15g) butter
grated nutmeg

RICE PUDDING

I have to confess that no two rice puddings ever turn out the same but they are always good! If you double the recipe allow another hour in the oven.

SERVES 4

Wash the rice and drain. Grease a 1 pint (600ml) ovenproof dish. Put the rice into the dish, add the sugar and butter and pour over the milk. Stir. Grate over some nutmeg.

2 Roasting Oven: with the grid shelf on the lowest set of runners cook for about 20-30 minutes until a pale golden skin has formed and the milk boiled. Transfer to the Simmering Oven for about 2-3 hours or until the rice is cooked.

4 Baking Oven: place the dish in the half size meat tin and hang near the top of the oven for about 25 minutes until a golden skin has formed and the milk boiled.

Simmering Oven: remove the pudding from the Baking Oven and stir in any skin, grate over some nutmeg and transfer to the Simmering Oven for about 2-3 hours, until the rice is cooked.

I N G R E D I E N T S

about 8 medium slices white bread
about 1¹/₂oz (40g) butter, melted
4oz (100g) currants and sultanas,
mixed
grated rind 1 lemon
2oz (50g) caster or demerera sugar
2 eggs
³/₄ pint (450ml) milk

BREAD AND BUTTER PUDDING

A great family favourite for a weekend lunch pudding. Far more exciting than it sounds. My recipe is not economical – just delicious. Ideally use an oblong dish as the bread fits in better. If you use thin sliced bread use 12 slices and you'll find you get 3 layers of bread instead of 2.

SERVES 6

Well butter a shallow ovenproof dish about 7 x 9 inches (18 x 23cm). Trim crusts off the bread. Cut each slice in three. Dip each in melted butter on one side. Arrange bread butter-side-down in the dish covering the whole of the base. Sprinkle over fruit, lemon rind and half the sugar. Cover with another layer of bread butter-side-up.

Beat eggs and blend with milk. Pour over the bread. Sprinkle with remaining sugar and leave to stand for about an hour if time allows.

2 Roasting Oven: with the grid shelf on the floor of the oven cook for
4 about 20-25 minutes until set, pale golden and crisp on top.

LEMON MERINGUE PIE

As this is such a family favourite I have tested two sizes for the AGA and also two different crusts. The first is a quick, easy and delicious crumb crust, it makes the pie slightly more difficult to serve but is so crisp and light that it is well worth it. With the pastry case it is such a joy not to have to line the pastry with foil or greaseproof paper and beans. Baking on the floor of the oven ensures a crisp brown crust.
If making a crumb crust add all the yolks to the filling.

To make the Crumb Crust: melt the butter in a pan and stir in the crushed biscuits and sugar. Stand a loose-bottomed fluted flan tin on a baking sheet and tip the crumb crust into the middle, then smooth over the sides and base using a metal spoon. Bake blind on grid shelf on third set of runners in the Roasting Oven for 6-8 minutes until pale brown at the edges.

To make the Pastry Crust: measure the flour and sugar into a bowl and rub in the butter until the mixture resembles fine breadcrumbs. Add the egg yolk and water and work to firm dough, – this may of course be done in the processor. Use to line a loose-bottomed fluted flan tin. Prick the base with a fork and freeze.

Cooking and timing for the Pastry Crust:

2▪ Roasting Oven: Stand frozen tin on a baking sheet and slide on to the
▪4▪ floor of the oven for 10-15 minutes, turning half way through cooking, until pale golden colour. Carefully lift out of the oven.

For the filling: finely grate the rinds from the lemons and squeeze out the juice. Put the rind, juice and cornflour in a small bowl and blend together. Bring the water to the boil, then stir into the cornflour mixture. Return to the pan and heat on the Simmering Plate, stirring until it is a thick custard. Mix the yolks and sugar together and stir into the custard. Heat on Boiling Plate, whisking till it bubbles a couple of times. Remove from the heat. Allow to cool a little then spread into the crumb crust or pastry case.

Next make the meringue. Whisk the egg whites until stiff then add the sugar, a little at a time, whisking hard until all the sugar has been added. Pile the meringue on top of the pie, taking care that there are not gaps.

Cooking and Timing for both the Crumb Crust and Pastry Crust Pie

2▪ Roasting Oven: Bake on the grid shelf on the third set of runners for
▪4▪ about 2-3 minutes till a gentle brown colour, then transfer to the centre of the Simmering Oven for about a further 15 minutes for 9" (23cm) pie and 20 minutes for the 11" (27.5cm) pie. The top should be a soft meringue and a little crisp on top. Allow to cool until warm, then turn out on to a flat plate.

11" (27.5cm) pie serves 12.
9" (23cm) pie serves 6.

INGREDIENTS

11" (27.5cm) Pie

CRUMB CRUST

10oz (350g) digestive
biscuits, crushed
4oz (125g) butter
2oz (50g) demerara sugar

or PASTRY CRUST

8oz (225g) flour
1oz (25g) icing sugar
4oz (100g) butter
1 egg yolk
about 2 tablespoons water

FILLING

4 large lemons
3oz (75g) cornflour
1 pint (600ml) water
4 egg yolks (5 if crumb crust)
6oz (175g) caster sugar

MERINGUE

5 egg whites
8oz (225g) caster sugar

9" (23cm) Pie

CRUMB CRUST

6oz (175g) digestive
biscuits, crushed
2oz (50g) butter
1½oz (45g) demerara sugar

or PASTRY CRUST

6oz (175g) flour
½oz (15g) icing sugar
3oz (75g) butter
1 egg yolk
about 1 tablespoon water

FILLING

2 large lemons
1½oz (40g) cornflour
½ pint (300ml) water
2 egg yolks (3 if crumb crust)
3oz (75g) caster sugar

MERINGUE

3 egg whites
4½oz (120g) caster sugar

Ingredients (left column)

I N G R E D I E N T S

3 eggs, separated
6oz (175g) caster sugar
1 pint (600ml) milk
1oz (25g) caster sugar
1 heaped teaspoon cornflour
½ teaspoon vanilla essence

I N G R E D I E N T S

5 egg whites
10 oz (275g) caster sugar
2 oz (50g) flaked almonds

f i l l i n g
½ pint (300 ml) double cream
grated rind and juice of 1 small lemon
2 tablespoons good, real lemon curd
8oz (225g) raspberries

t o   d e c o r a t e
A few raspberries

FLOATING ISLANDS
SERVES 8
Serve this with red fruit salad or simply on its own.

A shallow 9-10 inch (22-24cm) ovenproof dish, greased with butter.

Whisk the egg whites at full speed in an electric mixer for one minute then add the sugar gradually over an eight minute period keeping the whisk at full speed. Bring the milk to the boil.

In a separate bowl mix the egg yolks, the 1oz (25g) caster sugar, cornflour and vanilla essence. Using a balloon whisk, pour on the boiling milk very slowly and whisking all the time.

Return the custard to the heat and cook gently until the froth disappears and the custard is lightly thickened. Pour the custard into the dish and, using two tablespoons, arrange the meringues on top. Makes 10 meringues.

2 4 Simmering Oven: Bake for 15-20 minutes or until the meringues are set and no longer sticky.

RASPBERRY MERINGUE ROULADE
MAKES 8-10 SLICES
A meringue roulade is quick and easy to do and has proved a very popular dessert

Line a 13"x9" (33x23 cm) Swiss roll tin with greased non-stick baking paper, the corners mitred in th usual way.

Whisk the egg whites in an electric mixer on full speed until very stiff. Gradually add the sugar, a teaspoon at a time, and still on high speed,whisking well between each addition. Whisk until very, very stiff and all the sugar has been added.

Spread the meringue mixture into the prepared tin and sprinkle with the almonds .

2 4 Roasting Oven: Place the tin on the grid shelf on the floor of the oven with the cold plain shelf on the second set of runners and bake for about 8 minutes until very golden. Then transfer to the Simmering Oven and bake the roulade for a further 15 minutes until firm to the touch.

Remove the meringue from the oven and turn almond side down on to a sheet of non-stick baking paper. Remove the paper from the base of the cooked meringue and allow to cool for about 10 minutes.

Lightly whip the cream, add lemon rind and juice and fold in the lemon curd and raspberries. Spread evenly over the meringue. Roll up the meringue fairly tightly, from the long end, to form a roulade.Wrap in non-stick baking paper and chill well before serving. Decorate with raspberries.

PRESERVES

A SELECTION OF MY FAVOURITE LEMON CURDS AND MARMALADES

The great thing about preserving is that the word describes the act so precisely. What could be more wonderful than locking away the fruits of a golden summer to enjoy throughout the winter?
I find the whole process of preserving so satisfying. Those rows of warm jars packed with fruits either given to me by generous friends or from my own garden, the powerful aroma of jams and chutneys bubbling away on the Aga. It is irresistible.

TIPS FOR SUCCESS WITH JAM AND MARMALADE

EQUIPMENT

The heavy Aga preserving pan (22 pints (13 litres)) is most useful because it gives plenty of space for the jam to froth up when boiling, without boiling over. Pans should be only about half full.

Even though I have a preserving pan, I still prefer to divide, say, a 10lb lot of marmalade into two batches when I reach the stage of boiling the fruit with the sugar. This means that there is half the amount in the pan, it comes to a full rolling boil quickly, and as the pan is large it froths up but cannot boil over. A good guide for those making jam and marmalade without a large preserving pan is not to make more than an 8lb (4kg) yield in a 10 pint (5.5 litre) pan or a 6lb (3kg) yield in an 8 pint (4.5 litre) pan.

The best choice of pan is stainless steel, heavy aluminium or unchipped heavy enamel. Brass and copper can be used but they reduce the vitamin C in the jam. Cast iron should not be used for preserving. The base of pans may be rubbed with a little butter to prevent sticking.

LIDS AND JARS

I find it a great bore to use discs of waxed paper on top of the jam or marmalade and cellophane tops and elastic bands. Time consuming to do and after a few months the jam shrinks down the jar. Also, you have no proper lid once the jar is opened. I prefer to use screwtop lids on jam jars. The ideal ones are honey jars. The lids should be really clean. If the price label is still on the top, try to get it off by soaking. If not, dry well and remove with Copydex adhesive remover. The best jars I gather through the year and store them with their lids ready. If you are a WI member, you can buy new screw tops, and snap on plastic lids for the older type of jar.

Warm at the back of the Aga or in the Simmering Oven before use. Cover jars when jam or marmalade is first potted and piping hot or when cold – never when warm.

SUGAR

Choose granulated sugar for economical jams and marmalades, but take care to stir constantly when it is added to the pan and dissolving. It forms a dense layer, prone to burn on the bottom of the pan if heated without stirring.

Preserving sugar is more expensive, large grained and less prone to sticking on the bottom of the pan and so needs less stirring. It produces less scum and so a clearer jelly or jam. Choose this sugar for jelly jams and any special jam and marmalade you are making.

Jam sugar is a specially formulated sugar mixed with acid and pectin. It is ideal for fruits low in natural acid and/or pectin to give a perfect set. Use for Apricot, Blackberry, Elderberry, Cherry, Sweet Oranges, Pears, Peaches, Nectarines, Raspberry, Strawberry and Rhubarb. You may even use it to make cartons of fruit juice into quick and easy jelly jams, such as Pineapple, Apple, Grape and Tropical Fruits. All sugar may be warmed slightly in the Simmering Oven before use to speed dissolving.

FRUIT

Firm fresh fruit that is slightly under rather than over ripe will give the best "set" in jam. This is when the pectin level is at its highest. Most fruits need to be cooked gently and thoroughly before the sugar is added. Bring to the boil with water as given in the recipe, simmer on the top of the Aga for 5 minutes and then cover and continue to cook in the Simmering Oven until the fruit is pulpy.

USING FROZEN FRUIT

To ensure you have a good colour to the jam, cook the fruit straight from frozen, do not thaw first. Use the same proportion of fruit and sugar as in other jams and marmalades. Remember to use the high pectin jam sugar for low pectin fruit i.e. strawberry or raspberry but not for gooseberry, plum, blackcurrant and high pectin fruit. Use Seville orange marmalade wholefruit method for frozen Seville oranges. Do not thaw – bring to the boil then put in the Simmering Oven overnight.

SCUM

To reduce scum, add a knob of butter to the jam or marmalade before bringing to the full rolling boil.

REDUCING THE SIMMERED FRUIT

In my recipes I have cooked the fruit in the Simmering Oven with just the amount of water needed, with the lid on. Therefore, there is no need to reduce the jam or marmalade before adding the sugar. Less water to reduce means less condensation in the kitchen dripping down the windows and walls!

TESTING FOR A GOOD SET

Over-cooking causes jam to darken and lose flavour. Under-boiling will give a runny jam. Three methods may be used to judge the best setting point.

1. Use a sugar or cooking thermometer to test temperature in the centre of the pan. 105 deg C (221 deg F) is a good setting point.

2. When a spoon of jam is allowed to cool a little and the jam falls in a "flake" or large droplet from the edge of the spoon.

3. When a spoonful of jam is allowed to go cold on a cold saucer and forms a wrinkled skin when a finger is pushed through.

Continue to cook a further 2-5 minutes if a good set is not reached then re-test.

To ensure that fruit does not float to the top of the jar, cool 10 minutes before potting.

N.B. The Aga is wonderful for marmalade making but do make sure that you do the boiling part when the Aga is at its hottest i.e. in the morning or not after you have done a lot of cooking.

GOOSEBERRY JAM

The colour of the jam will depend on the maturity of the gooseberries. Green gooseberries make a greeny yellow jam. Ripe gooseberries make a pink jam. Also, lengthy boiling after adding the sugar makes a darker jam.

MAKES ABOUT 12LB (5.5kg)

Measure the gooseberries into a very large pan or preserving pan with the water. Bring to the boil. Cover.

2/4 Simmering Oven: transfer the pan to the floor of the oven for about 1 hour until soft and pulpy. Mash well with a potato masher to ensure that the fruit is really soft. Add the sugar and stir until dissolved.

Bring to the boil and boil for about 10 minutes, or until setting point is reached. Allow to cool for about 10 minutes. Pour into clean, warm jars, cover and label.

GOOSEBERRY AND ELDERFLOWER JAM

As above but add 12 large elderflower heads in a muslin bag to the fruit as it is softening before the sugar is added. Squeeze these out and remove bag before sugar is added.

INGREDIENTS
**6lb (2.75kg) gooseberries, topped and tailed
1½ pints(900ml) water
8lb (3.5kg) granulated sugar**

I N G R E D I E N T S

**3½lb (1.75kg) prepared
strawberries, equivalent to 4lb (2kg)
unprepared strawberries
2 x 1kg bag of jam sugar
knob of butter**

STRAWBERRY JAM

Strawberries are particularly low in pectin and acid so a sugar containing these is a boon for quick reliable results.

MAKES 7LB (3.5kg)

Check fruit, removing any over-ripe or bad strawberries. Place in a large pan. Crush with a potato masher or purée first in a processor. Add sugar, heat gently on the Simmering Plate, stirring continuously until sugar is dissolved. Transfer to the Boiling Plate to bring to a fast rolling boil, that will not stir down, for 4 minutes. Remove from the heat. Stir in the butter. Ladle into warm jars and screw down lids tightly as each jar is filled.

RASPBERRY JAM

As above but using raspberries.

STRAWBERRY CONSERVE

A whole fruit jam. Luscious served with freshly baked scones.

MAKES ABOUT 5lb (2.25kg)

Place the strawberries in a bowl. Cover with sugar. Wash the lemons well, cut in half and squeeze the juice all over the strawberries and sugar. Place the lemon halves in too. Cover with cling film and leave next to the Aga overnight. Next morning, place the strawberries, sugar and lemons into a large preserving pan.

2 Put into Simmering Oven to warm through, for about 30 minutes. Remove
4 the pan and place on the Simmering Plate to dissolve the sugar completely – approx. 20 minutes. Put the jars to warm in the Simmering Oven. Move the preserving pan to the Boiling Plate and boil until a soft setting point is reached (about 10-15 minutes).

Discard the lemon halves. A knob of butter will disperse any scum. Allow to cool for 10 minutes then place into the warmed jars and seal.

Tip: Serve the Strawberry Conserve with scones and clotted cream. Or, use to sandwich together a traditional Victoria Sandwich Cake, made with butter.

I N G R E D I E N T S

**3lb (1½kg) dry strawberries
3lb (1½kg) sugar, granulated
2 large lemons
Knob of butter**

FIRST-RATE APRICOT JAM

No need to buy whole or halved apricots for this, buy the odd pieces.

MAKES 5LB (2.25kg)

Snip the apricot pieces into quarters. Bring the water to the boil in a preserving pan or large pan, add apricot pieces. Remove from the heat and leave to stand covered on the floor of the Simmering Oven for about 3 hours until the apricot pieces have plumped up. Return to the heat and bring back to the boil, cover with a lid.

2 Simmering Oven: transfer the pan back to the floor of the oven for **4** about 1 hour until the apricots are tender.

Stir the sugar and lemon juice into the hot apricots and stir until the sugar has dissolved. Bring to the boil on the Boiling Plate and boil fast for about 10-15 minutes or until setting point is reached. Allow to cool for about 10 minutes then pour into clean warm jars, cover and label.

INGREDIENTS
**1lb (450g) dried apricot pieces
3 pints (1.75lt) water
juice 1 lemon
3lb (1.5kg) sugar**

CULTIVATED BLACKBERRY JELLY

If you do not have enough blackberries add half quantity of Bramley apples. For wild blackberries or brambles, add the juice of 1 large lemon when adding the sugar.

MAKES ABOUT 10LB (4.5kg)

Measure the blackberries into a very large pan or preserving pan with the water and bring to the boil. Cover.

2 Simmering Oven: transfer the pan to the floor of the oven for about **4** 1½ hours until soft. Mash well with a potato masher to ensure the fruit is really soft. Strain through a jelly bag for at least two hours or overnight.

Measure the quantity of juice and for each pint (600ml) allow 1lb (450g) sugar. Bring the juice to the boil and stir in the sugar until dissolved. Bring back to the boil and boil for about 15 minutes, or until setting point is reached. Pour into clean warm jars, cover and label.

INGREDIENTS
**8lb (3.5kg) blackberries
1½ pints (900ml) water
4-6lb (1.75-2.75kg) granulated sugar**

DEAD EASY RED CURRANT JELLY

This recipe was given to me by Mrs Block whose Aga was the first I knew, yonks ago. A devoted gardener she always has a mass of redcurrants to be preserved.

Tie redcurrants as picked in muslin and squeeze out juice with hands. Measure quantity of juice and pour into a large pan. For every pint (600ml) juice add 1lb (450g) of sugar. Heat gently until the sugar has dissolved then boil for 4-5 minutes or until setting point is reached. Pour into small jars.

As a variation add chopped mint to the hot jelly after setting point has been reached. This makes a delicious alternative to mint sauce or jelly with lamb.

INGREDIENTS

**3lb (1.5kg) Seville oranges
juice of 2 lemons
6lb (3kg) sugar
4 pints (2 litres) water**

SEVILLE ORANGE MARMALADE

*Softening of the fruit in the Simmering Oven is the method that most
Aga owners swear by – I do because it is so much easier to cut up the fruit
after the peel is cooked. I soften all the fruit together then divide it into
two batches – for the adding of the sugar and the final boiling.
I find this way you get a better set.
If using frozen fruit do not thaw the fruit beforehand and weigh down
with a pyrex plate.*

MAKES ABOUT 10LB (5kg)

Put the sugar to warm at the back of the Aga. Put oranges and lemon juice in a large pan. Cover with 4 pints water. If the water doesn't cover the oranges then use a small pan. If necessary weight the oranges down with a pyrex plate to keep them under the water. Bring the pan to the boil, cover. Transfer the pan to the Simmering Oven. Cook until tender, check after 2 hours.

Remove the lid. Stand a colander on a deep plate, lift out the fruit and put into the colander. Allow to cool enough to handle. Leave the orange liquid in the pan for the time being. Cut oranges in half. Scoop out all the pips and pith and add these to the orange liquid in the pan. Bring to the boil for 6 minutes with the lid off. Strain this liquid through a sieve, pressing the pulp through with a wooden spoon. This thicker liquid is high in pectin and helps to give the marmalade a good set. Pour half this liquid into the largest Aga pan or pre-serving pan.

Cut up the peel with a sharp knife as thin as you like it. Add half the peel to the liquid in the large pan with half (3lb) of the sugar. Stir on the Simmering Plate until the sugar has dissolved. Transfer to the Boiling Plate and boil rapidly for 15-20 minutes until setting point is reached. Leave in the pan for 10 minutes to cool a little then pot, seal and label. Repeat for the remaining batch.

VARIATIONS:

MUSCOVADO DARK SEVILLE MARMALADE: weigh 8oz (225g) less white sugar and add 8oz (225g) dark muscovado instead.

GINGER MARMALADE: add 8oz (225g) chopped preserved ginger after the sugar has dissolved.

WHISKY MARMALADE: add 8 tablespoons whisky to the marmalade just before potting.

INGREDIENTS

**4oz (100g) dried apricot pieces
1¼ pints (750ml) boiling water
1lb 14oz (850g) can prepared Seville oranges
5lb (2.25kg) granulated sugar**

FAST CHEAT APRICOT AND ORANGE MARMALADE

A quick and easy marmalade to make mid-season when there are no Seville oranges about. No need to use top quality whole dried apricots for this, buy the pieces if you can get them. I have made this with Mamade and Beech's canned prepared Seville oranges.

YIELD ABOUT 8LB (4kg)

If the apricot pieces are large chop them into smaller pieces. Pour over boiling water, cover and leave to soak in the Simmering Oven for 1 hour. Pour the contents of the can of oranges and sugar into a large preserving pan or very large pan, failing this 2 smaller pans. Add the apricots and soaking water. Heat on the Simmering Plate, stirring until all the sugar has dissolved. Transfer to the Boiling Plate, bring to the boil and boil briskly for 10 minutes. If using 2 pans, boil for 8 minutes. Remove from the heat and test for setting. If necessary, boil for further 2 minutes. Cool for about 10 minutes then pot, seal and label.

MINT SAUCE CONCENTRATE

When mint is prolific in June and at the point of flowering it has a superb flavour.
Bring the sugar and vinegar to the boil. Meanwhile chop mint leaves by hand and add to the hot vinegar or place in a processor with the vinegar and sugar and work to a smooth purée. The mint concentrate can be packed into screwtop jars and then stored in the cupboard to dilute with extra vinegar for a mint sauce to go with lamb.

I N G R E D I E N T S
½ pint (300ml) distilled vinegar
8oz (225g) granulated sugar
6oz (175g) mint leaves

LEMON CURD

The best way I know of using up egg yolks though I nearly always use whole eggs.
MAKES 3 SMALL JARS
Measure the butter and sugar into a bowl and stand over a pan of simmering water. Stir every so often until the butter has melted. Finely grate the rind and squeeze the juice from the lemons and add to the butter mixture with the eggs. Mix well together and continue to cook for about 25-30 minutes until the curd thickens. Stir from time to time. Remove from the heat and pour into warm, clean jars and cover. Keep in the refrigerator for up to 3 months.

I N G R E D I E N T S
4oz (100g) butter
8oz (225g) caster sugar
3 lemons
5 egg yolks or 3 eggs, beaten

ELDERFLOWER CHAMPAGNE

Store as a cordial in the refrigerator for up to three months.
Measure the sugar and water into a large pan, bring to the boil stirring until the sugar has dissolved. Remove from the heat and cool.
Slice the lemons thinly by hand, or in the processor, and place into a large polythene box or glass bowl. Add the elderflower heads and citric acid and pour over the cooled syrup. Cover and leave overnight.
Strain into bottles and store in the refrigerator. To serve dilute to taste with chilled carbonated water and ice.

I N G R E D I E N T S
3½lbs (1.75kg) granulated sugar
2½ pints (1.5lt) water
3 lemons
About 25 elderflower heads
2oz (50g) citric acid (Boots sell it)

Tomato Chutney P.136
Spiced Apple Chutney P.136
Rhubarb Chutney P.136

TIPS FOR SUCCESS WITH CHUTNEYS

A marvellous range of choices are possible when making your own chutney. A glut of marrows, windfall apples, rhubarb, or tomatoes, or bags of frozen plums, gooseberries or apricots forgotten in the freezer when the new season's fruit comes in, can all be converted into delicious chutneys. The presence of vinegar, salt, sugar and spices, not only gives the varied and distinctive flavours, but also preserves the chutney. The flavour usually mellows with age so improves after 1-2 months. Chutney may be kept for 2-3 years. The Aga is excellent for making chutney, a long slow simmering to reduce the mixture to a thick texture is often needed – about ³/₄-2 hours is normal.

EQUIPMENT

Choose the largest aluminium, stainless steel or enamel pan that you have with a ground base. Brass, copper or iron gives a metal flavour and should not be used. Chutney does not boil up and over like jam so pans can be ³/₄ full at the start of cooking.

JARS

A tight fitting lid to prevent drying out and shrinkage is needed so never cover with cellophane. Plastic lidded jars such as coffee or pickle jars are ideal as metal lids, unless lined with a plastic coating (as in pickle jars) tend to corrode with the presence of vinegar. Chutney is not prone to mould when jars are opened so large jars may be safe and suitable. Heat jars at the back of the Aga or in the Simmering Oven before potting.

SUGAR

Both white and brown sugars may be used. Brown especially the Muscavado impart both flavour and colour. Choose white or pale sugars where you do not wish the colour of the fruit to be marked, as in tomato, gooseberry or apricot chutney. Sugar and vinegar are added to the fruit and vegetables at the beginning of the cooking time.

FRUITS AND VEGETABLES

Fresh, frozen and dried fruits can all be used. The most suitable fresh and frozen being apples, pears and rhubarb, all stoned fruit, peach, apricot, mango and plum, and of the soft fruits, gooseberries are excellent but others less often used. *Frozen fruit* should be cooked quickly from frozen in the vinegar in a covered pan, then left uncovered as the remaining ingredients are added.
Oranges and lemons may be used to add flavour, the grated rind and juices only are added. The popular dried fruits are dates, raisins and sultanas plus candied peel or crystallised ginger.
Ripe and green tomatoes are the most widely used vegetable in chutney, along with onions, celery, marrows, courgettes, cucumber, garlic and fresh chillies and peppers for extra flavour.
Vegetables with a high water content like marrows, courgette and cucumber are best diced and salted overnight to draw out some water and so cut boiling time. Alternatively use these vegetables frozen then thawed and squeeze out extra moisture.

SPICES

A wide range of spices can be used in chutney. For convenience and economy I often use Mixed Pickling Spice. It may be tied in a muslin bag and put in during cooking but I prefer to grind it in a pepper or coffee mill or blender. It is very good to blend a variety of spices, 1oz (30g) will be sufficient to make 2 batches of 7-10lb quantity of moderately spicey chutney. If you prefer mellow chutneys, halve the hot spices given in recipes and add more to taste towards the end of cooking.

INGREDIENTS

4lb (2kg) cooking apples
2 red peppers
8oz (225g) stoned dates
1oz (25g) fresh ginger
½ (15g) mixed pickling spice
2 tablespoons salt
2 teaspoons mixed spice
1½ pints (900ml) malt vinegar
2lb (900g) dark muscovado sugar

INGREDIENTS

6lb (3kg) green tomatoes, sliced
3 red peppers, seeded and chopped
1½lb (675g) onions, sliced
1½lb (675g) apples, weighed when
peeled, cored and sliced
12oz (350g) sultanas
1½oz (40g) mustard seed
1½oz (40g) salt
1 large root ginger, bruised
1 teaspoon cayenne pepper
1½lb (675g) soft brown sugar
1¼ pints (750ml) malt vinegar

INGREDIENTS

4½lb (2kg) rhubarb
8oz (225g) onion
2 oranges
1 pint (600ml) vinegar
1 tablespoon ground allspice
1½lb (750g) molasses sugar
8oz (225g) mixed dried fruit

INGREDIENTS

2lbs (900g) tomatoes, skinned
and chopped
1½lbs (700g) onions, chopped
fairly small
1 large apple, peeled and chopped)
1 yellow pepper, seeded and
chopped)
about 2lb (900g)
3 red peppers, seeded
and chopped)
about 2lb (900g)
4 fat cloves garlic, crushed
1 tablespoon salt
1 tablespoon coriander seeds,
crushed
1 tablespoon paprika pepper powder
1 dessertspoon cayenne pepper
powder
½ pint (300ml) white wine vinegar
or distilled malt vinegar
12oz (350g) granulated sugar

APPLE, PEPPER AND DATE CHUTNEY

An excellent use for windfall apples.

MAKES ABOUT 8LB (3.5kg)

Peel, quarter and core apples. Chop in a processor or with a knife. Halve the peppers, discard the core and seeds and cut in dice. Chop dates. Grate ginger. Grind the pickling spice in a peppermill or coffee grinder or tie in muslin and lift out at the end of cooking. Place all the ingredients into a large pan. Heat slowly on the simmering plate until sugar dissolves, then bring to to a fast boil on the boiling plate. Return to simmer for 30-40 minutes until reduced to a thick pulpy consistency stirring regularly. Pot, seal and label.

GREEN TOMATO CHUTNEY

The red peppers give a bright fleck of red colour in the jars.

MAKES ABOUT 10LB (4.5kg)

Put all the ingredients into a large pan. Bring slowly to the boil on the Simmering Plate, stirring frequently.

2 / 4 Simmering Oven: cover then transfer to the oven for 3½ hours until the onion is tender.

Remove the lid, bring back to the boil on the Boiling Plate then simmer on the Simmering Plate until the mixture is thick and all the liquid has reduced. Remove the root ginger and pot in clean warm jars.

MARY'S RHUBARB CHUTNEY

Use the firmer mid-summer rhubarb rather than the spring or forced rhubarb with its high water content.

MAKES ABOUT 7LB (3.5kg)

Cut rhubarb into ½ inch (1cm) lengths, chop onion, grate orange rind and squeeze out juice. Place all the ingredients together in a large pan. Heat gently until the sugar dissolves and the fruit begins to soften, then bring to a fast boil on the Boiling Plate. Return to the Simmering Plate and cook for 30-40 minutes, stirring regularly until reduced to a thick pulpy consistency.

HOT TOMATO CHUTNEY

This chutney is a glorious colour. Make it at the end of the summer when the tomatoes are plentiful and cheap or when your own crop is abundant.

MAKES ABOUT 6LB (2.75kg)

Put all the prepared vegetables and the garlic into a large pan and bring to the boil, simmer for 5 minutes covered then transfer to:

2 / 4 Simmering Oven: simmer for 1 hour.

Add the sugar, vinegar, salt, coriander, paprika, cayenne and stir well until the sugar is dissolved. Bring to the boil and with the lid off return to the Simmering Oven for 1 hour. If still a bit watery boil fast, still with the lid off, until the right consistency.

Ladle into clean jars, cover with screw top lids and seal while hot. Leave for at least a month in a cool dark place.

BREAKFASTS

BAKED KIPPERS P.138 · BUCKWHEAT PANCAKES P.138 · APRICOT, PRUNES AND ORANGE P.138

*W*hatever you choose to eat for break-fast, the Aga takes over. You are never once required to stand over a spitting frypan frying eggs – not the pleasantest of starts to the day. Instead, let the family prepare Aga toast to their liking while an oven-grilled breakfast sizzles quietly in one tin in the oven or the kippers are cooking to perfection in foil.

No smells, no mess. Good Morning!

4oz (100g) dried apricots
1 pint (600ml) water
8oz (225g) prunes
1 thin skinned orange,
very finely sliced
³/₄ pint (450ml) orange juice from
a carton

2oz (50g) buckwheat flour
2oz (50g) plain flour
2 level teaspoons baking powder
1 teaspoon runny honey
1 egg
¼ pint (150ml) milk

a pair of kippers
2 good knobs of butter

herrings or mackerel
seasoning
buttered foil

APRICOTS AND PRUNES WITH ORANGE

No sugar is needed for this dish as the fruit is quite sweet enough on its own.

SERVES 6-8

Soak the apricots in water overnight. Put the apricots in a fairly large pan with the water, prunes, orange and juice. Bring to the boil on the Boiling Plate and cover.

2∎ **∎4**∎ Simmering Oven: transfer to the floor of the oven for about 20-30 minutes. Leave to cool and serve chilled.

BUCKWHEAT PANCAKES

Simple to make and lovely to serve with butter and honey or cherry jam.

MAKES ABOUT 16 PANCAKES

Put the flours, baking powder and honey in a bowl, make a well in the centre and add the egg and half the milk and beat to a thick batter. Stir in the remaining milk.

Grease the Simmering Plate lightly with lard or oil. Use a pad of kitchen paper for this. When ready to cook the pancakes, the fat should be just hazy, then wipe off any surplus with more kitchen paper. If your Aga is particularly hot, it may be necessary to lift the lid of the Simmering Plate for a few minutes to reduce the heat a little before cooking.

Spoon the mixture onto the plate in tablespoonfuls, spacing them well apart. When bubbles rise to the surface, turn the pancakes over with a palette knife and cook on the other side for a further 30 seconds or so until golden brown. Lift off and keep wrapped in a clean teatowel to keep them soft. Continue cooking until all the batter has been used and then serve them warm.

KIPPERS COOKED IN THE OVEN

No smells and delicious moist kippers result from this method of cooking.

SERVES 2

Put a knob of butter on top of each kipper. Wrap each kipper loosely in foil, folding the foil over but not sealing it. Place side by side in the small roasting tin.

2∎ **∎4**∎ Roasting Oven: hang the tin from the fourth set of runners, cook for 15 minutes or until cooked through. Serve straight away or transfer to the Simmering Oven until ready to serve.

OVEN FRIED HERRINGS OR MACKEREL

For those who love herrings but hate the smell all over the house!

Remove the heads from the fish and clean them under running cold water. Place the buttered foil in the roasting tin. Make three slashes with a sharp knife down each side of the fish. Season then place the fish on the foil.

2∎ **∎4**∎ Roasting Oven: hang the tin on the top set of runners and cook for about 10 minutes until the fish are nicely browned and the flesh flakes.

CROISSANTS

These take time and care to make and rise overnight in the fridge which gives one a breather in between processes!
The flavour is wonderful. They freeze very well. Bake and allow to cool then freeze in polythene boxes. To reheat from frozen, place on the grid shelf on the floor of the Roasting Oven for about 8 minutes, from thawed about 3 minutes.

MAKES 12

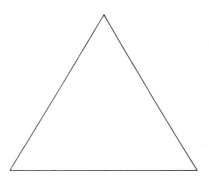

Measure flour and salt into a large mixing bowl. Rub in 2oz (50g) of butter into the flour until it resembles breadcrumbs, make a well in the flour mixture and crumble in the yeast followed by the sugar and liquid. Gradually mix in the flour with the hand and work until smooth. Put into an oiled polythene bag and leave in the fridge to rest for 2 hours.

Take the remaining butter at room temperature, spread out onto an oblong of greaseproof paper, about 8 x 5 inches (20 x 13cm), cover with a second piece of greaseproof and smooth this out with a rolling pin. Put into the fridge.

Roll out the chilled dough to a rectangle about 14 x 7 inches (35 x 18cm), peel the greaseproof off the chilled butter and place towards the top of the rolled out dough so that it covers the top two-thirds. Fold the bottom of the dough up over the butter then fold the top half down on top and seal the edges with a rolling pin. Put the dough back into the bag and leave to rest in the fridge for 30 minutes.

Roll out the dough again into a long rectangle, fold in three as before and seal the edges with the rolling pin. Replace in the bag and leave in the fridge overnight.

Next day: roll out in the same way, fold in three, seal the edges then roll out to a rectangle 14 x 21 inches (35 x 53cm), and cut into triangles as shown in the diagram.

Take each triangular piece and from one straight side roll into a sausage shape pulling the "tongue" to stretch it a little and finishing this with this piece underneath. Pull the ends round in opposite directions to make a crescent shape.

Lift six onto the cold plain shelf and six onto a baking tray and glaze with beaten egg. Leave for 45 minutes to prove.

Glaze again with a beaten egg.

2▪ / ▪4▪ Roasting Oven: put the croissants into the oven one above the other as low as possible in the oven. Bake for 12 minutes, swapping the trays over after 6 minutes or until golden brown.

INGREDIENTS

1lb (450g) strong plain flour
½ teaspoon salt
8-10oz (300g) salted butter
½oz (15g) fresh yeast
1oz (25g) sugar
¼ pint (150ml) milk
¼ pint (150ml) very hot water
beaten egg, to glaze

AGA YOGURT

Aga owner, Mary Francis's own yogurt recipe.

Cream the natural yogurt and dried milk together with a little of the milk. Heat the rest of the milk in a pan on the Simmering Plate to blood heat. Pour onto the yogurt mixture, mix and place into a 1½ pint (900ml) basin. Cover with a plate, then put a woolly cap or tea cosy on top to cover completely! (Alternatively wrap in a towel.) Stand in a colander on top of the Simmering Plate lid (protect lid with a tea towel). Leave all night to set. Transfer to the refrigerator, then use as required.

INGREDIENTS

1 tablespoon natural yogurt
1 tablespoon non-fat dried milk
1 pint (600ml) sterilised milk

SUNDAY MORNING BREAKFAST
SHOWN IN CAST IRON DISH P.141
AGA TOAST P.8/9

SUNDAY MORNING BREAKFAST

All cooked in the large roasting tin, only one pan to wash up, and no mess on the top of the Aga. If cooking for one or two, use an Aga cast iron pan on the floor of the Roasting Oven.

OVEN-COOKED BREAKFAST

Put the sausages at one end of the large roasting tin, having greased with a little bacon fat. Use the small tin if only cooking for 2.

2▪ ▪4▪ Roasting Oven: hang the tin on the highest set of runners and cook for about 10 minutes. Turn the sausages and cook again for about 10 minutes (5 will be enough for chipolatas). Add the tomatoes, cut side up, and the rashers of bacon, cook for 5-7 minutes. Turn the bacon and sausage and cook for a further 5 minutes. Add the mushrooms and cook for 5 minutes. If necessary add a little more bacon fat when turning the mushrooms. Break the eggs into one end of the tin, put the tin onto the floor of the oven and cook for 2-3 minutes.

GRILLED BACON

Grilling is done in the Roasting Oven. Either use the grill rack in the roasting tin, hanging the tin from the highest set of runners, or put the bacon straight into the tin with the tin on the floor of the oven. Timing again is very variable – about 3 minutes each side for thin bacon and up to 7 minutes either side for thicker cuts.

GRILLED SAUSAGES

Again in the Roasting Oven – put sausages onto the grill rack in the roasting tin hung on the highest set of runners. Turn every 5 minutes until done.

OVEN FRIED BREAD

The timing for fried bread varies according to the thickness of the slices and also depending if the bread is brown or white, as brown bread takes longer.

Spread bacon fat or other fat on both sides of the bread and put into a roasting tin on the floor of the Roasting Oven, turn after about 5-7 minutes.

AGA TOAST

Using the special Aga toaster is easy as it does not matter how thick or thin the slices of bread are. You can toast at least four slices at a time according to the size of the loaf. Time varies enormously according to the thickness of the slices and brown bread generally takes longer. Toast on the Boiling Plate leaving the lid up. For faster toast, put the lid down but watch it very carefully. This way is not quite so crisp.

IRISH SODA BREAD

Quick to make and often baked fresh for breakfast or tea.

Mix the dry ingredients together. Work quickly to a light dough with the buttermilk. Turn onto a board and knead until free of cracks, not too long or it will toughen.

Flatten into a round loaf and place onto a lightly greased baking sheet. Cut a cross in the top.

2▪ ▪4▪ Roasting Oven: with the grid shelf on the third set of runners bake for 30-35 minutes, turning once. When baked the loaf will sound hollow if tapped in the base. Wrap in a clean tea towel to cool, this stops the crust hardening too much.

INGREDIENTS

per person
a little bacon fat
1 sausage
1 tomato, halved
2 rashers bacon
2oz (50g) mushrooms, wiped
1 egg

INGREDIENTS

1lb (450g) plain flour
(or a mixture of wholemeal and plain flour)
1 teaspoon baking soda
1 teaspoon salt
Buttermilk to mix, about ½-¾ pint (300-450ml)

GUIDE TO AGA COOKING CHART

As the Aga cooker is heated differently from an ordinary cooker, exact conversions are not possible. Look in the Aga Book for a similar recipe.

Below is a quick guide to oven usage.

OVEN TEMPERATURE	2▪ TWO OVEN AGA	▪4▪ FOUR OVEN AGA
HIGH	**ROASTING OVEN**	**ROASTING OVEN**
GRILLING SCONES PASTRIES BREAD YORKSHIRE PUDDING ROASTS SHALLOW FRYING	Top – Grilling; 2nd runner – Scones, Small Pastries; 3rd runner – Bread Rolls, Yorkshire Pudding; 4th runner – Roasts, Poultry, Small Cakes in cases in the large meat tin. Grid shelf on oven floor – Loaves. Oven floor – Shallow frying, Quiche.	Top – Grilling; 2nd runner – Scones, Small Pastries; 3rd runner – Bread Rolls, Yorkshire Pudding; 4th runner – Roasts, Poultry. Grid shelf on oven floor – Loaves, Oven floor – Shallow frying, Quiche.
MODERATE	**ROASTING/SIMMERING OVEN**	**BAKING OVEN**
CAKES BISCUITS FISH SOUFFLÉS SHORTBREAD CHEESECAKES	Place grid shelf on floor of Roasting Oven. Protect food with the cold plain shelf slid on second or third runners. For cakes that require over 45 mins. use the Cake Baker. Alternatively with fish, cheesecake, start off in Roasting Oven, finish in Simmering Oven.	Towards top – Whisked Sponges, Some Biscuits, Small Cakes. Middle – Fish, Soufflés. Grid shelf on oven floor – Victoria Sandwiches, Shortbread and Cheesecake.
LOW	**SIMMERING OVEN**	**SIMMERING OVEN**
CASSEROLES STOCK MILK PUDDINGS MERINGUES RICH FRUIT CAKES	For Casseroles, Stock, Milk Puddings, bring to heat elsewhere on the Aga then transfer to Simmering Oven. (One exception is Meringues). Rich Fruit Cakes can be cooked for a long time here.	For Casseroles, Stock, Milk Puddings, bring to heat elsewhere on the Aga then transfer to Simmering Oven. (One exception is Meringues). Rich Fruit Cakes can be cooked for a long time here.

TEN GOLDEN RULES

1
COOK AS MUCH IN THE OVENS AS POSSIBLE

DO remember the Roasting Oven can be used for grilling and shallow frying too.

2
KEEP LIDS DOWN

DO keep the insulated lids down when plates are not in use to conserve the heat.

3
USE GOOD PANS

Do use thick ground base pans. Aga pans can be used both on the hot plates and in the Simmering Oven.

4
MOP UP SPILLS

DO wipe up spills as they happen.

5
TAKE CARE OF THE AGA

DON'T drag pans over the vitreous enamel surface, or slide the roasting tins etc. over the chrome lids as naturally they will scratch.

6
THE AGA CONTROLS ITSELF

DON'T alter the controls once the correct setting is showing in the heat indicator.

7
SERVICE REGULARLY

DO have your Aga always in tip top condition, have it serviced as recommended by your Authorised Aga Distributor.

8
2▆ KEEP THE PLAIN SHELF COLD

DO use the plain shelf, cold, to make a moderate oven in the Roasting Oven of the 2 Oven Aga. DON'T store the plain shelf in the oven.

9
2▆ USE THE CAKE BAKER

DO use the Aga Cake Baker in the 2 Oven Aga for cakes needing over 45 minutes cooking.

10
DO ENJOY YOUR AGA!